Something Borrowed
Something Blue

Principles of Jazz Composition
by ANDY JAFFE

Principles of Jazz Composition

by ANDY JAFFE

ISBN 978-3-89221-122-8

Cover Art by manx kommunikationsdesign, Essen, Germany

Layout and Musical Notation by T. Max Zentawer

Production: Veronika Gruber

Printed by Graspo Printing House, Czech Republic

Order No. 11207

TABLE OF CONTENTS

Foreword

First and foremost I wish to thank my publisher and friend, the late Hans Gruber, as well as Ms.Veronika Gruber and the staff of Advance Music, for their support of my work. Secondly I would like to thank my attorney and friend Steven Robinson, who secured the permissions for the use of the transcribed examples of copywritten material which form such an indispensable part of this text. Thirdly I must thank the numerous experts, mentors, and colleagues upon whose judgment and input I have relied in creating this text, chief among them the late Mark Tucker, Herb Pomeroy, William Russo, Horace Boyer and Bill Barron, as well as John Edward Hasse, Andrew Homzy, Fred Koch, David Berger, Tom McClung, Yusef Lateef, Fred Tillis, Bruce Diehl, Annie Kuebler, Dick Domek, Dave Demsey, Lewis Porter, Jeff Holmes, Walter van de Leur, Steve Lajoie, Jovino Santos Neto, Hermeto Pascoal, Jeff Friedman, Ted Pease, Johanne Cousineau, Billy Taylor, Father Peter O'Brien, Shannon Thomson, Eric Johnson, Tony Lada, Bill Lowe, Branford Marsalis, Alice Coltrane, Sue Mingus, Don Sickler, Doug LaRosa, Geoff Keezer, Art Lande, and Aida Garcia-Cole, among so many others. Thanks to Dave Reid for his assistance in editing the index. Regardless of the provenance of the musical examples in this text (published, archival, or transcribed), their accuracy has been verified by me and is my responsibility.

Also I must thank my family, who always so generously indulge and support me during these projects: my wife Gisele Litalien, and three children, Ceora, Lysander and Marty, musicians all.

This book is respectfully dedicated to the memories of my late friends and colleagues Hans Gruber, William Russo, Mark Tucker, and James Williams, as well as to my late parents Howard and Elizabeth Jaffe, who gave their children the invaluable gift of a musical home.

The philosophy of this book: I was motivated to write this book largely as a consequence of what I experienced while teaching jazz arranging and composition over the past thirty years. During this period I have been chagrined by the increasing trend toward genericism in composition and arranging in the jazz idiom. Notwithstanding the proliferation of jazz scholarship and education programs during this period (perhaps in part *because* of it?), I have found that students of composition and arranging, even at the graduate level, seem ever more disconnected from the experience of having studied the work of the historically important composers and arrangers firsthand. While no text can, nor does this text intend, to establish a "canon" of important composers or individual compositions, I do believe that there is no more valid approach to the study of composition and arranging than through the study of the repertoire itself. Like improvisation, writing in the jazz idiom is also an *aural* tradition.

Simply learning formulas or technique, without having an understanding of their provenance or evolution over time, is exactly what leads to the musical genericism to which I refer. Listening to and transcribing the work of our musical predecessors and colleagues will inevitably transform the music of those who make the effort to do so, resulting in the creation of a more idiomatic and personal musical vocabulary.

Philosophy aside, it is critically important to do all of the end of Chapter LISTENING and TRANSCRIPTION ASSIGNMENTS. In some cases these are directly correlated with material discussed in the text, while in others the material assigned will be different, but hopefully enlightening and relevant. Unfortunately it has not been possible for a variety of reasons to include all of the examples and composers I would have liked to represent here (most notably due to the economics of paying for permissions and/or the refusal of some composers to grant them or respond to our inquiries). It is expected of course that the individual instructor and student will supplement the examples I have included with those that are more closely related to their individual interests. In short, I believe that in many ways it is the assignments, and the process they represent, that constitute the backbone of the text. Listening is everything!

Andy Jaffe 2011

CHAPTER 1

General Questions
and Principles

As we begin our study of jazz composition, we pose several questions:

1.) What is jazz composition, and how does it *differ* from musical composition in other idioms?

2.) Conversely, what does it have in common with other compositional forms?

3.) How does jazz composition differ from *jazz improvisation?*

4.) What attributes does it *share* with jazz improvisation?

5.) Is the study of other closely related styles of composition and related repertoire (e.g. Broadway and *standards*) relevant?

6.) What influences have related musical styles exerted on the evolution of jazz composition?

7.) Can the work of the composer in jazz be separated from its performance or recorded documentation?

In answering these questions we hope to arrive at a series of underlying principles and techniques that describe the compositional process in jazz, regardless of the instrumentation or era involved. A few important notes before we begin:

· We are **not** attempting to establish the canon of jazz composition.

· Neither do we purport to establish a linear or historical approach to the subject.

· Rather, we are attempting to establish the existence of important underlying principles that are shared by representative compositions of a variety of composers whose work has contributed to the repertoire of the music. If you do not find your favorite piece or composer represented here, your challenge is to see whether or not these concepts apply to that work.

· This is *not* supposed to be a text on either arranging or jazz harmony (though each of these important and related disciplines is certainly relevant). So it is to your advantage to have a solid grounding in both.

· Neither is it a text about electronic music or the application of technology to the compositional process (notwithstanding the obvious fact that the proliferation of music software has greatly facilitated the documentation, storage, and distribution of music).

· **Method:** As we consider each of the individual topics related to this subject, we will reflect on the relevance of each to the issues raised above. We will see that it is difficult to separate the study of one compositional device entirely from others, because in context these rarely exist independently of one another.

A related goal of this text is to help you to understand that your favorite composers listened to and studied the work of *their* predecessors and contemporaries (both jazz and non-jazz) just as you are, so the process of emulating their style must begin with your examination of the music that influenced them. What you hear in their music was not created in a vacuum. We all must realize that there was a great deal of wonderful music written before we ourselves became involved with the music, and that in studying the compositional process we cannot separate technique from the stylistic and cultural context in which the music was produced.

The Principles

At the outset, we can say that the following principles seem common to the compositional process in jazz, regardless of era (these are not intended to be listed in order of importance):

1.) *Recapitulation:* Most compositions in jazz seem to share the universal impulse to return to the established theme after some sort of development. This may be thought of as being analogous to the literary principle of "beginning, middle, end".

2.) The form taken by this *development* may vary greatly from one instance to the next. Sometimes it takes the form of (an) improvised solo(s). Sometimes it is composed. Frequently it is a mixture of both.

3.) Regardless of the nature of its development or instrumental presentation, it is the *motivic identity* of the thematic material that makes the composition memorable. The motivic identity of a given theme is defined primarily by its *shape* and *rhythm*, though its associated harmony and form may also be factors. A colloquial term for the main motif of a piece would be its *hook*.

4.) Two compositions may sound similar because one has influenced the other, or due to common musical or cultural influences shared by their respective composers (this latter principle may be thought of as an adaptation of the principle of *consilience*, also the title of an eponymous work by E.O. Wilson[1]).

5.) Jazz has in large part created a musical world constructed of necessity from *appropriated musical materials*. This is true in matters of instrumentation, form, and even theoretical explication of the music. Most elements of the American musical heritage, of which jazz is a central part, predated its evolution. The evolution of jazz reflects the complex cultural milieu in which the music evolved. The African American musicians who created this music had no choice but to marry the musical attributes and traditions of the "New World" to those that they brought from their own.

[1] Wilson, *E.O. Consilience: The Unity of Knowledge*. Knopf, N.Y. 1998

6.) One of the most important African-based attributes of the music is *call and response*. One would be hard pressed indeed to find musical examples from the jazz repertoire where this principle is not in evidence. Listen to Thelonious Monk deconstruct his own melodies and convert them to spacious accompaniment riffs to which the soloist has no choice but to respond (for example, the beginning of Charlie Rouse's solo on "Well You Needn't" – see Ex.s 2.14). Listen to juxtaposition of Brass versus reeds in Don Redman's arrangements (for example, "The Stampede" – see Ex.s 5.33). Whether written or improvised, each is a compositional manifestation of the principle of call and response.

7.) Another important concept is that of *adaptation*. It was inevitable that as African-American music developed it resulted in new uses of extant materials, and new forms of making music by those participating in its evolution. These were influenced by, though not identical to, those practiced in antecedent cultures, both European and African. As the world has become more interconnected, and access to formal education has become more universal, the palette of adapted materials has been further expanded by imaginative musicians to embrace ever more diverse cultural, philosophical and technological influences. In other words, Jazz has not just developed from within, and the student of composition must always be mindful of the larger musical world.

8.) Related to the notions of both adaptation and appropriation is the notion of *signification*. Henry Louis Gates defines this as "repetition with a signal difference"[2]. When African Americans danced the cakewalk, for example, they were not merely imitating the formal dances of plantation owners, but rather adapting them, with implicit commentary. Many well-known jazz compositions, for example, borrow and recontextualize pre-existing melodic material. Instances of appropriation and signification can range from the oft-heard gesture of using a melodic quote in the middle of an improvised solo to the wholesale recasting of large sections of melodic and harmonic material, as seen, for example, in "Impressions" (see Ex.s 7.8), or the Ellington/Strayhorn version of the "Nutcracker"(see Chapter 8).

9.) Related to signification is the important notion of *recontextualization*, or imparting new meaning to a musical idea by changing the setting in which it is presented. One obvious example of a technical device illustrating this principle would be *reharmonization* (Chapter 4). *Rhythmic recontextualization* (Chapter 6) of thematic material may result from rhythmic *displacement* or changes in meter or the underlying rhythmic groove. Recontextualization may occur during thematic statements and/or as a developmental tool, and can enable the same musical idea to create points of either stability or instability depending upon the context in which it is reiterated.

[2] Gates, Henry Louis. *The Signifying Monkey: A Theory of African-American Literary Criticism*. Oxford, 1988

10.) Jazz is an *aural tradition*. As noted in the introduction, this is equally as true in composition as it is in performance. As such notation has not always necessarily been a criterion for the existence of a composition. Verbal directions and other cues are frequently used by composers (who are often bandleaders as well) to direct the development of their compositional materials in performance[3,4]. Further, central to the very notion of such a tradition is the concept of **learning through listening**. It is no more possible to become a jazz *composer* without listening to one's predecessors than it is to become a jazz *player* without having done so. There is no escaping the impact that the advent of recording technology and other forms of documentation has had in this regard. As a result we can reasonably ask the further question as to whether or not a given jazz composition is best defined by its *notated* or recorded form (as we will see, the answer to this question may vary from one case to the next).

11.) Implicit in the notion of an aural tradition is that of the role of *memory*. Since we learn by listening, our common practice and sense of musical style evolves from a collective cultural memory conditioned by our shared aural experiences, a fact that accounts for the presence of shared musical attributes of various compositions within a given era. Learning music without listening to music is impossible. To not listen is to divorce oneself from the tradition. In a society predicated on the notion of instant gratification, jazz is an anachronism in this regard. There are no shortcuts to its mastery or understanding. We are all students for life.

12.) There is no escaping the notion of *individuality of voice* in jazz composition (another important similarity with improvisation). Of course vocal influence also exists in a literal sense, due to the influence of both the Blues and of jazz vocalists, particularly Louis Armstrong, on the evolution of our collective sense of phrasing and idiomatic interpretation. This is also true metaphorically however, in that each jazz musician (composers and arrangers included!) must develop his/her own recognizable sound *(sonic signature)*. We know all of the great musicians within an instant of hearing them play. We identify them because of the personal sound and individuality of voice that they have achieved. This is also true of the great composers (and arrangers).

13.) We have all been influenced profoundly by the *Blues*. The Blues and jazz are inseparable. Technically this relationship may manifest itself in such devices as *Blue notes*, Blues-based harmonies, the Blues form, and other common practice phenomena. More generally, Blues influence can be heard in the *juxtaposition or coexistence of major and minor tonalities* afforded by the Blues, and in the pervasiveness of *chromaticism* in jazz composition. The Blues is therefore also one of many factors which have combined to condition our sense of consonance and dissonance in the jazz idiom.

[3] Coolman, Todd. *The Miles Davis Quintet of the mid-1960's: Synthesis of Improvisational and Compositional Elements*. UMI Dissertation Services, Ann Arbor, 1997

[4] Author's notes from talk by saxophonist Steve Lacy at Williams College, 1/7/04

14.) All of the principles outlined here are also equally valid regardless of the instrumentation or size of a given ensemble, and the same may be said in terms of the duration of a particular composition (i.e. a "tune" represents a *micro* compositional world, while an extended suite might be thought of as the *macro* world, but the same unifying principles define successful composition in each).

15.) Finally, it is impossible for any of these principles to exist in isolation or to be the sole defining factor in a given composition, even though one or more of them may be the most prevalent. Successful composition balances many of these elements, and the proportional emphasis between these factors differs from one piece to the next.

So perhaps our working definition of composition can simply be: *a predetermined and recognizable piece of music*. It is a *jazz* composition because it sounds and feels like jazz (and importantly not just because it provides a framework for improvisation, which *any* piece of music can do. Jazz is a way of playing and writing music that can be applied to any repertoire).

CHAPTER 2

Motivic Identity
and Reiteration

*M*otivic identity rests on two factors: *shape* and *rhythm*. Of course, each motif exists within a given harmonic context as well. Its relationship to the supporting harmony contributes to our sense of the motif as being "antecedent" (unresolved) or "consequent" (resolved). Implicit in the related notions of "antecedent" and "consequent" is the ubiquitous phenomenon of *call and response*. As a composition (or an improvisation) begins, its primary motif is stated. The subsequent reiteration, *transformation* and *recontextualization* of the motif helps to structure the music.

First, let's examine some abstract examples of various sorts of motivic transformation by way of definition, then illustrate these in real world musical examples.

Taking an arbitrary thematic idea:

Ex. 2.1

Playing it backwards is known as *retrograde:*

Ex. 2.2

Then we can play it upside down (or in *inversion):*

Ex. 2.3

Or we could perform both of these operations concurrently to render it "upside down and backwards" (or in *retrograde inversion):*

Ex. 2.4

We can *reharmonize* it:

Ex. 2.5

We can repeat it *sequentially*:

Ex. 2.6

We can *transpose* it:

Ex. 2.7

We can *displace* it rhythmically (i.e. change its relationship to the beat, the rhythmic analogue of *reharmonization):*

Ex. 2.8

We can *fragment* it (i.e. break it down into smaller component parts which can then be subject to all of these same manipulations):

It can be "embellished" (decorated melodically), either chromatically or diatonically, or both:

Embellishment or melodic alteration may also be blues-based ("bluesified"):

Here are some examples of the various techniques listed above from the real world. "Satin Doll", by Duke Ellington and Billy Strayhorn is illustrative of many of them, reinforcing the following notions:

1.) Not *every* technical device need be used in every composition (just as every improvised solo need not contain every technique or device) and, conversely;

2.) It is rare to find a single compositional technique used in isolation.

Ex. 2.11A

SATIN DOLL

Ellington/Strayhorn

The main motif (found in ms.A-1 and 2) has a clearly identifiable rhythmic and melodic contour. It also has clear tonal implications. At the end of its repetition in measure 2, it has acquired *antecedent (unresolved)* status by virtue of the fact that it did not return to its melodic anchor or point of stability (its second note, G natural).

Subsequently the main motif is *transposed* up a whole step in measures 3 and 4 (as is the accompanying harmony). This transposition is *literal*, i.e. the intervals and relationship to the supporting harmony remain the same (importantly and more generally however, a given motif retains its identity even in cases where the intervals it contains are altered to accommodate the harmony, or for other reasons).

Then it is *fragmented*, and only its second measure used in measure 5.

Subsequently that resultant motif is transposed, becoming *consequent* as the phrase concludes by returning via a chromatic (technically "substitute dominant") cadence to the tonic (measure 6).

This 8-bar phrase then repeats with a second ending, creating the first two A's of the AABA songform (see also Chapter 5).

A *bridge* is then created by transposing and *embellishing* the initial motif (note that both the A and B sections begin with the descending two eighth-note, whole step motif), and the resultant phrase is then transposed, up a step, to mirror the transposition which occurred in the first four bars of the A section.

Finally, we might also note that the *bridge* may be viewed as an *augmentation* of the A section insofar as the harmony is concerned (i.e. measures 1 and 2 of letter A are expanded in the bridge from two bars to four, through the addition of a temporary tonic, FΔ, which represents a resolution of the cadence found in measures B 1-2).

In other words the cadence with which the A section begins, D–7 to G7, has been transposed up a fourth, then doubled in length and followed by the temporary tonic, IV, as shown in Ex. 2.11B below:

Ex. 2.11B

"Satin Doll" bridge, first harmonic phrase

Chords in Ms. 1-4

In any event, it is clear that a variety of factors, working in balance, combine to create the desired forward motion and unity in the development of the initial motif throughout the composition. (Incidentally, it is interesting to compare this piece, written in 1953, with the late 40's Ellington extended work entitled "The Tattooed Bride", which employs essentially the same theme, in *retrograde*, to structure a through-composed multi-sectional work. See also end of Chapter LISTENING ASSIGNMENTS). (More discussion about motivically-based extended works follows in Chapter 8.)

These same principles may of course exist in an improvised solo as well. Transcribe and analyze the first chorus of Sonny Rollins' initial chorus on his well-known composition "St. Thomas" (See also end of Chapter ASSIGNMENTS. There is actually some dispute as to whether or not the melody is actually Rollins' own. Randy Weston had previously recorded the same piece with the title "Fire Down There"[1], and the melody is reportedly that of a Danish Folk Song, "Det var en lordag aften" as well). Note how Rollins skillfully establishes his two-note initial motif, then proceeds to *reiterate*, *embellish*, and then *depart* from it for a more boppish phrase of continuous eighth notes. He then returns to it at the end of the first eight bars, by which time it has achieved a consequent status.

As you listen to the Rollins solo, note how concise its development is. There is nothing gratuitous. Even though this solo was improvised, it illustrates the important compositional principle of getting the most out of a given idea, or *motivic economy*.

[1] Randy Weston, 1955 (Riverside)

It is also clear that the main motif appeared initially as an antecedent phrase, yet upon its return felt distinctly *consequent.* This dynamic is also in evidence in Wayne Shorter's blues-based composition "Witch Hunt", where the primary motif is varied to create a B idea, which is then transposed sequentially over cadential harmony before returning in fragmented form as a consequent phrase.

Ex. 2.12

"Witch Hunt" by Wayne Shorter

As mentioned earlier, Thelonious Monk often extended the compositional reach of his themes beyond their initial melodic statement by deconstructing *(fragmenting)* them into background riffs behind soloists. In the example we cited earlier, Monk segues from the melody of his "Well You Needn't" into saxophonist Charlie Rouse's solo by paraphrasing his own melody and integrating it into his harmonic accompaniment.

Main melodic motif of "Well, You Needn't"

Ex. 2.14

Monk's comping paraphrase

(This excerpt is found at the very beginning of Rouse's solo, immediately following the melody – see also DISCOGRAPHY.)

Note that Monk not only demonstrates the principle of *motivic economy* here, he also is creating a *call and response* dynamic between himself and the soloist in the process. Rouse's opening between the rifflike melodic paraphrases in Monk's comping is clearly delineated, thereby enabling his solo to become a musical and compositional conversation. (Of course, one of Monk's best known characteristics as both a player and a composer, his creative use of space, is also in evidence here.)

These last two examples each show why it is important for composers to listen carefully to good improvisers and accompanists. There is great benefit in emulating (orchestrating) such interactive dynamics in our writing. Listen for example to Gil Evans' 1958 version of "King Porter Stomp"[2], and you will clearly hear how the accompaniment role has been assigned to the trombones.

Ex. 2.15

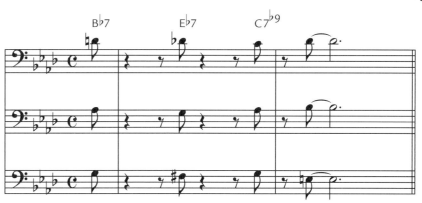

[2] Transcription, see also Sturm, Fred. *Changes Over Time: The Evolution of Jazz Arranging*. Advance Music, Rottenburg, Germany, 1995

Common practice drumset patterns may likewise prove useful in orchestration. The following stereotypical swing drumset pattern employs accents on the cymbals and in the bass drum, while the intervening eighth notes are articulated on the toms and/or the snare drum.

Ex. 2.16

In his well-known composition "Stolen Moments" (from the 1960 album "Blues and The Abstract Truth"), Oliver Nelson seems to be orchestrating this very interactive dynamic in the consequent phrase melody of his melody:

Ex. 2.17

Ms.13 & 14 of initial melodic statement

This is also an example of *oblique motion*, or a static melodic line being supported by moving harmony, a very common phenomenon in blues-based music in which reiteration of the tonic is so frequent. Thelonious Monk's "Thelonious" is perhaps the best example of the use of this device in the jazz repertoire (Antonio Carlos Jobim's "One Note Samba" is another obvious example). Note that oblique motion is generally accompanied by *reharmonization* as well.

Ex. 2.18

"Thelonious" A section

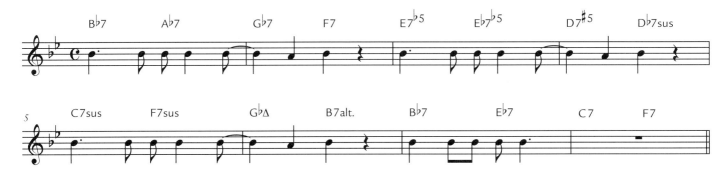

(Bill Holman's "Dial 1" is another great example of a composition based on a single note motif, as is the B section of Joshua Redman's "Heading Home" on the album "Mood Swing", which is also a good example of oblique motion – see DISCOGRAPHY).

Clearly, then, it is crucial for the jazz composer to draw inspiration from what happens on the bandstand in an improvised context. Good composition in jazz often "sounds improvised", in large part because our composers have sought to emulate this interactive dynamic between soloist and accompanist(s) in their orchestration, and such orchestration of these interactive roles often includes the drums as well.

Of course it is obvious that such motivic manipulation is an important part of structuring extended pieces and arrangements. Gil Evans, in his arrangement for the Claude Thornhill band of "What Price Love" (Charlie Parker's original title for the piece that would later become more popularly known as "Yardbird Suite"), primarily employs *augmentation* and *displacement* of the main thematic motif in structuring his startling coda, but also *embellishes* and *reharmonizes* it.

Ex. 2.19

Original theme statement

Ex. 2.20

Theme in augmentation in the coda

(This is reminiscent of Strayhorn's drastic reworking of the theme of Tchaikovsky's "Arab Dance", also accomplished in part by means of augmentation – see also Chapter 8)

In his seminal early 30's masterpiece "Creole Rhapsody" Ellington, in rapid succession, establishes an initial motif, transposes it up a minor third (Blues influence), then creates a consequent phrase by *embellishing* it (by adding notes before this final reiteration, a device he would return to in "Tone Parallel to Harlem" – see also Chapter 8.)

Ex. 2.21

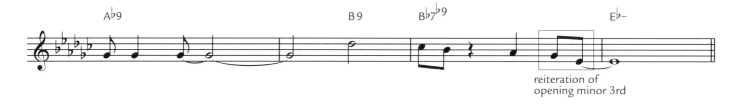

reiteration of
opening minor 3rd

In a later section of the piece, an ABAC songform is created out of this consequent phrase, presented in fresh harmonic, rhythmic, and instrumental settings. This resultant "sweet" theme is presented first by trumpet in its simplest and harmonically most basic form, then subsequently reharmonized in a duet between piano and clarinet. Both iterations follow.

Ex. 2.22

The "sweet" theme (from Ellington's sketch score at the Smithsonian)
original presentation

Later reharmonized presentation

Ellington frequently used the same material in this manner to create contrasting "sweet" and "hot" themes. This provided continuity and contrast to the music without creating new material, the ultimate in economy of means. As we will see in Chapters 7 and 8, there are many such examples to be found in the work of great jazz composers such as Duke Ellington and Charles Mingus.

Stylistic Characteristics Found in the Work of Jazz Composers

Finally, although we have said that the same mechanical manipulations of melody, harmony and rhythm may exist in the work of both jazz and popular composers, it is worth noting that there are stylistic markers which tend to be relatively more prevalent in the work of jazz composers. These might for example, include:

· A greater reliance on *harmonic richness* (use of color tones such as 9ths, 11ths, and 13ths) as expressed in either *melody* or the accompanying *harmony*.

· A proportionally greater reliance on riff-based and/or rhythmically reiterative thematic material;

· A greater degree of *angularity* and/or *rhythmic density* in melodic contour (this is perhaps due to the fact that many jazz compositions are *instrumental*, rather than *vocal*, in conception).

ASSIGNMENTS

Before going any further, three assignments are in order:

1.) **Listen** to all of the examples cited in this Chapter.

2.) Second, find your own examples of pieces illustrating the techniques of motivic manipulation discussed in this Chapter.

· One example should be from an extended or multi-movement piece (for any type of ensemble – note that extended motivically-based compositions need not necessarily be for large ensemble! – "A Love Supreme" is for quartet, for example, see also Chapter 8). This assignment could be summarized as follows: find a "Macro" application of motivic organization.

· One example should be of this technique as used in a "tune" (i.e. a 32-bar *songform* or a Blues, as was seen in "Satin Doll", or "Witch Hunt", for example). This assignment, in other words, is to find a "Micro" application of motivic structure.

3.) Find two contrasting examples, one by a jazz composer, the other a "standard" (Broadway show tune or movie theme that has become a part of the Jazz repertoire), which demonstrate contrasting approaches in terms of degree of melodic or harmonic tension and rhythmic density as a function of style (as illustrated in Ex. 2.22).

4.) Do a writing exercise where you compose a simple 8 or 16-bar melody, developed entirely from a simple motif of no more than 4 notes.

5.) Listen to the main theme of Ellington's "Tattooed Bride" and analyze its motivic similarity to "Satin Doll".

6.) Transcribe Sonny Rollins' first chorus on "St. Thomas". Note how in each case the initial motivic statement returns at the end of the chorus as a *consequent* phrase.

ADVICE

Some important points to consider in doing this exercise would be:

A.) Sometimes it makes sense to apply a variety of developmental devices to your motif before beginning to compose. In other words, don't just write "left to right". The first thing you think of needn't be the first thing the listener hears. I often begin by trying out a given idea in a variety of *rhythmic* settings (different meters, on the beat, off the beat, etc.) and over a variety of harmonies (or even with no harmonic accompaniment at all!). Regardless of how long a piece you are writing you might want to start in this manner by "establishing your palette". Then you can decide what order to put things in, and when a complementary or contrasting musical idea is necessitated to connect these ideas. Remember, the listener doesn't always need to hear your core idea in measure 1.

B.) **Keep it Simple.** Successful (memorable) motifs are more often than not simple, and as such inherently more manipulable than more complex ideas, whose potential for use in diverse harmonic and rhythmic settings may be circumscribed by their complexity. Simple ideas are also easier to establish and remember, and will therefore be more effective for you in communicating with your listeners.

C.) **Emphasize different elements from one piece or thematic statement to the next.** Some compositions, or developmental episodes within a composition, place more emphasis on harmony than rhythm, and vice versa. Challenge yourself to change the emphasis and proportional importance of these various musical elements each time you write a new piece, or with each restatement of your initial motif within a given composition.

D.) As you gain experience, try not to compose exclusively at your instrument. Especially when writing for ensembles, the ideal soundworld exists in your inner ear, and is inevitably compromised by your limitations when you attempt to reproduce the music at your instrument (not to mention at the computer[!]), no matter how well you play. As you listen to and compose more music, this will become easier. Most of what we hear in our mind we have heard before. It is the new combinations of this input that we are listening for and trying to give voice to when we compose. If you are having difficulty hearing your ideas for a given instrument or instrumental combination, the key is to listen to more music employing this instrumentation, rather than depending upon electronic playback to condition your ears.

CHAPTER 3

The Blues

O f course much has been written about the origins of the Blues. Given when it took place, this evolution is really impossible to document precisely. However, most scholars seem to agree that over time what was initially a marriage of African vocal practice to the basic harmonic elements found in English hymns[1] evolved into two related musical forms: Gospel Music (which was *sacred*) and the Blues (which was *secular*)[2]. Eventually the vocal form of the Blues evolved into a parallel instrumental form. This form carried with it many of the same key elements of its vocal precursor. And while the Blues also evolved into a distinct genre of music, separate from jazz and other popular forms, its primary musical elements (form, harmony, melody, and rhythm) have exerted a pervasive influence on them all.

Harmony of the Blues

Although not all Blues forms are uniform in length or structure (including the earliest of notated Blues, such as "St. Louis Blues" by W.C. Handy, the "Father of the Blues"[3]), for the contemporary jazz musician, the "Blues" is generally taken to mean its most commonly used *12-bar form*. The 12-bar form may have many harmonic variations, depending upon how it is interpreted (or even within a single performance). The general formula, however, usually involves the following basic harmonic structure:

Ex. 3.1

[1] Schuller, Gunther. *Early Jazz, Its Roots and Musical Development.* Oxford, 1968, p. 34
[2] Boyer, Horace Clarence. *How Sweet the Sound, The Golden Age of Gospel.* Elliott & Clark, Washington, D.C., 1995
[3] Handy, *W.C. Father of the Blues: An Autobiography.* Da Capo, New York, 1941 (1969)

The most important events in this harmonic scheme are:

1.) The arrival at the IV chord in measure 5, and

2.) A cadence of some sort (most commonly ii–7 - V7 or V7 - IV7) in measures 9 and 10, followed by...

3.) a return to the tonic in measures 11 and 12 by means of stylized "Blues endings" or by using a *turnaround* (I - vi - ii - V or one of its many common practice variants – see also Chapter 3 of "Jazz Harmony"[4]).

Of course, depending upon the era and individual composition involved, many harmonic variations are possible, as mentioned above. Here is a basic paradigm for the most commonly used harmonic variations of the standard 12-bar Blues:

Ex. 3.2

Major Blues paradigm (key = F major)[5]

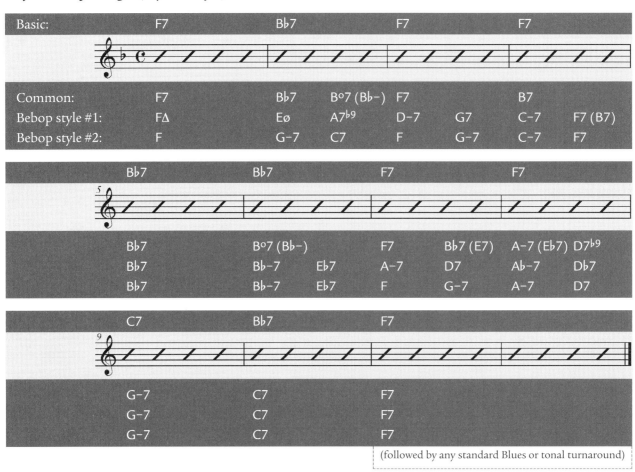

Basic:	F7		Bb7		F7		F7	
Common:	F7		Bb7	Bo7 (Bb–)	F7		B7	
Bebop style #1:	FΔ		Eø	A7b9	D–7	G7	C–7	F7 (B7)
Bebop style #2:	F		G–7	C7	F	G–7	C–7	F7

	Bb7		Bb7		F7		F7	
	Bb7		Bo7 (Bb–)		F7		Bb7 (E7)	A–7 (Eb7)	D7b9
	Bb7		Bb–7	Eb7	A–7	D7	Ab–7	Db7
	Bb7		Bb–7	Eb7	F	G–7	A–7	D7

	C7		Bb7		F7	
	G–7		C7		F7	
	G–7		C7		F7	
	G–7		C7		F7	

(followed by any standard Blues or tonal turnaround)

(Of course these basic variants will all be further modified through the use of such common practice devices as "sideslipping" and "substitute dominants".)

Bebop style #1 and #2 above may be found in such compositions as "Blues For Alice" and "Au Privave".

---

[4] Jaffe, Andy. *Jazz Harmony, Second Edition*, Advance Music, Rottenburg, Germany, 1996, p. 37

[5] ibid., p. 147

In comparing, for example, the chord progression of "Blues for Alice" (corresponding to the "Bebop Style Variation", above) with that of "West End Blues" *(basic)*, we find that the latter emphasizes a relatively basic three-chord format, not even employing the dominant seventh chord until bar 4, while the former has replaced the stereotypical tonic seventh chord with a major chord, after which it progresses directly through the cycle of fifths, *backcyling*[6] to its ultimate goal of arrival at the IV chord in measure 5 ("backcycling" is the process of working backwards through the cycle of 5ths to find an alternative starting point for a chord progression that will still arrive at the predetermined goal.)

This greater proportional emphasis on harmony over melody is typical of Bebop – given the harmonic complexity of such progressions these melodies often sound like an improvised solo. In contrast to Parker's instrumentally-inspired tune, Armstrong's melody, as is so often the case, shows *vocal* influence.

Ex. 3.3

"West End Blues"[7]

[6] Pass, Joe. *Chord Encounters for Guitar, Book 1: Blues, Chords, and Substitutions.* Charles Hansen, Los Angeles, 1979
[7] Jaffe, p. 38

Ex. 3.4

"Blues for Alice" chord changes[8]

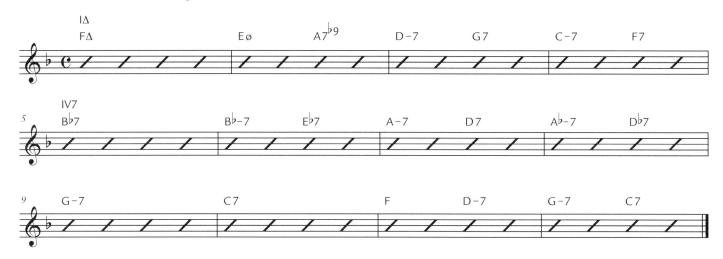

Of course, many other harmonic variations are possible within this basic framework, and it would be incorrect to state that Parker's tunes or improvisations demonstrate a universal reliance on harmonic content (listen also to "Au Privave" or "K. C. Blues" for example), or that the reverse was necessarily true of Armstrong.

Minor Blues

Minor Blues is also a common form, differing from its major counterpart in that its tonic chord and iv chord are of minor quality, while its cadential options are those found in minor tonality (most commonly either iiø in measure 9, followed by V7♭9 or (♭9, ♭13) in measure 10, or ♭VI7 in measure 9, followed by the minor key dominant in measure 10):

Ex. 3.5

Minor Blues schematic

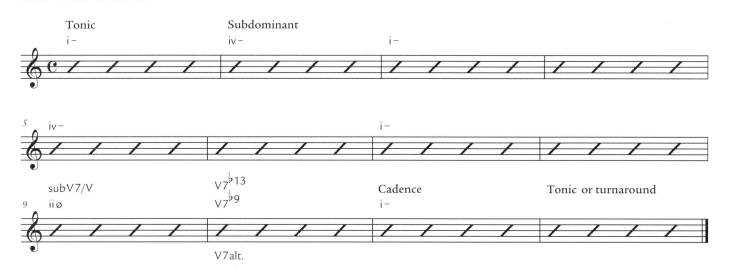

8 ibid., p. 144

Another possible variant on the *minor Blues* is a *modal Blues*, in which the chords are neither purely dominant, nor primarily in a minor mode. Such an example would be the well known Miles Davis blues, "All Blues", from the album "Kind of Blue", which is not only modal, but also in triple meter (yet another example of "paradigm inversion" from this incredibly influential recording).

Ex. 3.6

"All Blues"

Of course a Blues could be in any meter, with the 3/4 meter being the most common other than 4/4. Frank Foster's "Simone" is another example of a 3/4 modal Blues (see DISCOGRAPHY and end of Chapter ASSIGNMENTS). Note that the 3/4 blues, if notated in 6/8, will still have 12 bars, while if it is notated in 3/4 it will have 24, with all of its landmark events occurring in comparably augmented rhythmic values (i.e the IV chord will appear in measure 9, the cadence in measure 17, etc. – see also end of Chapter ASSIGNMENTS):

Ex. 3.7

Triple meter Blues form schematic

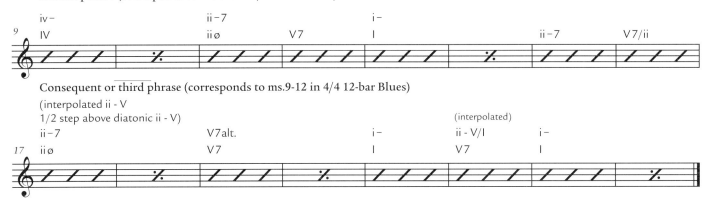

Thad Jones' "Ahunk, Ahunk" is an example of a Blues in 5/4. (Be sure to review this piece again when you are reading the upcoming section on "Phrase Structure".) The modernity of this piece is evidenced not just in terms of its meter, but also in its angular melodic contour (unsurprisingly Monkish, given that Jones had previously worked with Monk) and *through-composed* melody (again, with regard to the phrase structure, this piece is neither AAB, AA'B, nor riff-based):

Ex. 3.8

"Ahunk, Ahunk"[9]

[9] Jones, Thad. pub. Kendor Music, Delevan, N.Y., 1974

Harmonic Implications of Melodic Content

Of course a great deal has been made of discussing the so-called "Blues Scale". What we think of today as the "Blues scale" is probably as much a pedagogical convenience as anything else. That having been acknowledged, most students and practitioners of the music would probably at least agree that the Blues scale involves some "tempering" of the diatonic scale through the presence of "Blue notes" (chromatically lowered versions of the diatonic *scale tones* 3, 5, and 7):

Ex. 3.9A

Blue notes in the key of C

Sometimes these notes coexist with their diatonic counterparts, while on other occasions they may replace them, as illustrated by the following two typical Blues melodic phrases.

Ex. 3.9B

Ex. 3.9C

It is particularly interesting to note that in the major form at least, both thirds, major and minor, often coexist (as shown above in Ex. 3.9B).

Many of our characteristic jazz sonorities have evolved because of the superimposition of Blue Notes on the three primary chords of the basic Blues progression, I, IV and V.

Ex. 3.10A

I7$^{\sharp 9}$

C7$^{\sharp 9}$

Ex. 3.10B

IV7

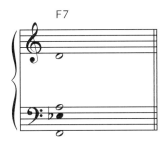

Ex. 3.10C

$V7^{\flat 13}$

Indeed, it is arguable that both the I and IV chords evolved into seventh chords, as opposed to triads, precisely in this way. In any event, it is important to understand that this process of "Bluesification" can also affect other, more tonally-based, harmonies. Still in the C Major Blues tonality, here are some other examples of the tonal effects of the superimposition of Blue notes on various other commonly used chords:

Ex. 3.10D

$V7^{\flat 9, \flat 13}/V7$

Ex. 3.10E

V7alt./ii

A7alt.

Often, a secondary tonal axis for the Blues scale can be found on the sixth degree of the major scale. Sometimes referred to as the "Major Blues scale", this version was favored by Lester Young and many other Swing-based players.

"C Major Blues scale"

Of course, in the minor tonality this variation would not include the major third:

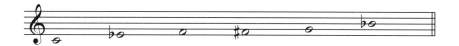

As the previous examples (3.10) illustrate, superimposing the primary Blue notes on the primary harmonies (I, IV, and the various cadential seventh chords outlined above) yields characteristic color tones. This is true in minor tonality as well. In fact the commonly used subdominant option in minor, ♭VI7, is often voiced in such a way that it is comprised almost exclusively of characteristic notes from the "Minor Blues scale".

A♭7⁹,¹³

A♭7

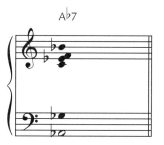

Indeed, this "♭VI7" dominant chord is frequently found in minor key compositions, not just the Blues. Of course, the same can be said of the characteristic major Blues sonorities described earlier. This enrichment of the tonal palette of jazz composers through the embrace of these "borrowed" common practice Blues sonorities has been employed throughout the history of the music to impart a Blues flavor in tonal settings.

♭VI7 is used commonly for this purpose, whether the primary tonality is major or minor (see Ex. 2.21, the intro of "Creole Rhapsody", where the piece is in E♭ minor and the B7 functions as ♭VI7, and Ex. 2.19 "Yardbird Suite", where the piece is in E♭ major and the C♭ or B7 functions as ♭VI7 once again).

Charles Mingus' "Goodbye Porkpie Hat" (see end of Chapter Assignments) illustrates that using Blues-based material is one time-honored method for the jazz composer to assure that his or her work remains accessible, without compromising harmonic interest. Given the harmonic confluence between the minor modes and minor Blues, the advent of the "modal" period in the late 1950's resulted in many 12-bar Blues compositions where the tonic and iv chords were voiced in ways which emphasized this similarity. So a piece like John Coltrane's "Equinox", for example", is informed by the modal aesthetic, stylistically speaking, while it is a minor Blues in form.

Finally, Blues-based harmonic and melodic gestures have been equally pervasive in virtually all popular styles. The Blues form is ubiquitous in both "Rhythm & Blues" and "Rock & Roll" (see end of Chapter Assignments).

The opening phrase of the A section of Hoagy Carmichael's "Stardust" illustrates the Blues-based proclivity for emphasizing on the IV chord which is so common in popular song:

Ex. 3.14

The melody of this piece also exploits the common Blues-based juxtaposition between major and minor thirds:

Of course, Duke Ellington (and Bubber Miley's) "It Don't Mean a Thing If It Ain't Got that Swing" also incorporates the common practice Blues-based melodic device of the flatted 5th in its melody.

Ex. 3.15

Each of these examples demonstrates one or more stylistic aspect of the Blues being brought to bear on the construction of popular standards, though clearly some of these examples sound "jazzier" than others do. Other interpretive factors, especially the rhythmic context, are clearly at work in shaping our perception of their respective musical styles.

Such examples reinforce the notion that there are indeed specific elements of melodic, rhythmic, and harmonic content in a given composition that make it "sound like jazz". Given the fact that, with regard to melodic and harmonic technique (see also Chapter 4), there is little distinction between the resources of Jazz and popular composers prior to the so-called "modal" period, it is indeed phrase structure, packaging, and the use of rhythm that distinguishes the work of a jazz composer from that of others employing comparable harmonic materials. French musicologist Laurent Cugny differentiates between *bona fide* jazz compositions, and "standards", which have been embraced by jazz players to become a part of our repertoire, by describing the latter as pieces "pour le jazz"[10]. This is in a sense another way of saying that jazz is perhaps better defined in terms of process than in terms of repertoire. There is no doubt, for example, that composers such as Gershwin and Hoagy Carmichael were profoundly influenced by jazz in their compositional process, and that we find similar harmonic practice at work in their music as in that of Ellington. It must also be noted that whether or not a given performance of one of their pieces "sounds (and feels) like jazz" of course rests as much with the manner in which it is interpreted as it does with its notated content.

10 Cugny, Laurent. *L'analyse de l'oeuvre de jazz. Specificites theoriques et metho-dologiques*, Doctoral Thesis, Sorbonne, Paris, 2001, p.66

Phrase Structure of the Blues

The ubiquitous influence of the 12-bar Blues is not confined to its harmonic implications however. Its phrase structure is also very significant. By far the most common form of 12-bar Blues is that which is found in the commonly used "storytelling" (or narrative) AAB structure. In this format, one line is repeated over the first eight bars of the progression, followed by a consequent ("B"), or "response" phrase that accompanies the cadence in measures 9-12:

Ex. 3.16

Lyrics to the first chorus of Bessie Smith's "Backwater Blues"

A1:   *When it rained five days the sky turned dark as night;*
A2:   *When it rained five days the sky turned dark as night;*
B: *Then trouble takin' place in the lowlands at night.*

Of course, this AAB strophic dynamic can be found in instrumental Blues as well. Note how the following example, while clearly a 12-bar Blues in both harmonic and strophic form, features a melody that is primarily diatonic save for a single Blue note:

Ex. 3.17

Blues in the style of "Creole Love Call"

As the instrumental AAB form evolved on its own, a frequent scenario resulted in which the second "A" was varied, as in "Straight, No Chaser", or "Bessie's Blues":

Bessie's Blues

Certainly the AAB or AA'B phrase structures are not the only formats to be found in the Blues. Especially during the Big Band era, "riff" Blues were often used, in which the same simple idea was repeated three times over the 12-bar form:

Riff Blues in the style of "C Jam Blues" or "Sonny Moon For Two"

One exemplar of the variety of available non-12-bar formats used would be Nat Adderley and Oscar Brown, Jr's "Work Song". Certainly this piece is Blues in melodic and harmonic content, though it has a 16-bar form. And a piece like Bobby Timmons' "Moanin'" is also assuredly Blues-based in melodic and harmonic content, though not in form *per se*.

Finally, the argument can be made that it is indeed the phrase structure, more importantly than the harmonic format, which defines the Blues. The listener's intuitive sense of expectation was surely being exploited by Charles Mingus in "Nostalgia in Times Square". The melody of the piece has a clear AAB phrase structure, yet its unique harmonic structure is hardly arbitrary, but rather results from its multi-tasking "♭VII7" (D♭7 in its E♭ minor tonality) chord. The chord initially appears as an auxiliary chord in a vamp figure with the tonic (ms.1-3), then resolves down a fifth to the G♭–7 chord (ms.4-5), and finally down a half-step to a C–7 (ms.8-9), to begin a cycle of fifths based series of cadences to that returns to the tonic via reiteration of the chord's initial auxiliary role.

Ex. 3.20

Nostalgia in Times Square

Mingus exploited the familiarity of the Blues form to create a study in the use of a single, dominant seventh chord (E♭7) that functioned as a multifarious harmonic pivot point, leading in each of its successive resolutions to a different strategic landmark in the overall phrase structure of the piece (see also ASSIGNMENT 9 below).

ASSIGNMENTS

1.) Listen to all the examples cited in the chapter.

2.) Find comparable examples of your own of AAB, major, and minor Blues (vocal or instrumental).

3.) Find examples of "standards" which illustrate the use of common practice melodic or harmonic elements from the Blues.

4.) Find an example of a non-12-bar Blues or a 12-bar form with atypical harmony (like "Nostalgia in Times Square").

5.) Write a 12-bar AAB Blues.

6.) Find an example of a modal Blues or a Blues not in 4/4.

7.) Transcribe Frank Foster's "Simone" (see discography).

8.) Write a 24-bar Blues in triple meter (see Ex. 3.7 and accompanying discussion).

9.) Analyze the relationship of melody to the supporting harmony of Charles Mingus' "Goodbye Porkpie Hat", ms.1 and 2 (i.e. melodic function; 7, 9, ♯11, 13, etc.). Also do a complete harmonic analysis of the composition's first 5 chords. How does the composer move from the first chord (i−) to the iv− chord two bars later? (Transcription found in Ex. 8.42).

10.) Transcribe an example of a Rock & Roll or Rhythm & Blues tune that features the prominent use of Blue notes in its melody (one such example might be the Beatles' "Taxman").

CHAPTER 4

Harmony

Jazz composers have primarily employed three types of harmonic systems: Tonal, Modal, and Blues-based (Blues-based harmony was just discussed in Chapter 3). In compositions from the late 1940's and forward (i.e. prior to the advent of the popularity of the so-called "modal" style *per se*), examples of mixed modal and tonal harmonic progressions are commonly found, as are chord progressions employing modal sonorities in the more rapid harmonic rhythm associated with more complex tonal progressions. Similarly, the so-called "Hard Bop" style of playing often integrated the Blues-based harmonic and melodic practice of "Rhythm & Blues" into existing formal structures. In other words, these "new" sounds were rapidly incorporated into existing common practice forms, as has been the case throughout the development of the music. Bearing in mind, then, that the examination of harmony as an isolated study does not divorce it from the larger context of the musical style within which it exists, an overview of these general harmonic building blocks follows. (This is a good time to be sure that you have reviewed your understanding of tonal harmony and its analysis.)

Changing the harmonic context in which a given melodic phrase is placed can drastically change its role within the piece. This process, known as reharmonization, will be discussed in this Chapter as well.

Tonal Harmony

The prevalence of tonal harmony in jazz reflects the common practice of the music of the 19th century that initially formed the harmonic foundation for the earliest jazz improvisers and composers. Early jazz musicians were familiar with the music of opera composers, and they also knew popular dance tunes of the day, and of course they were familiar with Rags, Marches and Church music as well. The harmonic characteristics and practices of this music remained essentially unchanged in the music of Tin-Pan Alley composers in subsequent years. (In fact, as noted in Chapter 3, in matters relating to functional harmony there is not a great deal of difference between the Tin Pan Alley and jazz composers of the 20's and 30's. This cross-pollination is hardly surprising given the frequent intermingling of the two groups and the embrace of the Tin Pan Alley and Broadway repertoire by jazz musicians.)

Most of this music employs diatonic harmony, enhanced by secondary and occasional substitute dominant sevenths, passing diminished seventh chords, and the odd Blues-based harmony.

It is not unusual to find Gershwin and Ellington each employing similar harmonic devices. Compare the following two examples (the first by Gershwin, the second by Ellington):

Ex. 4.1

"Nice Work If You Can Get It"

Ex. 4.2

Bridge of "Sophisticated Lady"

In both of these cases the composer is employing the common technique known as "extended dominant sevenths", or a chain of dominant chords in the cycle of fifths. This was one way in which composers of this era were able to step outside of the realm of the purely diatonic, and exhibits the frequently used scenario of supporting the diatonic, singable melody, with a chain of non-diatonic dominant chords (usually, though not always, ending on the V7 of the key). The use of secondary dominant seventh chords not only enables this chromatic enrichment of an otherwise diatonic texture, it also provides horizontal momentum to the piece as a result of the need for resolution created by these dominant seventh chords. Imagine either of the above examples accompanied by diatonic harmony on the same roots (better yet, play them and compare), and the comparative lack of richness and harmonic momentum is evident. For example:

Ex. 4.3A

Of course, sometimes the secondary dominant is used to support non-diatonic melody to equally good effect. An example from one of Ellington's most famous pieces illustrates the marriage of these two devices (in Ex. 4.3B the chromatic alteration is also a "bluesified" one, as suggested by the title of the piece):

Ex. 4.3B

First four bars of "Mood Indigo"

This is not to say that purely diatonic chord progressions or melodies are uncommon.

Turnarounds (chord progressions based on the I‑vi‑ii‑V7 progression or any of its commonly used substitutions) are one of the most common building blocks in jazz and popular composition. The following well-known examples (4.4‑4.6) of pieces from the repertoire illustrate the use of this device, and in each case the harmony is diatonic.

Ex. 4.4

"I Got Rhythm" (Gershwin)

Ex. 4.5A

"Rockin' in Rhythm"(Ellington)

The consequent phrase of the A section of "Rockin' in Rhythm" is a good example of the use of parallel diatonic harmony.

Ex. 4.5B

The chord progression to the bridge of "Moten Swing", which is based on the harmonic progression to "You're Drivin' Me Crazy" (a more thorough discussion of the "contrafact" can be found in Chapter 7):

Ex. 4.6

As the use of substitute dominant seventh and modal interchange chords became more prevalent among jazz and popular composers, the turnaround often took on more chromatic root motion and began to employ a variety of these non-diatonic chord substitutions for the diatonic chords employed in the previous examples. However the same underlying effect of a four-chord sequence ending on the dominant or its most common substitutes ("subV7/I", or "♭IIΔ") is maintained.

Ex. 4.7

Well-known "substitute dominant" root motion as seen in Tadd Dameron's "Ladybird" turnaround

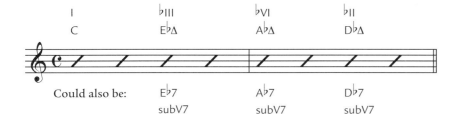

This common practice device (the turnaround) may be expressed in so many different ways that it becomes more of a gesture than a technique, wherein virtually any sequence of 4 chords at the end of a phrase creates this effect, regardless of harmonic function (Strayhorn's "Isfahan", for example, employs a turnaround of parallel descending major seventh chords at the end of its first A section – see End of Chapter ASSIGNMENTS).

It is worth reiterating that most of these devices were in use from the very beginnings of the music (even though they may be generally associated with later styles), and that the tonal resources available to the jazz composer had not changed appreciably from the beginnings of the music through the 1950's.

Consider Jelly Roll Morton's "King Porter Stomp", in which the opening bars employ the "♭VII7" chord (G♭7) preceding the V7/ii chord (F7):

Ex. 4.8

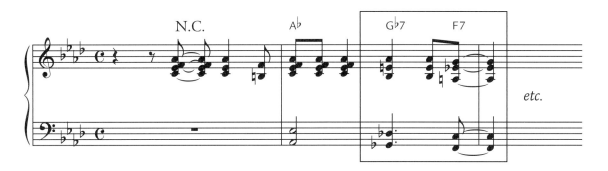

The coda of James P. Johnson's "Carolina Shout" (1918) illustrates the use of substitute dominant seventh chords (compare with the "Ladybird" cadence, shown in Ex. 4.7 above):

Ex. 4.9

Substitute Dominant Harmony and Sideslipping

Of course in later years such harmonic practice was unquestionably more commonplace. It can be found frequently in the work of both Ellington and Monk.

Ex. 4.10

Opening bars of Monk's "Pannonica"

And pieces like Ellington's "Who Knows" and Monk's "Ask Me Now" (see discussion, p. 56-59) employ the technique of backcycling to create their progressions.

Even such common practice devices as the well-known "Count Basie Ending" were in existence long before their popularization by the artist with whom they are most associated. To review, the distinctive sound of the "Basie Ending" is produced through the use of *chromatic connecting chords*, usually diminished 7ths, based on Blues-based voice-leading (i.e. the non-diatonic notes in the middle chord are also Blue notes in the key):

Ex. 4.11

Revisiting "King Porter Stomp" (circa 1906[1]), we see this same device at work, this time to approach the dominant (V7) chord:

Ex 4.12

The "Carolina Shout", written some dozen years later, used nearly the identical chord progression in the parallel measures of its introduction to ornament its dominant chord, D7:

Ex. 4.13

[1] Dapogny, James. *Ferdinand "Jelly Roll" Morton, The Collected Piano Music.* Smithsonian Institution Press, Washington, D.C. (and G. Schirmer, New York), 1982, p. 496

The examples above clearly exemplify the practice of Blues-based voice-leading. However, it should be noted that the use of passing diminished sevenths and other connecting chords, like most other common harmonic devices in jazz, could also be said to have been inherited from the Western Classical tradition. Two examples of such cadences may be found in Chopin's "Prelude #4 in E minor", and Mozart's "Fantasia in C minor" (K575), respectively (see end of Chapter ASSIGNMENTS).

Of course these progressions are frequently found in the popular repertoire as well. For example, the following generic chord progression may be found in the first four bars of many standards, including "Ain't Misbehavin'", "Makin' Whoopee", and "You Took Advantage of Me", among others:

Ex. 4.14

Generic formula

Though these connecting diminished 7th chords are most commonly found in the *ascending* form (as shown above), they may also occasionally *descend* chromatically, as in Jobim's "Wave" for example, in the very first measure (see end of Chapter ASSIGNMENTS).

Another ubiquitous harmonic building block is the use of the ii-V7 cadence to "tonicize" a major seventh chord other than the tonic. Most frequently it is the IV chord that is targeted in this manner, as in the bridge of "Satin Doll" for example – see Ex. 2.11, p. 18). Here the generic progression would be ii-7-V7/IV to or in the key of C: G-7-C7-FΔ.

Ex. 4.15

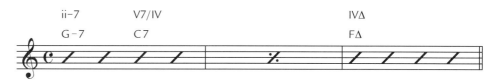

The use of "modal interchange" major seventh chords (so-called "borrowed" harmonies) allows for the option of further expanding the tonality through the tonicization of other non-tonic major seventh chords:

Ex. 4.16

Ms.9-12 of "Blue Bossa"

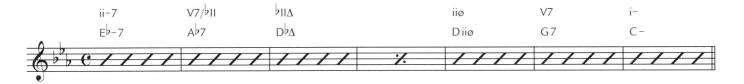

Modal Interchange

"Modal Interchange" may be globally defined as the juxtaposition or integration of diatonic harmonies from parallel modal forms (in the "Blue Bossa" progression illustrated above, for example, the D♭Δ chord is "borrowed" from the parallel C Phrygian mode, as well as having been tonicized by its own ii-V7, although the overall tonal center of the piece clearly remains C). Most commonly, these progressions are created when harmonies are "borrowed" from parallel minor modes in progressions and used in the parallel major key.

For example, in the generic progression illustrated below (as found in such standards as "What's New" and "Do You Know What It Means to Miss New Orleans", among many others), almost all of the harmonies in the A section are borrowed from and/or used to tonicize chords from various forms of C minor, although the tonality of the piece remains C major.

Ex. 4.17A

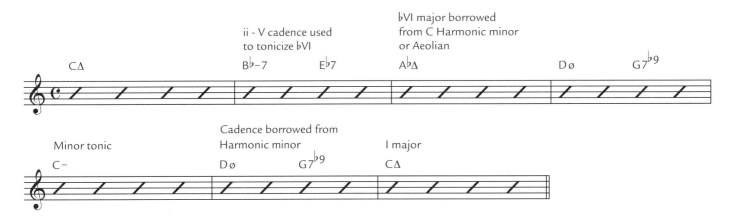

Composer/pianist Art Lande's "Waltz for A" (see DISCOGRAPHY) illustrates the deliberate formal juxtaposition of diatonic and modal interchange materials. In the first 12 bars, both the melodic and harmonic material are completely diatonic to the key (F major, notwithstanding the lack of key signature), while in the second half (final 12 bars) of the piece *both* the harmony and melody are derived from parallel minor modes (Aeolian and Phrygian), thereby creating an increasing level of harmonic tension as the piece unfolds. Analyze this piece harmonically, being sure to review the modal sources for each of the chords used in the final 12 bars:

Ex. 4.17B

WALTZ FOR A.

Art Lande

This is a process which one can find at work in the music of Bach as well (indeed one of the best-known common practice harmonic gestures in Baroque music is the use of the "Picardy" third, or ending a minor key composition on the parallel major tonic).

Thelonious Monk famously employs this device at the conclusion of the A section of "Round Midnight". The entire A section has been in Eb minor,

Ex. 4.18

...but then ends in the parallel major (based on the solo piano recording on Columbia):

Of course, many of these examples beg the question of the boundary between modulation and *tonicization*. There is no absolute distinction between the two, other than the application of the combined resources of one's musical intuition and aural perception. The bridge of "In a Sentimental Mood" for example, goes from the primary key of the A section, F major, directly to Db. Most musicians would consider that to be a *modulation*, while the move to Ab Major in measure 3 Ex. 4.17A above seems not to be. We probably hear the two cases differently as a result of such common sense factors as the duration of the chords and their strategic location within the form of the piece.

"In a Sentimental Mood" analysis of changes

IN A SENTIMENTAL MOOD

Duke Ellington

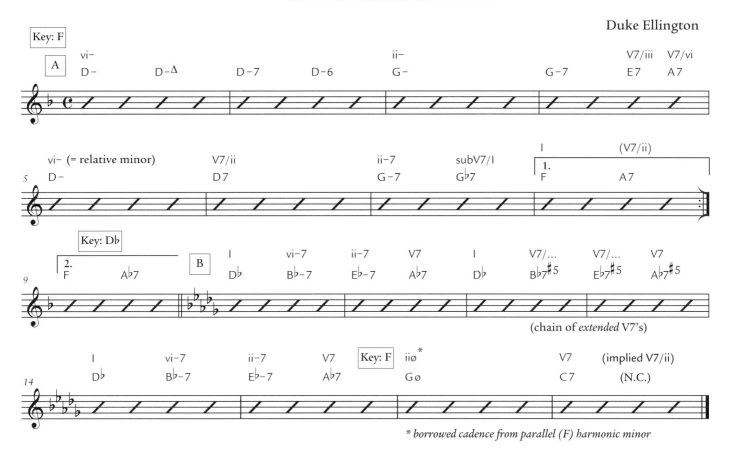

(chain of *extended* V7's)

* *borrowed cadence from parallel (F) harmonic minor*

Another type of modulation, based on the concept of the *pivot chord* (or chords), works based on the potential for a given chord or cadence to work in both the old and new keys. "All the Things You Are" works in this manner, for example, exploiting the fact that the Db∆ chord in measure 5 is at once the diatonic IV chord in the primary key (Ab) and the bII∆ in the new key C.

Ex. 4.20

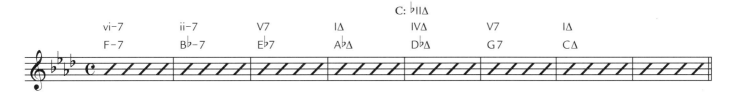

Another type of indirect modulation can occur when a chain of cadences is used to prepare a new key. In such cases, sometimes called *transitional* modulations, the new key is established when one of the cadences in the sequence finally resolves to a different key than the one in which the progression began:

Ex.4.21

Excerpt from "Dersu", by the author

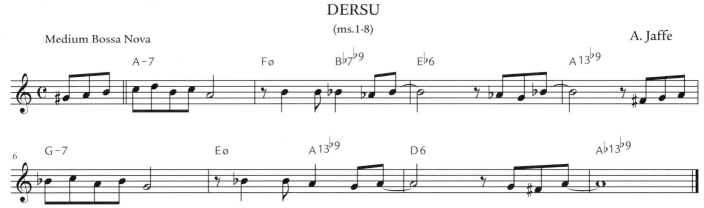

DERSU
(ms.1-8)

Medium Bossa Nova

A. Jaffe

Note the way in which the melodic sequence combines to create a sense of logic in the phrase structure, deemphasizing, perhaps even concealing, its modulatory character (This sort of effect also occurs in the first 8 bars of "Along Came Betty" by Benny Golson – see end of Chapter ASSIGNMENTS).

The concept of repeating a melodic motif in a different key area to create a series of temporary modulations can be found in the work of jazz composers in many styles. For example, Wayne Shorter's "Wildflower" and the bridge of Benny Carter's "When Lights Are Low" both use this device to great effect (see also end of Chapter ASSIGNMENTS AND DISCOGRAPHY).

Of course there are occasions when modulations occur abruptly in the middle of a melodic phrase, but these are much less common. The most famous such example from the Jazz repertoire follows:

Ex. 4.22

"Giant Steps" initial three bars with harmonic analysis

(Much more on "Giant Steps" to follow in Chapter 8.)

Regardless of the formal location or harmonic rhythm, however, there can be no doubt that the device of modulation is one which composers have used throughout the history of tonal music to provide formal contrast.

As alluded to earlier (see also Ex. 4.10), a commonly used harmonic phenomenon that became especially prevalent during the Bebop Era is often referred to as "sideslipping". In sideslipping, the commonly used ii-V7 progression is moved chromatically, often from a half step above the primary ii-V7 in the key as a way of creating horizontal momentum and delaying the obvious move to the expected cadence:

Ex. 4.23

Use of "sideslipping" (as found in tunes like Miles Davis' "Half Nelson"*)

(* Davis' "Half Nelson" is actually a contrafact on the chord progression to Tadd Dameron's "Ladybird". In jazz, the term contrafact refers to the common practice, generally associated with, but definitely not innovated during, the Bebop era, of composing a new melody on an existing set of chord changes – see further discussion in Chapter 7. For the time being we note that both the practice and the descriptive term for it have their origins in 9th century Gregorian Chant![2].)

Monk's "Ask Me Now" (as well as "Pannonica", discussed earlier in Ex. 4.10) illustrates an entire composition built on the notion of sideslipping. In typical Monkian gesture, the forward motion of the piece is created by confounding the listener's expectations. Monk's mastery of harmony and knowledge of standard repertoire enabled him to manipulate and confound the harmonic expectations of fellow musicians and listeners alike.

Ex. 4.24

First, Monk establishes his "premise":

Secondly, he creates a sequence of descending chromatic reiterations of the initial motif:

[2] Posch, Michael, and Ambrosini, Marco. *Notes to "Music of The Troubadours"*, Ensemble Unicorn, Naxos Records, Franklin, Tennessee, 1999

Thirdly, he prioritizes the final iteration of the motif by expanding its harmonic rhythm to two beats per chord from one:

Now that he has let us know that this ii-V is the one that finally establishes the tonality (of D♭), he delays the obvious resolution to the tonic by interpolating a deceptive resolution of the V7 chord:

Finally, in order to establish that this is the first ending, Monk's turnaround (ending on the substitute dominant, D7) unexpectedly resolves down a fifth (instead of the expected half step, as it "normally" would, to the tonic), to connect it to the G-7 in the first measure of the second A section to start the entire cycle over again:

(Note: The turnaround chords in ms.8 may vary depending on the recording. On some recordings, Monk plays: B7♭5 - B♭7♭5 - A7♭5 - A♭7♭5, or the tritone substitutes for the chords shown above.)

Monk's understanding of the fact that the substitute dominant 7th chord normally resolves down a half step to the tonic enabled him to exploit this element of surprise in "Ask Me Now" (not only did he know that, but Monk could be sure that his listeners and colleagues, whose expectations of tonal function had been comparably conditioned by the repertoire of the American Songbook, knew to expect it as well, at least intuitively).

A less common version of "sideslipping" occurs when the ii-V7 cadence ascends. Here are three such examples:

Ex. 4.25A

The opening bars of Coltrane's "Moment's Notice"

Ex. 4.25B

Bars 17-25 (beginning of the second A section) of Hermeto Pascoal's "Vale da Ribeira"
illustrate a slightly different variation of this concept,
ascending chromatically to the ii–7 chord of the upcoming cadence

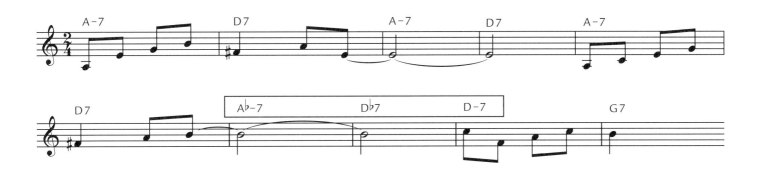

Of course we are much more accustomed to having root motion descend, rather than ascend to begin with, since that is what occurs in any sort of cycle of fifths-based root motion. As a result the ascending effect is inherently more dramatic. It should also be noted that Ex. 4.25B used the indicated chords only on the second repetition of the A section, so in effect it is also an example of reharmonization (harmonically-based recontextualization). The bridge of Kenny Barron's "Voyage" is another excellent example of the use of ascending chromatic harmony (see Discography and end of Chapter Assignments).

Modal Harmony

Although the use of modal harmony is widely and stereotypically thought of as representing a new stylistic innovation in jazz in the late 1950's (said to have begun with "Milestones" by Miles Davis, according to one such interpretation[3]), the concept of modal harmony is in fact another one which predates the jazz idiom. Throughout the world, a variety of musical cultures play music that employs static harmony, or the reiteration of a given mode or scale. The *trouveres* of 12th century Provence essentially played "modal" music. Many Irish traditional reels are of modal quality ("What Do You Do With a Drunken Sailor?", is in the dorian mode for example). Other examples abound in non-Western music. What was "new" about the use of the modal concept in jazz was its attempt to invert the dominant musical paradigm of the time, which in jazz was Bebop. Many of the musicians involved, like Miles Davis, were already acknowledged masters of Bop but sought a less encumbered environment for their musical explorations. By slowing tempos down, simplifying harmonic progressions and melodies, extending the length of improvised solos, and challenging stereotypical paradigms of form, meter, instrumental roles, and instrumentation itself, these musicians drastically altered the landscape and creative possibilities of the music.

Their experiments constituted a real departure in terms of the harmonic resources of the music. While Bebop had essentially continued to use the same harmonic language of the American Songbook and the Blues, with Modal Jazz came a diminution in harmonic complexity.

[3] Kirchner, Bill. *Introduction to "Miles Davis, Kind of Blue"*. Hal Leonard Corporation, Milwaukee, 2001, p.7

To begin this discussion, let's review the basic "church modes" of the diatonic major scale[4].

Ex. 4.26

Diatonic modes of a major scale (C major)

C Ionian (parent scale)

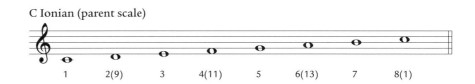

| 1 | 2(9) | 3 | 4(11) | 5 | 6(13) | 7 | 8(1) |

D Dorian (2nd mode)

| 1 | 2(9) | ♭3 | 4(11) | 5 | 6(13) | ♭7 | 8(1) |

E Phrygian (3rd mode)

| 1 | ♭2(♭9) | ♭3 | 4(11) | 5 | ♭6(♭13) | ♭7 | 8(1) |

F Lydian (4th mode)

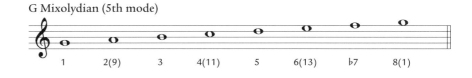

| 1 | 2(9) | 3 | ♯4(♯11) | 5 | 6(13) | 7 | 8(1) |

G Mixolydian (5th mode)

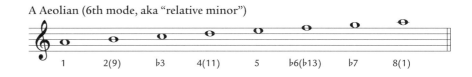

| 1 | 2(9) | 3 | 4(11) | 5 | 6(13) | ♭7 | 8(1) |

A Aeolian (6th mode, aka "relative minor")

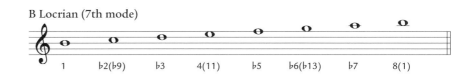

| 1 | 2(9) | ♭3 | 4(11) | 5 | ♭6(♭13) | ♭7 | 8(1) |

B Locrian (7th mode)

| 1 | ♭2(♭9) | ♭3 | 4(11) | ♭5 | ♭6(♭13) | ♭7 | 8(1) |

Some important notes:

· Each mode obviously represents the parent scale, displaced to each make each of its successive degrees the "root".

· Note use of compound interval nomenclature (i.e. 9, 11, 13) were appropriate.

[4] Jaffe, Andy. *Jazz Harmony, Second Edition.* Advance Music, Rottenburg, Germany, 1996, p.21

Of course a mode of a given scale results from playing its notes in the same order, but starting from a different note. As illustrated above, each scale therefore has as many modes as it has notes. (These modes are named in relation to the new root, for example we say F Lydian when a C scale is started on F). Each of these modes (and conceptually speaking, any of the modes of the various minor scales as well, or any other given set of notes, whatever their source) may be employed constitute a self-sufficient tonal world of any duration, exploiting the characteristic sound that results from the lateral shift to the new tonic.

While the best known "pure" modal compositions such as "So What", for example, employ exclusively modal materials, as previously mentioned many contemporary composers employ close juxtaposition of modal and tonal resources within the same composition or section of the form (Horace Silver's "Yeah" or Cedar Walton's "Ugetsu" are such examples).

A mode may be tonicized by means of reiteration (i.e. by being employed in a static way, without a chord progression), or by means of a *modal cadence*. A modal cadence generally moves to or from the tonic chord from a neighboring chord in the mode. A modal cadence always involves the tonic chord and a diatonically adjacent neighbor because this combination yields all of the notes in the mode.

For example, a dorian cadence can move from i− to either ♭VII or ii−:

Ex. 4.27

This is the case in "So What", in which the effect is enhanced through the use of quartal (fourth-based) voicings in the harmonic accompaniment.

Ex. 4.28

Note the other elements of the modal style at work, both harmonically and aesthetically. The "melody", or "call" (in the bass) outlines most of the notes in the mode, and reiterates the tonic. The responsive cadence goes from the ii– chord to the tonic. Thus, both the cadence and the melody emphasize the tonic. Just as Monk knew what his listeners' expectations were in his manipulations of cadential harmony, Miles Davis was equally conscious of stereotypical jazz performance roles. By giving the melody to the bass he was challenging the aesthetic protocol of his time, and the use of modal harmony by his generation of musicians may be seen in that context as well.

Just as the dorian cadence goes from I to ii– or ♭VII, so the characteristic Phrygian cadence moves from I to either ♭II or ♭vii–, or in the case of "Spanish Phrygian" (an octatonic scale originating in the Iberian peninsula and used characteristically in Flamenco Music), from i– to ♭II to ♭III and back. Because the Spanish Phrygian mode features both thirds, its tonic can be major or minor, or both:

Ex. 4.29A

Phrygian Scale

Ex 4.29B

Spanish Phrygian Scale

This juxtaposition of major and minor thirds is similar to that found in the Blues. The following cadence can be found in both Coltrane's "Olé" and Chick Corea's "La Fiesta", though both compositions are likely adapted from a Spanish folk song[5].

Ex. 4.29C

Compound Spanish Phrygian Cadence

5 Porter, Lewis. *John Coltrane, His Life and Music.* Michigan, Ann Arbor, 1998, p.212

Similarly, a Lydian cadence would move back and forth between its tonic and II chords:

Ex. 4.30

Lydian cadence (commonly found in introductions and codas in Brazilian Jazz – see also end of Chapter ASSIGNMENTS)

Note that pedal points and ostinato are also frequently used in this style of composition to reinforce the tonic. Though perhaps obvious, it is also worth noting that a corollary of the inherent parallelism found in modal harmony is the absence of voice-leading as commonly found in diatonic cycle of fifths-based chord progressions.

The Modes of Melodic Minor

The modes of melodic minor, particulary the fourth, (aka the "Lydian dominant" scale), sixth (sometimes known as the "Locrian natural nine" scale), and seventh (best known as the "Altered" scale, though also referred to in some texts as "Superlocrian" or "Diminished whole tone"), are frequently employed as modal sonorities as well as in their more common tonal usages, either cadentially or in modal interchange settings.

Diatonic modes of a Melodic minor scale (C Melodic minor)[6]

C Melodic minor (parent scale)

| 1 | 2(9) | ♭3 | 4(11) | 5 | 6(13) | 7 | 8(1) |

D Dorian ♭9 (2nd mode)

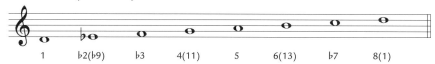

| 1 | ♭2(♭9) | ♭3 | 4(11) | 5 | 6(13) | ♭7 | 8(1) |

E♭ Lydian augmented (3rd mode)

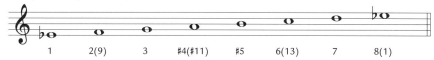

| 1 | 2(9) | 3 | #4(#11) | #5 | 6(13) | 7 | 8(1) |

F Lydian ♭7 (4th mode, aka "Lydian dominant")

| 1 | 2(9) | 3 | #4(#11) | 5 | 6(13) | ♭7 | 8(1) |

G Mixolydian ♭13 (5th mode)

| 1 | 2(9) | 3 | 4(11) | 5 | ♭6(♭13) | ♭7 | 8(1) |

A Locrian ♮9 (6th mode)

| 1 | 2(9) | ♭3 | 4(11) | ♭5 | ♭6(♭13) | ♭7 | 8(1) |

B altered (7th mode)

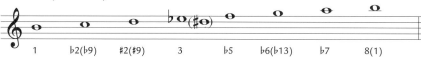

| 1 | ♭2(♭9) | #2(#9) | 3 | ♭5 | ♭6(♭13) | ♭7 | 8(1) |

Some important notes:

· Each mode obviously represents the parent scale, displaced to each make each of its successive degrees the "root".

· Note use of compound interval nomenclature (i.e. 9, 11, 13) were appropriate.

(Note: In jazz theory,"melodic minor" refers only to what would be called the "ascending" form of melodic minor in traditional Classical parlance.) Some examples follow.

6 Jaffe, p.22

The following example illustrates the use of modal interchange lydian dominant (a similar example may be found in the coda to Milton Nascimento's "Gira, Girou").

Ex. 4.31B

Lydian sound produced by superimposition of triad
one step higher on major or dominant chords

An incomplete Lydian dominant sound (implies the full dominant 7th (#11) sound but in fact leaves the 3rd out in order to employ all three of the triadic extensions of the chord; 9, #11 and 13. A favorite of Horace Silver (see end of Chapter ASSIGNMENTS).

Ex. 4.31C

Incomplete B♭7#11 chord implies the complete chord sound
but does not include the 3rd

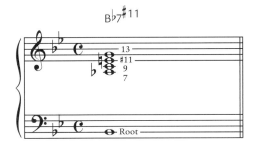

Hermeto Pascoal's "Arapuá" illustrates many uses of parallel modal harmony over an ostinato with a different tonal center, creating both *polytonal* and *polymodal* implications (see DISCOGRAPHY).

A mode may also be established through nothing other than reiteration, which may take a linear or harmonic form. And sets of notes other than those comprising modes of the major and melodic minor scales may also be employed similarly. Related in concept, though not in origin, these so-called "synthetic scales" and modes may also be treated in this same fashion. This group of scales or modes include diminished (aka octatonic), whole tone, hexatonic, and even modes from non-Western music (for a fully detailed discussion of these possibilities, consult Dr. Yusef Lateef's "Repository of Scales and Melodic Patterns"[7]).

[7] Lateef, Yusef. *Repository of Scales and Melodic Patterns.* Fana Music, Amherst, MA. 1981

The ability of jazz to transform itself through the absorption of new materials and aesthetic approaches resulted in the adaptation of existing forms to the new sounds. Blues could now be modal or tonal, and new instrumental combinations changed the sound palette available to composers and arrangers through the influential innovations of Gil Evans and Miles Davis, among others.

Mixed Modal and Tonal Compositions

As mentioned earlier, there are many examples of modal and tonal harmonies being integrated into the same composition, hardly surprising, given the intrinsic potential for formal contrast that the juxtaposition of the two harmonic concepts provides. The use of this compositional device predates the modal period per se, as evidenced by such compositions as Juan Tizol's "Caravan" (1936), Dizzy Gillespie's "A Night in Tunisia" (1944), and Bud Powell's "Un Poco Loco" (1953), all of which create formal contrast in an AABA form based on the juxtaposition of a modal A section with a tonal bridge. Mary Lou Williams' "Aquarius" (from the 1945 "Zodiac Suite"), is another example of a composition featuring mixed modal and tonal elements (primarily in triple meter as well, unlike the other examples mentioned above). Indeed, the influence of various "Latin" styles on the evolution of jazz has been profound, and much of Afro-Caribbean and Brazilian music could be said to have been modal long before the so-called "modal" period began.

Joe Henderson's through-composed 16-bar tune, "Recordame" (see also Chapter 5), employs this device while retaining the underlying "Latin" feeling throughout, alternating between a dorian vamp and a series of ii - V progressions to delineate its two halves.

Ex. 4.32

The chord progression to "Recordame"

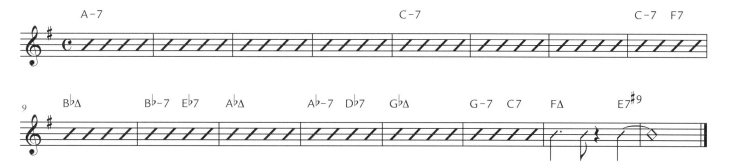

Horace Silver's "Yeah" works in similar fashion, providing a lydian dominant-sounding vamp in its introduction and at the beginning of the A section, then continuing on to a series of ii‑V cadences that coincide with a change to a swing-based rhythmic feel, as with "Un Poco Loco" or the other examples cited previously. This juxtaposition is a favorite device of Horace Silver's, and is also in evident in such compositions as "Nica's Dream". Both "Nica's Dream" and "Yeah" are available on the 1959 Blue Note recording "HoraceScope", a must for the collection of any serious aspiring jazz composer. Silver's influence in popularizing the compositional technique of juxtaposing "Latin" and "Swing" rhythms in conjunction with delineation of the form (usually AABA) cannot be overstated, though of course this technique was not one which he invented, as noted earlier (see end of Chapter ASSIGNMENTS).

Of course a modal sonority is a sonic resource for the composer, first and foremost, and there are many examples of pieces where a characteristic modal sound is used in transposition, or what is sometimes referred to as "constant structure" (aka "planing", as described by Rayburn Wright in "Inside the Score"), as in Ex. 4.32 above. The resultant reiteration imparts a modal flavor to the section of the composition in which it is used. In the bridge of "Chorinho Pra Ele", Hermeto Pascoal transposes a modal melody in parallel minor thirds over a stop-time rhythmic figure:

Ex. 4.33

Charles Lloyd's "Forest Flower" is another mixed modal/tonal piece employing this device to connect the surrounding sections of the form, though the accompanying melodic line is much simpler (see end of Chapter ASSIGNMENTS). Basically, any melodic sequence extracted from the harmony can be handled this way, regardless of the degree of simplicity or variation as the harmony is repeated:

Ex. 4.34A

Example of parallel melodic and harmonic modal sequence

Example of variable melodic and harmonic modal sequence

We see this latter device at work in Joe Henderson's "Inner Urge" also, which is based on transposed lydian sounds. Note that unlike "Forest Flower", which is more like Ex. 4.33 above, "Inner Urge" features more variability in the contour of the various melodic expressions of the mode.

Ex. 4.35

"Un Poco Loco" by Bud Powell, referred to earlier, also illustrates the use of parallel lydian sonorities (the descending chromatic bassline adds further harmonic implications not considered here).

Ex. 4.36

We also find modal sounds chained together to create progressions in ways that are not functional in the traditional sense. Herbie Hancock's "Speak Like a Child", a composition that clearly exemplifies this concept, will be analyzed in greater detail in Chapter 8, but for purposes of the current discussion it is interesting to note this particular aspect of the piece. Each of the following chords as found in "Speak Like a Child" may be represented by a transposition of the identical intervallic structure (a tritone supporting a perfect fourth).

Ex. 4.37

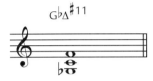

In such an example, the normal tonal relationships between chords (ii-V-I, etc.) cannot be readily discerned from merely examining the chord symbols used to describe these sonorities. The progression is nonetheless organized, due to the fact that each of these chords represents a reiteration of the same voicing over relatively different roots. Thus as we listen to the piece we hear the same sound over and over in different contexts, so that we have the effect of tonic (or "home"), but it exists in the purely sonic realm. Traditional analytical tools do not account for it. In Chapter 8 we will re-examine this piece and others in which the composers have created equally original structural premises. This process of reiterating the same harmony over changing root relationships may be regarded as a structural form of reharmonization.

Reharmonization

Let's now address the important technique of reharmonization of a melodic idea. Because it implies a change in the context in which a melodic idea is being presented, reharmonization is an extremely useful compositional tool. Reharmonization might be thought of as the process by which a given melody or melodic fragment is recontextualized harmonically. The principle is based on the concept that any note could fit a wide variety of harmonies, depending on the function it is given within the chord. For example, a C natural would be the root of a C chord, the ninth of a B♭ chord, the ♯11 (or ♭5) of an F♯ chord, and so on. Within a given tonality, however, the chord that is chosen to support a given melody will have an expected tonal function. That tonal function is synonymous with our conditioned expectations for its most commonly heard resolution within the tonality. This means that in choosing a reharmonization in a given tonal setting, it is important to consider not only the vertical richness of the new harmony, but also its normal resolutional tendency within the key (in modal settings, of course, that may not matter). For example, the first 8 bars of the standard "Just Friends" would normally have the following harmony:

Ex. 4.38

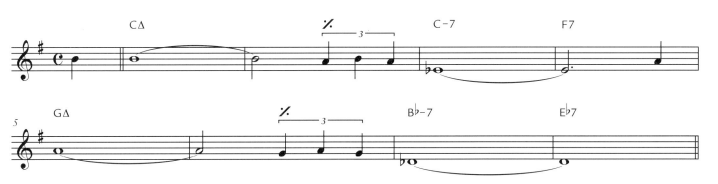

It might be reharmonized as follows:

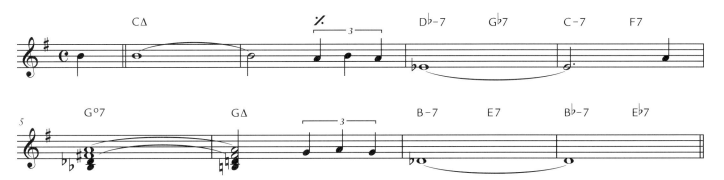

In this second case the device of sideslipping is employed to create horizontal interest in measure 3, allowing the melody note (E♭) to sound richer vertically as a result of the reharmonization (E♭ becomes the ninth of the D♭–7 chord, instead of the third of the original C–7 chord). Then in measure 5 the tonic chord is converted (bluesified) into a diminished seventh by flatting its third and fifth, thereby delaying the expected resolution to the tonic one measure and further enhancing the horizontal momentum. In each case, of course, these reharmonizations afford a richer harmonic setting for the melody. Additionally, given the tonal context, as soon as we hear the new chords, we expect them to proceed to the original ones according to normal functional expectations.

Reharmonization is useful in structuring original compositions as well, and is in fact one of the most commonly used techniques. Consider the following example by Duke Ellington, at the beginning of the bridge of his composition "Heaven", from the "Second Sacred Concert".

Ex. 4.39

Ellington first plays the melody over a relatively obvious tonal scenario of a cadence to the E♭ chord. Immediately he repeats the motif with harmony a half-step lower, cadencing into D minor, in the process creating much richer vertical relationships between it and the supporting harmony. Just as in Ex. 4.38 above, the vertical relationships are made richer by moving the harmony chromatically. Secondly, it is important to note the simple, pentatonic nature of Ellington's motif. Simpler ideas are inherently more manipulable since they are less restrictive harmonically.

A similar example is found in Hermeto Pascoal's "Bebê". In the first A section, his melody remains in the aeolian mode throughout, while in the second A section he reharmonizes it dramatically (and chromatically) in the eighth bar to link its tonal and modal sections[8].

Ex. 4.40

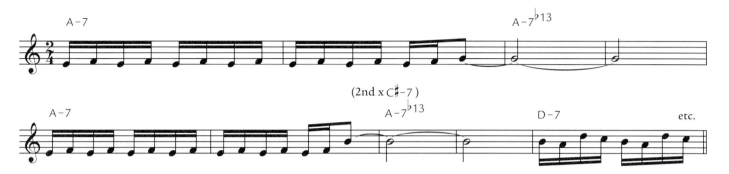

(The piece then continues much like "Recordame" does, by repeating the same melodic and harmonic sequence at different pitch levels.)

Each of these last two examples also illustrates the inherent drama of the rarely used gesture of ascending root motion.

This seems to be a favorite technique of Pascoal's (we also saw it used in Ex. 4.25B in his "Vale da Ribeira" – see p.59).

Notice that in many of these examples, the goals of creating vertical tension and linking harmonically contrasting sections are both achieved by means of the related devices of ascending root motion and chromatic approach chords. Also note that most such technical devices are equally useful whether employed in the closely related disciplines of arranging or composition.

Extended Triads

Another technique that can be used in either tonal or modal situations, for purposes of primary or reharmonization, is the use of extended triads (also sometimes referred to as "bitonality"[9]). Of course the notion of "extended" triads is really just another way of saying that a given mode can be treated as a seven-note tertian vertical entity, with the lowest four notes comprising the primary seventh chord with which it is associated, while the upper three constitute the available "extensions".

[8] Pascoal, Hermeto, Ed. Jovino SantosNeto, Tudo E Som, *The Music of Hermeto Pascoal*. Universal Edition UE70045, 2001, p.16

[9] Schuller, Gunther. *The Swing Era*. Oxford, N.Y., 1989, p.361

The following examples illustrate what has become common practice in this regard:

EX. 4.41A

Minor 7th chord

C Dorian

EX. 4.41B

Major 7th chord

C Lydian

EX. 4.41C

Unaltered dominant chord

C Lydian ♭7

EX. 4.41D

Sus4 dominant chord

C Mixolydian

EX. 4.41E

Half-diminished chord

C Locrian ♮9

EX. 4.41F

Minor 6th or minor/major 7th chord

C melodic minor

EX. 4.42

Commonly used extended triads for the "altered" scale

The same process may be applied to *symmetric scales:*

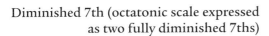

Ex. 4.43A

Diminished 7th (octatonic scale expressed as two fully diminished 7ths)

Ex. 4.43B

Distinctive extended triads found in the octatonic scale

Ex. 4.44

Extending the whole tone scale (by expressing it as two augmented triads a step apart)

Alternating between the tonic chord and its extended triad, may of course create the effect of a modal cadence.

Ex. 4.45

See also Ex. 4.44

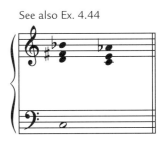

These extended sonorities are especially common in big band writing, and in fact may have originated in trumpet section writing for large ensembles (giving the trumpets a triad to play enables them to play better in tune, especially in the high register situations where the dynamics are often louder and it is difficult for them to hear the harmonic underpinnings of the voicing being played by instruments seated in front of them).

Horace Silver's "Adjustment" from the album "Silver and Brass", is one typical example of the kind of sound resulting from the employment of *polytonal* cadences such as the following:

Ex. 4.46

IV7 - V7 - I7 cadence using extended major triads from the octatonic scale, based on the 6th degree and containing the distinctive (♭9,13) combination (see end of Chapter ASSIGNMENTS also)

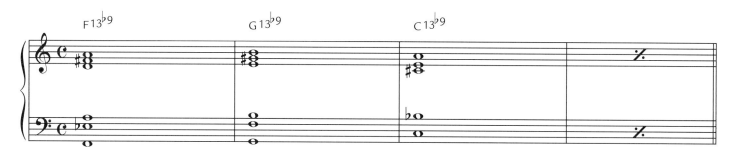

Billy Strayhorn's "Take the A Train" features a dramatic pyramidal use of this same voicing (at 2:14-15 of the famous Blanton-Webster band version) as well.

A related sound results when the extended triad is superimposed on the root note of the mode, but with one or more of the primary chord tones which normally support it being left out (see also Ex. 4.31C). The result is a tonally ambiguous sound. This sound has been used effectively by many sextet composers/arrangers, since it is an effective way to orchestrate harmonic richness within the horn section. The timbral difference between the horns and the rhythm section support (even if the latter is harmonically complete) is striking enough to lend a distinct identity to this sound:

Ex. 4.47A

Ms.A-3 horn voicing from Slide Hampton arrangement of "What's New" on Dexter Gordon's "A Day in Copenhagen", used to represent Ab∆

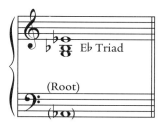

Ex. 4.47B

Final cadence in Cedar Walton's "Ugetsu", using extended triads to imply an A7alt. dominant

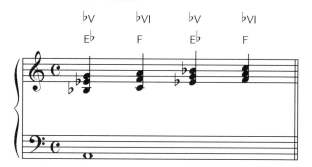

Certainly this sound can be employed in non-cadential contexts as well. The following example demonstrates its use in a piano trio composition by Bud Powell from 1956:

Ex. 4.47c

Bud Powell's "Glass Enclosure", Ms.A1 & 2

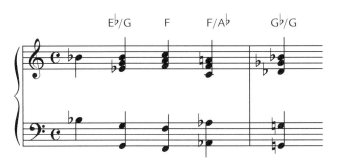

This sound is also closely related to that produced by the "Baser" in Gospel music. The "Baser" is an exhorative, improvised bassline that moves toward a predetermined cadential goal, often creating passing vertical clashes with the parallel triadic harmony above it[10,11]. This same principle can be employed for instrumental harmonization. For example, given then following melody:

Ex. 4.48a

A bassline could be constructed which moves in contrary motion to arrive on the primary chord (in this case the dominant of the key):

Ex. 4.48b

[10] Schuller, Gunther. *Early Jazz, Its Roots and Musical Development.* Oxford, 1968, p.41

[11] Author's conversation with Dr. Horace Clarence Boyer, 2002

Then a final step would be to harmonize the top line in parallel triads (when available, inverted triads generally work better than those in root position because they contain the resonant interval of a fourth – more on intervallic content of harmony in Chapter 7):

Ex. 4.48c

The resultant passage creates tension through a series of temporarily dissonant vertical moments, which is resolved at the appropriate and inevitable cadential moment.

Some of these individual vertical moments, if analyzed in "freeze frame", might seem not to show any common modal source. This is because their vertical function is coincidental to their horizontal one. As such this is not real *polytonality* (coexistence of more than one key).

Polytonality

As distinguished from *bitonal* sounds, which essentially exploit the triadic interrelationship between consonant extensions from a common chord scale as discussed previously (see Ex.s 4.41), polytonal chords or passages involve the coexistence of material from different tonal sources. The following examples, all by Billy Strayhorn, illustrate this principle, as does Ex. 4.31C shown earlier. (Consult Walter van de Leur's definitive book on the music of Billy Strayhorn for a transcription of "Strange Feeling"[12], which is certainly one such example.)

[12] van de Leur, Walter. *Something to Live For; The Music of Billy Strayhorn.* Oxford, 2002, p.79

The final chord of "Northern Lights", which Strayhorn contributed to "The Queen's Suite", is another such example. (There is an element of text painting here as well-the dissonant overtones "shimmering" to evoke the image suggested by the title of the piece. See also discussion of "The Queen's Suite", Chapter 8.)

Ex. 4.49A

Juxtaposition of major and minor tonic chords at the end of "Northern Lights"

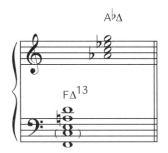

Ex. 4.49B

From Strayhorn's coda to the "Overture" (Mv't. 1 of the Ellington/Strayhorn version of Tchaikovsky's "Nutcracker"), use of parallel triads (including many parallel fifths) to harmonize a descending scale

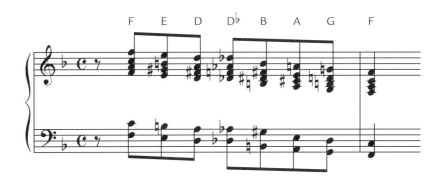

From the second tenor part in the main theme of "Ko-Ko" (ms.A9 and 10), Ellington's famous use of the Major 7th of the chord (B♭) against the cadential B7 chord:

Ex. 4.49C

Ellington's piano solo on "Ko-Ko" is another example of Ellington's deliberate use of polytonal pitch sets, in this case he runs the E whole tone scale above the predominant E♭ minor tonality of the piece (this moment is found during the fourth chorus of the piece, excluding the 8-bar introduction):

Ex. 4.49D

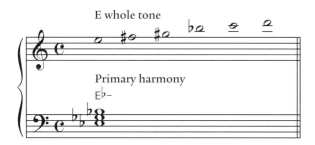

The solo backgrounds to Sun Ra's "Brainville" similarly impose whole tone harmony, in the form of augmented triads, on a traditional tonal cadence (see DISCOGRAPHY).

Polytonal chords may also be derived by combining two different diatonic chords from the same tonal system. For example, superimposing a major triad on a minor triad may result in an "extended triad" situation where the resulting compound chord does not conform to any of the traditional tertian scenarios outlined earlier (see Ex. 4.31C):

Ex. 4.49E

From the author's "So You Say" (see DISCOGRAPHY), the final chord

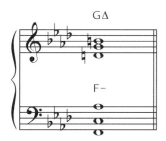

Note that although this last sonority may technically be derived from C harmonic minor (i.e. the V triad superimposed on the iv triad), the tonality of the piece is actually F− in this case. Therefore such a derivation is somewhat theoretical. Still, this is a useful and somewhat dramatic final sound. I have also employed this sound in vamp figures such as the following:

From the author's "Theme for the New Sixties"

A similar polytonal sound is produced by superimposing the major triad 1/2 step below the tonic above it. This sound is dramatically effective when use as the final chord for pieces in major keys. The following chord might be represented by the chord symbol "D/E♭", or described by means of parenthetical terminology as "E♭Δ(♯9,♯11). Generally speaking when the former description is used, a vertical, rather than a horizontal, slash is used in the chord symbol to indicated two triads as opposed to a triad over a bass note. Again, from the author's "P. St" on the recording "An Imperfect Storm" (see DISCOGRAPHY):

Ex. 4.49G

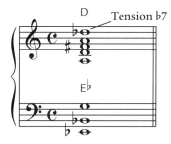

(Note also the use of the flatted seventh [D♭] above the major seventh [D] at the top of the chord, which seems to imply a further triadic extension of D♭. Why not C above that, then B, etc.? This particular hierarchical triadic sequence is made possible by the fact that any "♭9" interval becomes a major seventh interval when the relationship between the two voices is inverted.)

Use of Non-Harmonic Tones
to Create Intentional Dissonance

Occasionally composers use melody notes that do not seem to fit the chords deliberately. This also might be thought of as being related conceptually to the notion of bi- or atonality, though the effect is not always drastically dissonant. For example, Charles Mingus' "Self Portrait in Three Colors" contains an E♭ in one of its three melodies over an E7 chord. This coincides with the only 2/4 bar in the piece as well, so it also subtly reinforces a key structural point in the piece:

Ex. 4.50A

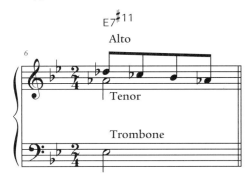

(Mingus further explores the notion of polytonality in the 5th and 6th bars after this, when the tenor saxophone part outlines the roots and thirds of C and D major chords against harmonies of F−7 and B♭7 respectively). See also Ex. 6.30.

Of course, Thelonious Monk's music is full of harmonic sounds that seem to exist outside of the realm of conventional tertian harmony. For example in "Coming on the Hudson" we find the following in measures 2 and 3. Note the "cross relation" of the A♭ in the harmony against the A natural in the melody, a favorite dramatic device of Monk's:

Ex. 4.50B

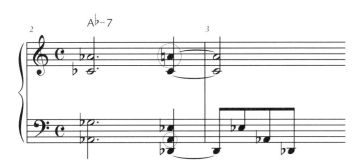

Similar examples of linear harmony can be found in "Crepuscule with Nellie". Such examples as the following (the cadence going from the fifth to the sixth measure of the Bridge) illustrate the importance of every moving voice in the establishment of Monk's harmony.

Chord symbols are often insufficient to describe the resultant harmony (and of course discerning Monk's harmonies exactly is further complicated by variations between performances, in addition to his extremely idiosyncratic use of pedaling and a uniquely percussive attack, which combine to create overtones that may sound as loud as notes which are actually played):

Ex. 4.50C

In his riff-based contrafact on the standard "Just You, Just Me" (which he also recorded) entitled "Evidence", Monk also seems to be using several sounds that defy description in terms of commonly used chord symbols.

Is the following chord, which concludes the A section, supposed to represent the tonic (E♭), or the dominant (B♭7)? If it is meant to be the former, then why was its third (G natural) used as a neighbor tone to the more rhythmically emphasized G♯ that follows? If it is a B♭7, then why an A natural in the left hand to support the A♭ in the right? In such examples Monk seems to be effectively reversing the paradigm between the normal role of *approach notes* to their expected targets, using the expected *consonance* to lead to the *dissonance* instead of the other way around. Though the expected tonic chord is E♭, the E♭ triad is implied for only an eighth note before leading to E and F triads in quick succession:

Ex. 4.50D

(As if to reiterate this conundrum, Monk ends the "Evidence" on this same sound, as played on "Thelonious Monk, The Columbia Years, '62-68; Disc 3.)

Of course Monk's greatness came in large part from his ability to integrate and balance a variety of techniques concurrently. His sense of harmonic dissonance is often complemented by a rhythmic sense of dissonance as well, which is created through the extensive use of rhythmic displacement, and occasional asymmetric phraselengths as well (see also Chapter 5). These elements worked in conjunction with Monk's unique performance practice to create his "signature sound" (see also Chapter 7). Such is the case in "Off Minor".

In measures 5-7, Monk seems to be again treating chord tones as *approach notes*, as the notes G and B♭ move up 1/2-step:

Ex. 4.50E

As if this were not enough, Monk's coda reiterates this ambiguity, reharmonizing these final notes with an implied B♭7(♭9) chord:

Ex. 4.50F

Coda

Sequential Harmonization

Many composers have effectively employed the device of sequence as applied to harmony (refer again to Ex. 4.21). What is interesting is the way in which sequential repetition of a given motif can unify a chord progression in the absence of traditional tonal or modal function. The sequence makes the music sound organized, notwithstanding the unorthodox harmonic relationships. In the following examples, you may find that conventional harmonic analysis is not fully effective in explaining the underlying organizational logic. This speaks not only to the overriding organizational strength of melodic and harmonic sequence vis a vis conventional norms of harmonic function, but perhaps also to the inadequacy of our appropriated European models of harmonic and formal analysis to fully describe our music.

Ex. 4.51A

"Dersu" opening eight bars

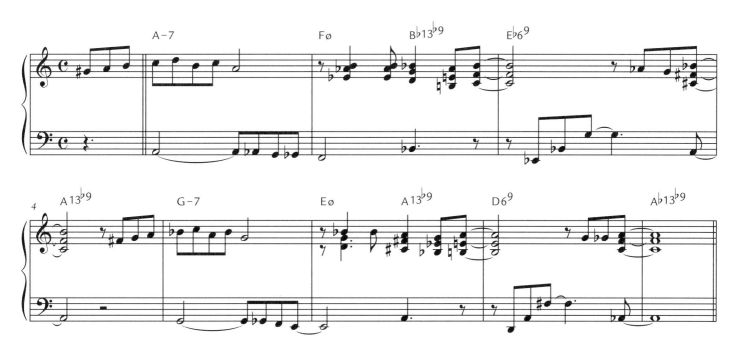

What is the tonality of the opening 4-bar phrase? Does that change in the second 4 bars? What about in the next four? Is there a primary overall tonality to the phrase?

Ex. 4.51B

"Dersu" ms.9-12

Finally, as the second half of the tune begins, the third and fourth bars of A are reharmonized:

Ex. 4.51C

(This example may be found on the author's CD "Manhattan Projections", see DISCOGRAPHY.)

The following example starts with a section based on "constant structure", yet progresses from there to employ a variety of chord types. The lyrical, sequential flow of the melody unifies it, however, in spite of the less than conventional tonal relationships.

Ex. 4.52

First four bars of Hermeto Pascoal's "Aquela Valsa"

Opening phrase of Herbie Nichols' "The Third World"

In this last example the harmony may also be thought of being a part of a rhythmic riff. As such its inherently idiomatic and motivic qualities are strongly identifiable, so much so that factors such as harmonic function become relatively less important in organizing the phrase (In fact, the G♭ chord at the end of the transcribed phrase acts more like a dominant chord than tonic, creating a *transitional modulation* to B major as a result. Because of the strong sense of motivic coherence created by the sequential nature of the *phrase structure*, the modulation does not seem jarring. See also end of Chapter Assignments).

What each of these examples demonstrates is that cadential and modal harmonies can be effectively combined, especially when they support a lyrical, sequential and rhythmic melody.

Conclusion

Constructing the harmonic palette for a given melodic *motif* is easily done, especially if the motif itself is not too specific harmonically. (This process might be rendered more difficult if the motif involved were as complex as, for example, the first four bars of Miles Davis' "Donna Lee"[!]). It is simply a matter of finding various harmonies that can support the motif. When and where to use the resulting harmonizations, and how they are connected and contrasted, is where the Art is. For a composer, creating the palette is as important to writing music as having the correct ingredients is to a good cook.

ASSIGNMENTS

1.) Listen to the Examples discussed in the Chapter.

2.) Find comparable Examples of your own illustrating the following harmonic techniques:

- · Diatonic melody supported by non-diatonic harmony.
- · Chromatic or Blues-inflected melody.
- · Modal harmony.
- · Mixed modal/tonal harmony.
- · Reharmonization of a motif within a melody.
- · Examples of "extended triadic" harmony.
- · Examples of non-functional harmony used in support of a melodic sequence.
- · Find an introduction or coda from a recording by a Brazilian artist that employs a tonic pedal tone supporting the progression I-II to create a Lydian cadence (cf. Ex. 4.30).
- · Analyze the diminished chord found in measure 2 of the A section of Jobim's "Wave".
- · Transcribe the voicings found in the 3-chord cadence in ms.5-8 of the A sections of Horace Silver's "Adjustment" (found on the album "Silver and Brass" – see DISCOGRAPHY).
- · Analyze the melodic / harmonic relationships in the final 6 bars of the form of Charles Lloyd's "Forest Flower" (cf. Ex. 4.34).
- · Listen to the modulations in the bridge of "When Lights Are Low" by Benny Carter and examine the reuse of the primary motif of the tune over this series of direct modulations to temporary keys.
- · Analyze the melody / harmony relationships of the first four bars of Herbie Nichols' "Third World" (cf. Ex. 4.53). Transcribe the rest of the A section of the piece and analyze it harmonically.
- · Analyze the harmony found in the variant Blues progressions to Charlie Parker's compositions "Au Privave" and "Blues for Alice".
- · Listen to the turnaround at the end of the first half (ms.15-16) of Strayhorn's "Isfahan" (cf. Ellington's "Far East Suite"). See discussion p.48.
- · Analyze the harmony of the Bridge of Kenny Barron's composition "Voyage".

3.) Transcribe and analyze Benny Golson's "Along Came Betty" (both in terms of harmony and phrase structure – how does the phrase structure serve to "soften" the impact of the modulations?).

4.) Transcribe the piano voicings from the introduction to "Where You At" by Horace Silver, from the album "HoraceScope" (see DISCOGRAPHY and Ex. 4.31C).

5.) Transcribe the introduction to "Yeah" by Horace Silver from the same album. How is the melodic "pedal" tone (repeated note) reharmonized by the two chords used in the introductory vamp, and how does its melodic function change as a result?

6.) Write an AABA 32-bar tune that uses a mix of modal and tonal harmony, and which employs at least two of the other techniques listed above.

7.) Analyze the following examples of vii°7 to i– cadences as used in classical harmony: Mozart's Fantasia in C Minor, K575, ms.4; and Chopin's Prelude in #4 in E minor, 17th complete measure (not including the pickups).

8.) Bring in examples of two compositions, one a "standard", the other a piece by your favorite jazz composer, for comparative analysis of the following:

· Relative degree of harmonic richness in the chords used;

· Relative degree of harmonic richness in the melody (i.e. prevalence or absence of color tones);

· Degree of melodic angularity and percussiveness in the melodic/harmonic structure.

CHAPTER

5

Form

As the jazz idiom has developed, it has always embraced available forms from the wider musical culture of which it was a part. Indeed, other than the Blues and Rag forms, the process of *adaptation* of extant formal structures has been the norm. In Ragtime and early Stride piano we find the *Strain form*, while AABA, Blues, and ABAC forms are ubiquitous from the Tin Pan Alley era forward. A variant of these common 12 and 32-bar forms could be called the "through composed" *songform*, in which formal repetition was not literal, but in which the reiterative impulse still served to organize the piece. Composers like Ellington, writing extended works for large ensembles, created "compound" forms by subsuming the commonplace 32-bar and Blues forms into larger formal schemes.

Jazz composers have also adapted various formal structures from European Classical music, including *Fugue*, *Rondo*, and the instrumental suite, among others (and, contrary to prevalent jazz history mythology, this process was *not* new in the 1950's, but rather has been an ongoing one since the beginnings of the music. Indeed, as Carl Atkins put it "jazz has always been Third Stream music"[1]). Jazz composers have also created musical forms by deriving extramusical inspiration and organizational concepts from literary, poetic, religious, philosophical, numerological, and even astrological models.

Finally, extended works may also be organized in "through-composed" fashion, based on the exploitation of a single *motif* as an overriding organizational force. Examples from these various categories of extended works will be analyzed more fully in Chapter 8, but in order to understand the work of composers involved in such formal experimentation it is important to begin by acquiring an understanding of the common practice forms with which they themselves were familiar.

As discussed in Chapter 3, the Blues form and its variants is one of the common practice templates exploited most frequently by jazz composers. As demonstrated by a piece like "Nostalgia in Times Square", the adaptability of the Blues to the formal experiments of imaginative composers derives from the ubiquity of its key paradigmatic elements: its *harmony* and, more importantly, its implicit "call and response" *phrase structure*.

One question asked by the contemporary jazz composition student might well be: "Why study Ragtime"? There are a number of good reasons to do so, regardless of whether or not one aspires to write music in that style.

[1] Author's notes, lecture by Atkins at Williamstown Jazz Festival, April 2002

First, paraphrasing Branford Marsalis[2], "if you want to sound like 'Trane you've got to listen to what he listened to". In other words, it is not enough to listen only to the musician you wish to emulate. Only by absorbing the influences on that musician can you truly understand where they were 'coming from'. (Of course you ultimately need to put your personal areas of musical interest into that mix as well in order to be able to cultivate a truly individual sound.) To fully understand 'Trane, for example, listening to Ragas, Bartók, and Rhythm & Blues would all be essential[3]. Similarly, if we aspire to write like Ellington, an understanding of Stride piano would be one essential element in the complex equation of influences that interacted in his development. Someone interested in writing like Gil Evans would want to listen to the music of Louis Armstrong (which he knew thoroughly[4]), as well as that of Prokofiev and other 20th century composers. If you aspire to write like Cedric Dent (of "Take Six" fame), a solid grounding in earlier forms of Afro-American vocal music, both sacred and secular, is essential. And so on. These arbitrarily chosen examples are not meant to constitute any sort of definitive list of the key influences on these great writers, but rather to reinforce the point that as composers we are always in the process of looking backward in order to better understand the forces at work in the development of our musical role models. It is only through such an understanding that we can fully appreciate how they moved the music forward.

Secondly, the evolution of Ragtime represents a significant direct link between African music and the evolution of African American music. It has often been said that the adaptation of the banjo, and especially its characteristic rhythmic figurations, to the keyboard, was a key element in the evolution of Ragtime[5]. The banjo, in turn, was an indigenous African instrument, either brought from Africa or recreated on American soil (Thomas Jefferson reported the playing of the Banjo by his slaves[6,7]). Thus this pianistic adaptation is important because it is one of many manifestations of the way in which African musical practice created new approaches to playing European instruments (the evolution of Blues piano styles may be thought of as being similarly adaptive of the idiomatic practice of Blues guitar). The creation of new ways of playing existing instruments, as well as the imaginative adaptation of previously non-musical equipment to create new modes of performance practice, have both been important trends throughout the evolution of jazz. The evolution of the *plunger mute*, *brushes*, the *Diddley-bow*, and the modification of *oil drums* into percussion instruments, are among many further examples of this phenomenon.

[2] Author's notes, Marsalis' remarks during Williams College residency, November 2003

[3] Porter, Lewis. *John Coltrane, His Life and Music.* Michigan, Ann Arbor, 1998

[4] Author's notes, lecture by historian Phil Schaap at Williams College, October 2003

[5] Schreyer, Lowell. "The Banjo in Ragtime" in Hasse, John Edward. *Ragtime.* Schirmer Books, New York, 1985, p.58

[6] Oliver, Paul. *Savannah Syncopators, African Retentions in the Blues.* Stein and Day, New York, 1974, p.22

7 Schreyer, p.55

Thirdly, compositional practice in Ragtime illustrates ubiquitous vestiges of African music found in virtually all indigenous American musical forms regardless of era: the use of such devices as "call and response", "riffs", and the particular set of non-diatonic tones that we have come to call "blue notes".

Finally, in Ragtime we find evidence of other significant underlying principles in the music's evolution, including both "consilience" (the existence of similar musical ideas in the work of different composers, which may or may not reflect direct influence on or knowledge of one another's work) and "signification" (implicit commentary or acknowledgement in the reuse of the work of one's predecessors). Ultimately, this last notion gives evidence that the development of jazz composition owes a great deal to the fact that it is a self-referential tradition.

The Strain Form

The Strain form of Ragtime, as epitomized in the work of Scott Joplin and others, could best be described as ABACD, wherein the initial A theme is repeated only in its first appearance, and with a modulation to the subdominant (key area of IV) for the C strain. The return to the primary key for the D strain is optional, and the final strain may be repeated in variation, as a sort of precursor to the "shout chorus" found in many Big band arrangements. This formal scheme has been said by Gunther Schuller to reflect the influence and characteristics of both the *minuet* and trio and march forms[8], which were common in late 19th-century American Music. In any event the overall architectural sense of key structure and thematic repetition is clearly important to this form.

As mentioned earlier, both melodic and rhythmic characteristics of Ragtime represent adaptations from the *Banjo*, including the use of both "Blue" and "crushed" notes, duple meter, and a prevalent use of the "cakewalk" rhythm. (The "cakewalk" rhythm, in evidence in the following example, features the sixteenth-eighth-sixteenth, or "short, long, short" subdivision of the beat, which is also characteristic of the Brazilian style known as *Choro*. To Brazilian musicians this rhythm is referred to as "the fork"[9].)

[8] Schuller, Gunther. *Early Jazz: Its Roots and Musical Development.* Oxford, New York, 1968, p. 33

[9] Author's notes of lecture by Jovino Santos Neto, Williams College, September, 1999

Joplin's illustrious "Maple Leaf Rag"[10] from 1898, illustrates these various characteristic elements:

Ex. 5.1

The cakewalk rhythm in the A theme (labeled "Tempo di Marcia")

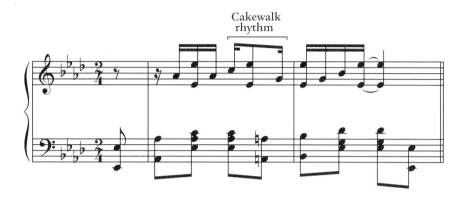

The cakewalk rhythm in the B theme

The cakewalk rhythm in the C theme (note the modulation), labeled "Trio"

Ex. 5.2

Use of Blue notes

[10] Joplin, Scott. The Best of Scott Joplin. Charles Hansen, New York, 1972, pp. 6-8

Typical banjo-influenced rhythmic figuration

Presence of call and response

Note also the presence of the ubiquitous "clave" based rhythm (two dotted pulses followed by a single beat pulse) – see also Chapter 6.

Jelly Roll Morton's oft-recorded "King Porter Stomp" (1906) illustrates these formal principles and melodic and rhythmic attributes as well. The form of the piece is Intro/AABB/transition/CCCC, with the third strain modulating up a fourth to D♭ from A♭ (the same primary key areas as "The Maple Leaf Rag"). Unlike many *rags* the A theme does not return subsequent to its initial statement. Also unlike "The Maple Leaf Rag", "King Porter" includes an introduction, as well as a modulatory *transition* to the C theme (often found in both rags and marches). Finally, the repeated C theme definitely imparts a dramatically climactic, quasi-"shout chorus" sense. Perhaps this implicitly orchestral feeling accounts for the fact that this piece became such a favorite of later Big band arrangers, a thorough comparative study of which can be found in Fred Sturm's "Changes Over Time"[11]).

[11] Sturm, Fred. *Changes Over Time: The Evolution of Jazz Arranging.* Advance Music, Rottenburg, Germany, 1995, pp. 56-66

Ex. 5.6

A theme of "King Porter Stomp"

B theme of "King Porter Stomp"

Modulatory transition and C theme of "King Porter Stomp"

C Theme

Note the use of "Blue notes" and "call and response" as well, similar to the "Maple Leaf Rag".

Ex. 5.7

Blue note ("♭3") in "King Porter Stomp"

Ex. 5.8

Call and response in "King Porter Stomp"

Of course, the "clave" based rhythm, famously described by Morton as the "Spanish tinge", is pervasive as well.

Ex. 5.9

The "Carolina Shout", by James P. Johnson (1918), became a famous test piece for the pianists of the day. While it owes a great debt to the ragtime style, the piece also presages the evolution of Stride piano. The formal structure of "The Carolina Shout" is roughly that of a standard rag, similar to "King Porter Stomp", in that it has three thematic strains, with the final one modulating to the key of IV (C in this case). As in "King Porter", the final strain appears in multiple variations. The balance in the form is also achieved in part through the similar use of variations on the harmonic progression in the repeated A and C sections (these sound like *composed variations*, another time-honored tradition in jazz composition which is definitely in evidence in the work of John Coltrane for example[12]). Unlike the previous examples, this composition exhibits more complex and elongated first and second endings for repeated strains. It also has a wonderfully original, and harmonically forward-looking, coda. Another device found in this piece is what Mark Tucker and others have referred to as "secondary ragtime"[13] (see Ex. 5.10B, below), or the 3 + 3 + 2 subdivision of a bar (this characteristic Ragtime and Stride piano rhythmic device may be thought of as clave in augmentation). The "Carolina Shout" shares with its predecessors such idiomatic devices such as the use of Blue notes and call and response.

Ex. 5.10A

The introduction of "Carolina Shout"

Ex. 5.10B

"Secondary Ragtime" in accompaniment pattern

12 Demsey, Dave. *John Coltrane Plays Giant Steps*. Hal Leonard, Milwaukee, 1995
13 Gillis, Frank. "Hot Rhythm in Piano Ragtime", in Hasse, John Edward. *Ragtime*. Schirmer Books, New York, 1985, pp. 229-30.

Comparison of the 3rd measure of the respective introductions of
"Carolina Shout" and "King Porter Stomp" – consilience or signification?

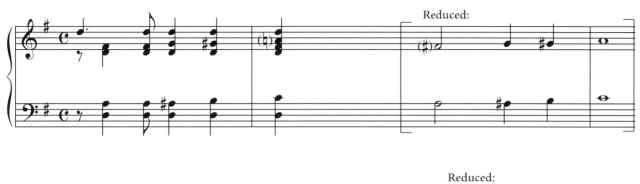

A theme #1 of "Carolina Shout"

Variation of A (same harmony but with embellishment and featuring the "secondary ragtime" rhythm in accompaniment):

Ex. 5.13

The B theme of "Carolina Shout"

The C theme

Ex. 5.14

Blue notes in "Carolina Shout"

Ex. 5.15

Call and response in "Carolina Shout"

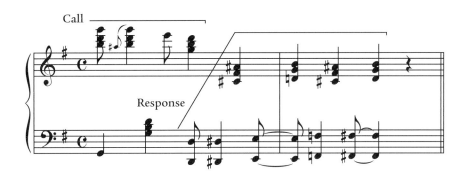

Finally, as mentioned in Chapter 4 (see Ex. 4.9), The coda of "Carolina Shout" contains *substitute dominant* root motion similar to that found in much later compositions such as "Ladybird" and "Satin Doll".

Comparison of the root motion:

"Carolina Shout"

Coda, "Satin Doll" (ms.A-6)

"Ladybird" (ms.15 & 16)

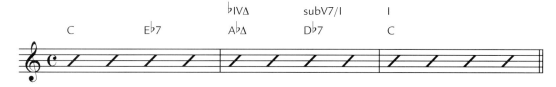

(Another important characteristic of the "Carolina Shout" coda is its blantant use of the "Spanish tinge", reinforcing the point that clave-based rhythmic devices were present from the earliest days of the music*, due at least in part to the historically strong connections between New Orleans and the Caribbean – see also Chapter 6).

(* The 1908 Joplin/Chauvin Rag "Heliotrope Bouquet" prominently features "clave" in its underlying rhythm as well.)

Finally, in "The Carolina Shout", we see the characteristic "shout chorus" effect, this time in both the variations of the C theme.

Another piece which shows the further evolution and adaptation of this form is Bix Beiderbecke's idiosyncratic "In a Mist" (1928). By the time it was composed the development of ensemble music in jazz (of which Beiderbecke was of course a participant) was fully underway. And although the basic multithematic structure of the *strain form* can still be found in "In a Mist", the themes are interrupted by frequent interludes and tempo changes. Further, the incorporation of the technical device of parallel ninth chords and related harmonic vocabulary shows at least as much influence of the French impressionists (and the pianistic tricks of the "novelty piano" genre[14]) as it does of the Blues. Finally, the return of the A theme to separate the subsequent thematic material is perhaps more *Rondo-like* than strain-based (in this sense an appropriate formal companion might be Ellington's 1930 composition "Rockin' in Rhythm").

[14] Riddle, Ronald. "Novelty Piano Music" in Hasse, John Edward. *Ragtime.* Schirmer Books, New York, 1985, pp. 290-92

EX. 5.17A

The A theme of "In a Mist" illustrating the use of parallel 9th chords

EX. 5.17B

Examples of use of "whole tone" based harmony

The form of "In a Mist" is roughly:

A | Interlude | B | Interlude | C | A | D | Interlude | A | Coda,

with the D section this time consisting not of a "shout chorus", but rather a rhapsodic, *rubato*, section. The brief, rubato, coda recapitulates ideas from the earlier slower sections, which are similar in mood and more developed than *transitions* in comparable pieces, although they eschew literal repetition. In this sense, the piece resembles those from the "through composed" realm. There is no modulation in this piece *per se*, though implicit in the A theme is the move from the *subdominant* (F) on which it starts to the *tonic* where it concludes (C).

The following examples illustrate the way in which the piece creates a sense of continuity between its slower sections by reusing prior material.

From the interlude connecting A and B,
and from measures 7 and 8 of "Soft and Rhythmic" (or C)

5th and 6th measures of B theme

Two excerpts selected from the eight bars
preceding the final statement of the A theme

Idiomatic Blues piano devices such as the use of "crushed note". Blue notes are in evidence in the piece as well.

Ex. 5.18B

(Listen to "Sagittarius", the 9th movement of Mary Lou Williams' "Zodiac Suite", especially between 00:41 and 1:00, to see if you can hear any references to "In a Mist"![15])

Even though the *strain form* did not continue to be as widely used as the 32-bar and Blues forms which gradually supplanted it, studying these early pieces shows us much about the ubiquity of the underlying organizational principles that characterize jazz composition, regardless of era.

Let us now turn our attention to those more familiar 32-bar forms and their common variants.

AABA

The AABA 32-bar songform is arguably the most common in American popular music. (The 32-bar forms, especially those having their genesis as showtunes, were often preceded in their original versions by an introductory section referred to as the "verse", not to be confused with the "verse" as used in choral or folk music idioms, wherein the same term is taken to mean different stanzas sung to the same music.) Many Tin Pan Alley and Broadway show composers used the AABA form, as did their counterparts in early jazz composition. Of course, there has always been a great deal of overlap between the work and repertoire of the two groups. Both "Satin Doll" and "I Got Rhythm" are examples of AABA songforms. (In its original version, "I Got Rhythm", like "Nice Work If You Can Get It", was a 34-bar form, resulting from the variation of its final A to accommodate a built-in "turnaround" in the final A section. However, as embraced by jazz practitioners the tune has usually been played in its truncated and familiar 32-bar form.) AABA forms often feature a modulation to the B (bridge) section, which in turn serves to link the first two A's to the last one. This dynamic can be found at work in the majority of Ellington tunes in this format, including "Prelude to a Kiss", "In a Sentimental Mood", "Sophisticated Lady", etc.

[15] Mary Lou Williams, "The Zodiac Suite" (1945)

Let's compare the aforementioned Gershwin tune, "Nice Work If You Can Get It", with Ellington's "It Don't Mean a Thing If It Ain't Got That Swing".

"NICE WORK IF YOU CAN GET IT"

As mentioned previously (see Ex. 4.1), in "Nice Work If You Can Get It", Gershwin establishes a main A idea that is essentially diatonic in character, which is made to sound successively *antecedent*, then *consequent*, as a function of the supporting dominant seventh chords, thereby achieving a balance between diatonic and non-diatonic elements:

Ex. 5.19

First (antecedent) phrase

Second (consequent) phrase

Of course the melodic component, though essentially diatonic, also contributes to our sense of antecedence and consequence by virtue of the harmonic implications normally associated with the terminal notes of each of these phrases (the "*antecedent*" ends on the leading tone, which is inherently unstable in tonal harmony, while the "*consequent*" conversely ends on the tonic).

The Bridge of "Nice Work" establishes a contrasting identity by employing more Blues-based material, in the closely-related secondary key of the relative minor. Note the use of the "Blue note" in the melody, as well as the associated Blues-based "♭VI7", F7 (in the key of the bridge, A minor).

Ex. 5.20

Once established, this new idea is then transposed to complete the bridge.

"IT DON'T MEAN A THING IF IT AIN'T GOT THAT SWING"

In "It Don't Mean a Thing If It Ain't Got That Swing", Ellington establishes a Blues-based *antecedent* idea beginning in the key of G minor, then creates a *consequent* phrase for it which is essentially rhythmic in character, reflecting the title in its musical content (see also Chapter 6, uses of rhythmic motifs).

EX. 5.21A

Antecedent and consequent ideas in the A section

(The consequent idea also performs a secondary function of enabling the transition to the relative major, Bb, to complete the A section.) The bridge of "It Don't Mean a Thing" is similar in its mechanics to that of "Nice Work If You Can Get It", establishing a new idea, then treating it *sequentially* to set up the return to the last A. It is worth noting that there is a wonderful "verse" to the piece as well, included on the original 1932 Ellington version, though not often heard when the tune is performed as a standard. Note that the bridge of the tune is based on a common practice harmonic formula of using two phrases a step apart (in the Gershwin tune these were minor, whereas here they are IV and V in relation to the final tonality of the A section, Bb).

EX. 5.21B

Harmony to the bridge

ABAC

The ABAC 32-bar form is equally common in the Jazz and popular repertoire. An ABAC form essentially uses common material for the beginning of each of its halves, then establishes what are in effect extended first and second endings for this shared initial material. Both Gershwin's "Our Love Is Here to Stay" and "But Not For Me" exhibit this form.

Ex. 5.22

"Our Love Is Here to Stay"

Note how, in the first eight measures above, Gershwin once again employs the technique of presenting his initial idea in *sequence* in the first four measures, using harmony to great effect in making *both* of these iterations feel unresolved (*antecedent*).

Then he creates a B idea, which is essentially sequential in both its melodic and harmonic components (second eight bars in Ex. 5.22 above).

This material is shared by both A's, but then ends differently in each case, thus defining the "ABAC" form. In the first half of the tune, the primary (A) idea is extended beyond the initial sequence to create an *antecedent* ending (on the dominant chord, C7), while the second half of the tune truncates the A idea so as to create space for the concluding *consequent* motif supporting the tune's lyric "hook" (its title), and the accompanying resolution to the tonic (last line of Ex. 5.22 above).

The following narrative should be used as an adjunct to the aural analysis of Horace Silver's "Strollin'" (see end of Chapter ASSIGNMENTS as well):

"Strollin'" provides a similarly structured example of the ABAC form. Silver's primary theme begins with a lyrical opening motif over a relaxed *two feel* (see also Chapter 6), subtly infusing the phrase with a bit of harmonic tension via the use of "sideslipping" in ms.3 and 4, before concluding on the V7 chord with the leading tone in the melody. The repetition of the opening four-bar phrase becomes a *consequent* phrase when its second final bars are varied melodically. The device of "sideslipping" is once again used in the accompanying harmony, this time to target the iii– chord where the B section (second eight bars) begins. The B section is contrasted with the A by its more rhythmically defined motif, as well as an accompanying change in the rhythm section's dynamism as expressed in both volume and use of swing (i.e. the rhythm section is used reinforce the formal boundaries of the tune, a fact that must be heard to be appreciated – once again, see ASSIGNMENTS).

AA'BC

The AABA form may be varied in a number of ways without sacrificing its basic organizing principles or musical effect. One means by which this frequently occurs is in the transposition of the A material for the second A section. A good example of this is Clifford Brown's composition "Joy Spring".

EX. 5.23A

First A section

EX. 5.23B

Second A section

Typically of the mid-50's small band compositions of the time (as was also the case with "Strollin'"), we again see a significant role being played by the use of rhythm to reinforce the form. The harmonic accompaniment to the B section provides contrast in its accents (see Chapter 6 as well).

Ex. 5.24

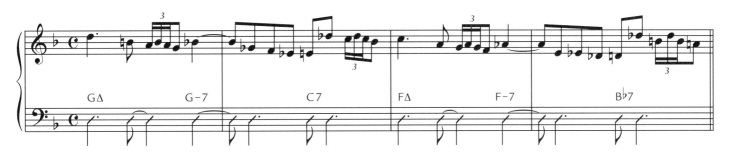

It should also be noted that the introduction of the piece illustrates the use of a rhythmic motif as a means of orchestrating for the ensemble as well presenting the main ideas of the piece.

Ex. 5.25

The introduction of "Joy Spring", showing the A and A' motifs

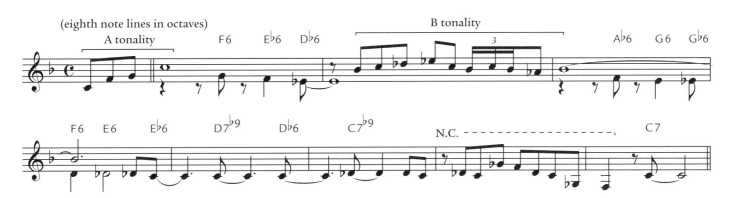

(The coda of "Joy Spring" employs the common practice device of repeating the first part of the final phrase two extra times before resolving it. With the exception of the break and corresponding written line in the penultimate measure, this device is essentially the same as what might have happened had the coda been improvised – listen to it and see if you agree.)

"All The Things You Are", by Jerome Kern, is one of the best known "standards" embraced by the jazz repertoire. It also shows the use of a transposed second A, or A', but has the further variation in its form of an extended (or varied) final A as well. Thus, in "All The Things", the A is never repeated literally. Yet there can be no doubt that the reiterative impulse is at work in organizing the form. Whether it is described as AABA, or AA'BA'' is an after the fact, clerical discussion, one which has no bearing on the creative variation of the well-known form that is illustrated by such compositions.

The Through-Composed Standard

Victor Young's "Stella by Starlight" provides a slightly different example of such a "standard", since its second 8 bars has completely different thematic material than its first 8. However, the return to the A material in the final 8 bars provides s a definite sense of recapitulation, even though its ending differs from that of the first 8. Also, the middle eight bars (ms.17-24) definitely have the sound and feeling of a B ("bridge") as traditionally found in an AABA form.

Ex. 5.26

Form of "Stella by Starlight" (consult a leadsheet of your choice)

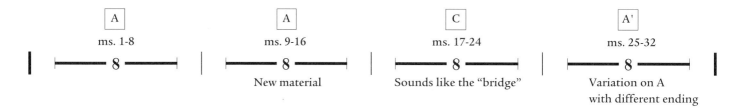

(The Stan Getz/Kenny Barron performance referred to in the DISCOGRAPHY is recommended.)

This device, which we might refer to as being a sort of varied recapitulation of the A material, is found in many compositions from the standard and jazz repertoire.

Cole Porter's "You Go to My Head", for example, has an AABA form in which the final A is extended by what might be described as a built in tag ("Dear Old Stockholm", as recorded by Miles Davis, does the same).

Wayne Shorter's "Delores" (as recorded by Miles Davis' on "Miles Smiles"), features an 8-bar melody which is repeated three times, separated by 8-bar sections that have no written melody. Interestingly, the second of the three iterations of the theme has the same rhythmic shape as the first, but features a varied (but recognizable) melodic contour and different harmonies. In other words, the rhythm and shape of the melody remain the same, but the notes and chords are different. Still, the material sounds related and *sequential*. Like Coltrane's "Impressions", it sounds initially as if the melody is being transposed, but the transposition in this case is not literal in any sense.

Like "Stella by Starlight", "Delores", and the other pieces analyzed above, "The Dolphin", by Brazilian composer Luis Eca, also creates a through-composed melodic form by reiterating its initial motif over a series of reharmonized phrases, concluding with a final 12-bars that start out sounding like a "last A" and is then extended and varied through the use of a *pedal point*.

Thus we might describe such compositions as "through-composed" in order to account for the fact that none of their 8-bar phrases is repeated literally, though clearly the piece sounds organized due to its motivically reiterative internal organization.

Many Wayne Shorter compositions may be thought of as being organized around reharmonizations of reiterated phrases or riffs ("Infant Eyes", "Wildflower", "Speak No Evil", are but three examples among many others – see end of Chapter ASSIGNMENTS and DISCOGRAPHY). The repeated phrases lend motivic coherence to the piece, while their relationship to the supporting harmony (especially at the end of each phrase) creates a feeling of *antecedence* or *consequence*, providing a sense of forward motion in each thematic statement.

Having examined these primary songforms we may now proceed to their combination and juxtaposition in what are known as "compound forms".

Compound Forms

A *compound form* is by definition one in which more than one discrete formal structure can be said to coexist. There are many such examples, and as with any of the principles being discussed in this book, it is important for the aspiring composer to realize that this formal device need not be a function of style or era. The implications of this principle for composers of extended works of the use are obvious. For the purposes of this chapter we will examine relatively simple and accessible examples of it (in Chapters 7 and 8 this will be an important premise for our examination of selected extended compositions).

JACQUI

Richie Powell's "Jacqui" (recorded by the Max Roach – Clifford Brown Quintet) is a good example of a compound form. Using the recording as your guide (DISCOGRAPHY), note the following formal elements:

Following a Blues-based introduction over a simple *pedal point*, the A sections are primarily *diatonic* in their (implied) harmonic and melodic content, continuing the "stop-time" feel that the introduction establishes through the end of the A section. In this section the ensemble is completely orchestrated. Note also the contrary motion in the final three notes of the saxophone *counterpoint* at the conclusion of each phrase.

The final phrase of the A section rises sequentially a half-step above the primary dominant of the key, from F7 to F♯7. The reason for this device becomes apparent at the bridge, when the F♯7 chord resolves. The Bridge is actually a 12-bar Blues in B. Further, the main motif of the Blues is created from the rhythmic motif of the melody at A.

As was the case with "Joy Spring", the ornamentation of the introduction presaged the further chromatic development of the bridge. After the bridge the A section returns as before.

So, although it is fair to say that "Jacqui" is an AABA form, it is also true that it is a compound form, because its B section is a "form within a form", in this case a Blues. Another piece that employs this device is John Coltrane's "Locomotion", from the album "Blue Train". In "Locomotion", it is the A sections which are Blues forms, connected by a variant of the "I Got Rhythm" bridge (much more about "Blue Train" to follow in Chapter 8). (See also End of Chapter ASSIGNMENTS.)

ST. LOUIS BLUES

"St. Louis Blues", by W.C. Handy, is an example of an earlier composition that might also be considered to "compound", alternating between 12-bar Blues and a repeated 8-bar second strain in the parallel minor:

Ex. 5.27

The formal scheme of "St. Louis Blues"

CLARINET LAMENT

An early example of compound form written for specifically for a larger ensemble can be found in Ellington's 1936 composition, "Clarinet Lament". The piece is often regarded as Ellington's first "concerto"-style piece, in that it featured one soloist juxtaposed against the orchestra. As such it also represents an adaptation of the European "Concerto Grosso" form by a jazz composer (see also Chapter 8), and as we will see the piece is also an example of *appropriation* (see also Chapter 7). So while our focus here is on the form of the piece, clearly there are many compositional forces at work here beyond that single element.

Creole clarinetist Barney Bigard is featured on this piece, which is in many ways a tribute to Bigard's native *New Orleans*. This is one of many Ellington's compositions that were based on a musical evocation of a particular place, scene or mood. It is also one of many examples of his ability to structure complex formal designs of three minutes or less in duration (early recording technology imposed this limitation on recording artists of the time[16]). Not surprisingly, Ellington recasts musical material associated with the Crescent City to create the piece.

[16] Hasse, John. *Beyond Category: The Life and Genius of Duke Ellington.* Simon and Schuster, New York, 1993, p. 115

The piece opens with composed three-part *New Orleans style* polyphony, a clear example of the use of a signature stylistic device to establish the "venue" of the piece, as it were. Additionally, this shows Ellington's ability to convincingly compose music that is in effect the recreation of a common practice improvised device.

Ex. 5.28

The 3-part counterpoint effect in the Clarinet Lament intro

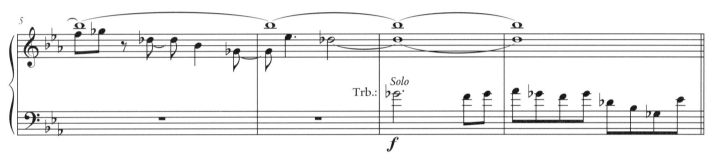

(Ellington's antiphonal introduction may actually be a paraphrase of the famous "National Emblem" march by E.E. Bagley.)

Following in the introduction we have a modulatory transition of 8 bars featuring plunger muted brass that establishes the tempo of the piece.

Having established the tonality and tempo, Ellington's compound form begins with a large A comprised of a 12-bar Blues form featuring a Bigard solo over spare backgrounds. Then follows a 2-bar modulatory transition (a vestige of Ragtime and March form, as mentioned earlier), this time moving up a fourth to the key of Ab.

(Key relationships in Ellington "concerti" tend to be more Blues-based, such as IV, bVI, etc., rather than dominant, in relation to the primary key). The modulation to Ab signals the beginning of the second section of the form, or large B. This second section is actually an AABA songform built out of the appropriated chord progression from Spencer Williams' "Basin St. Blues" (another geographically appropriate choice[!]).

Ex. 5.29A

Progression of the A section of the AABA songform of large B

Each of the A sections of large B are demarcated through the use of a solo break to feature Bigard in measures 7 and 8.

Ellington then composes simple backgrounds to create a bridge to complement the "Basin St. Blues" A section (up another fourth, this time to D♭) before returning to the final A of the form. The last A section becomes rhythmically more active in its final two bars, which actually constitute a modulatory transition that returns us to the original key of E♭. The return to E♭ is not only a recapitulation of the initial Blues form (large C), but includes orchestrated backgrounds based on the "Basin St." material, in diminution.

Ex. 5.29B

The backgrounds to large C

These backgrounds are not only significant for their intrinsic relationship to the composition, but also because they provide a "call and response" platform for the soloist to work off of. They also modulate appropriately to fit the chord changes of the 12-bar Blues in E♭. And as if that weren't ample exploitation of the recycled "Basin St." harmony, Ellington completes the piece with a two-bar coda that reiterates it one final time in yet further diminution:

Ex. 5.29C

The Coda

Ellington's clever integration of the "Basin St. Blues" harmonic material during his return to the Blues concurrently provides elements of both *recontextualization* and *recapitulation*. This is a concept to which he would frequently return in so many of his extended works, and one which bears strong similarity to the developmental process found in European classical Sonata form as well (see also Chapter 8).

Another excellent example of this process in Ellington's work may be found in the 1943 piece "Black, Brown and Beige". In its opening movement, "Black", the "sweet" theme (popularly known as "Come Sunday"), and the more rhythmically active "Work Song" (the opening theme of the movement), are recapitulated and intertwined in similar fashion, as predicted in Ellington's introductory remarks[17] (see also Chapter 8).

Because Ellington's career lasted so long, and due to the inextricable linkage of many of his signature sounds (see also Chapter 7) with those of his longserving players, these formal concepts and adaptations were continually reworked and refined throughout his career. Unlike some musicians whose careers underwent a variety of contrasting style periods, Ellington showed an uncanny knack for recycling compositional concepts and "devices"[18], as he liked to call them, and in the process frequently appropriated and recontextualized not just the material of others, but his own as well.

Ellington's 1928 "Swampy River" is another early example of a *compound* piece. Though on the surface level this piece seems to reflect Ragtime and early Stride piano performance practice, formally it is not in *strain form* per se, but compound.

The piece clearly combines two separate AABA songforms, while retaining vestiges of the "strain form" such as the modulatory interlude.

Ex. 5.30

The Formal Scheme of "Swampy River"

Introduction	Rubato
AA	Two 8-bar A phrases (major tonality).
1st AABA	BB: Two 8-bar minor strains (rhythmically featuring the "Spanish tinge"). C: 8-bar "Bridge" of the AABA songform defined by the B's. B: Now functions as "last A" of AABA songform.
Interlude	A: Extended by 4-bar interlude establishes *ostinato*.
2nd AABA	DD: Two 8-bar strains over the ostinato bassline (functioning as AA). E: "bridge" of the AABA songform defined by the preceding D's. D: Final "A" section of the second AABA form; extended two bars to create a "tag ending".
BB	Restatement of the B theme with a 4-bar intro gives sense of *recapitulation*.
C	Bridge of the first songform used as a coda.

[17] "Black, Brown and Beige", Carnegie Hall Concert, Jan. 1943
[18] "A Duke Named Ellington", PBS Documentary, 1988

Ellington's 1947 composition "The Clothed Woman" is another piece in which he uses variations on the Blues, appropriated materials, and even an angular, Monkish interlude (though, interestingly, Ellington had not yet acknowledged having heard Monk's music[19]). The piece begins with what seems to be an atonal multi-octave run, that upon repeated listening reveals a Blues form cloaked in extreme *dissonance*.

Ex. 5.31A

(Based on the Ellington manuscript score found in the Smithsonian collection.)

[19] Dance, Stanley. *The World of Duke Ellington.* C. Scribner's Sons, New York, 1970, p.139)

Following this Blues form, the Monkishly spare, riff-based interlude, establishes a medium bounce tempo.

This abruptly leads to an appropriated Willie "The Lion" Smith (one of Ellington's mentors) stride piano piece[20] in AABA form, the theme of which follows.

Finally the original distorted Blues theme returns, adding a common practice ending before reiterating the initial run of the piece for its coda.

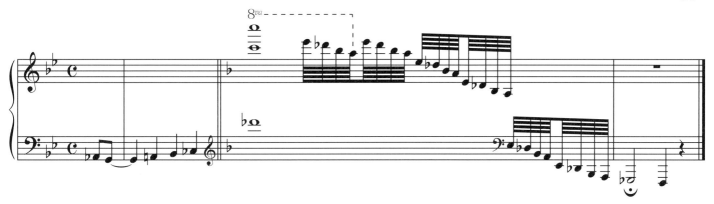

Don Redman's "The Stampede", as recorded by Fletcher Henderson, is another example of an early Big Band composition that created *compound* form by combining discrete *songforms* within the same piece, while retaining the use of modulatory interludes and other such signature stylistic devices of its time as the *whole tone scale*, duple time feel, and *call and response* between the instrumental sections. ("The Stampede" may be heard on the Smithsonian Collection of Classic Jazz.)

[20] Hasse, *Beyond Category*, p. 301

Ex. 5.32

The formal outline of "The Stampede"

Introduction	Call and response between sections (ms.1-4). Trumpet solo over rhythm section (in "2" feel ms.5-9). The resultant first 8-bar phrase repeats, but this does **not** turn into the first two A sections of a songform.
1st chorus	ABAC songform (32 bars) in A♭.
2nd chorus	ABA form repeats for tenor solo with simple backgrounds. Then reiterates the C from the first chorus to conclude the solo chorus.
Interlude	4-bar whole tone passage.
4th chorus	ABAC songform (30 bars) in relative minor key (F−), truncated to enable the *elision* of the previous Interlude beginning in ms.31 of the minor key form (see also Chapter 6).
Final chorus	Reprise of the initial ABAC songform, with some variation, notably the final 4 bars, which deftly *recapitulate* both the opening and closing figures of the 1st chorus to create the coda.

The following examples illustrate some of the interesting points in the form described above.

Ex. 5.33

The call and response between sections in the first four bars

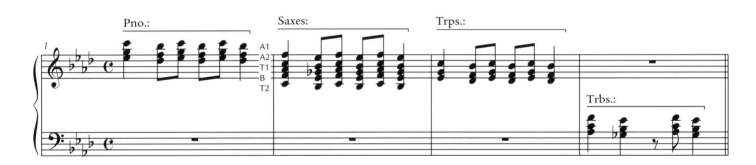

Use of retrograde "cakewalk" rhythm in background riff figures responding to the trombone theme in the first chorus

Use of "break" figures to conclude the both halves of 1st chorus

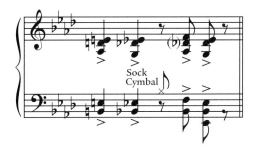

Whole tone break between the first and second ABAC forms

(Not just "whole tone", but also varying intervallic content within the scale, including the use of "cluster voicings" – see also Chapter 6.)

To be sure there are other details that unify the composition, most having to do with the reiteration of its riff-based thematic material throughout the arrangement.

Of course the *compound form* is not limited to use in the jazz idiom. The Lennon/McCartney tune "Can't Buy Me Love" has an AABA form in which the A sections are 12-bar Blues (i.e. like Coltrane's "Locomotion" or the previously discussed "Jacqui").

The Chorus Form

Finally, especially with reference to the compositional and arranging realms of Big band music, it is possible to postulate one additional form, which we might describe as the "chorus form". In the chorus form, the songform involved might be any of the commonly used ones, AABA, ABAC, or Blues. As the form is repeated, development occurs by means other than those associated with the formal combinations seen in *compound forms*. This development of necessity is a result of changes in texture, use of varying solo voices, backgrounds, and climactic *shout choruses*. Generally speaking, in this formal scheme, the *shout chorus* or the reiteration of the principle theme of the piece (or both in combination) may be used to conclude it. One such example is Mary Lou Williams' "Scratchin' in the Gravel", written for Andy Kirk and his Clouds of Joy, and recorded in 1940.

Ex. 5.34

The Formal Outline of "Scratchin' in the Gravel"

Introduction	4 bars
1st chorus	AABA 32-bar songform established, with the trumpet soloing over the A's, tenor over the bridge, and the piano over the last A (each with simple backgrounds in the complementary sections; brass behind the tenor; saxophones behind the piano).
2nd chorus	AAB "shout chorus" featuring "call and response" between the sections. Final A section recapitulates the first theme in the trumpet.
Coda	Featuring "stop-time" rhythm and reiteration of the *call and response* between the trumpet solo and the ensemble.

Some interesting moments among those outlined above include:

Ex. 5.35

Concerted rhythm between the trumpet solo and the accompanying reeds
to conclude the first A section of the melody

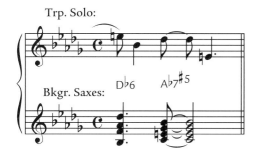

Use of "tutti" figure (in effect a "rhythmic cadence") to demarcate the end of the tenor solo

(i.e. the answer is not literal, but varied, including the use of rhythmic *displacement*). Note: This excerpt begins at approximately 2:18 of the recording.

Another wonderful example of the use of this form in an original composition is Ellington's 1932 masterpiece, "Lightnin'".

Ex. 5.36

Formal synopsis of "Lightnin'"

Introduction	8 bars featuring descending *diminished* 7th chords in the trumpets (joined by "Tricky" Sam Nanton on trombone).
1st chorus	ABAC 32-bar chorus in C, featuring ascending *dominant seventh* chords starting on the dominant in the same four brass as appeared in the introduction (and not arriving at the *tonic* until measure 31 of the form[!]), supporting a Harry Carney baritone solo.
2nd chorus	Change in solo voice to Sam Nanton, using complementary sax backgrounds, increasing tension in the background harmony to include a ♭9 (combining the melody with this harmony implies the *octatonic scale*, see Ex. 5.37A below).
3rd chorus	Brass revert to background role to support clarinet solo with rhythmic plunger mutes a seemingly "incongruous" 16-bar stride piano solo.
4th chorus	"Shout chorus" juxtaposing unison saxophones in a written line against static, then plunger muted brass (when the brass become active the saxes play trills to provide contrast).
5th chorus	*Modulation* up a minor third with the saxophones returning to the "♭9" backgrounds they played behind Nanton in 2nd chorus builds the tension further, while the theme is harmonized in the brass. Now the *octatonic* harmony which is only implied earlier is fully voiced in the brass, in the form of a B♭13♭9 chord that not only functions as the *dominant* in the new key (E♭), but actually incorporates the dominant from the original key, G7, within it (see Ex. 5.37C, below). Piece ends at the end of the chorus, with no coda.

Among the more interesting musical moments outlined above include:

EX. 5.37A

The octatonic harmony implied in 2nd chorus in the combination of melodic and accompanying harmonic material

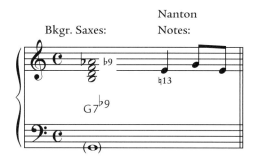

(Although this has actually been misinterpreted in other analyses of this piece, there is clearly no error in this combination of harmony and melody![21])

[21] Schuller, Gunther. *The Swing Era.* Oxford, New York, 1989, p. 57

The "call and response" between the brass and reeds in the second four bars of
the 4th chorus, featuring harmonized plunger muted brass against unison saxes

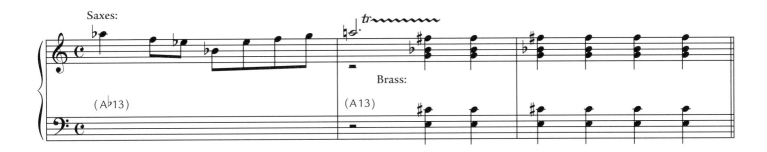

The "dominant within a dominant" harmony at the beginning of
the 5th chorus the Bb13♭9, showing the G7 within the Bb7,
a function of the octatonic harmony at work here

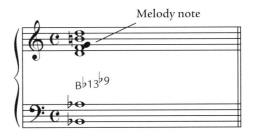

Finally, it is important to understand the integrative motivic nature of the structure of "Lightnin'" (this is a concept to which we will return during the discussion of "A Tone Parallel to Harlem", to follow in Chapter 8 as well). Ellington's initial minor third motif (first established in the descending diminished 7ths found in the introduction) is reiterated in various of ways throughout the piece. After the introduction, the minor third interval reappears in the primary melodic motif. It next appears when the basic *dominant* 7th harmony is extended to include the ♭9 (its newly extended structure now includes the *diminished* 7th chord from the introduction), and finally in the *modulation* itself at the beginning of the 5th chorus (from C to E♭). So although this piece is in "chorus form", it is also an example of a motivically-based composition.

Ex. 5.38

The descending diminished 7ths in the brass in the intro

etc.

The ascending minor third motif of the theme

The extended ("♭9") background harmony in the saxophones,
reiterating the diminished 7th chord from the introduction

Finally, the interval of the final *modulation* for the ensemble *shout chorus* is also a minor third, from G7 (V7 in C) to B♭7(V in E♭).

Conclusions

The issue of form encompasses all manifestations of the compositional process in jazz, regardless of era or style. Whether we are dealing with one of the basic songforms, or complex multisectional composites, reiterative and organizational imperatives are omnipresent. By studying the ways in which our predecessors have used elements of melody, harmony, rhythm, and orchestration to organize their work in both micro and macro frameworks, we will inevitably enhance our own ability to do so.

The most commonly used songforms are the 32-bar AABA and ABAC forms, the 12-bar Blues, and their respective variants (including the "through-composed" form). Ragtime music employed the "strain" form. The notion of "compound" form refers to the coexistence (juxtaposition) of discrete songforms within larger pieces to create their structure, while the "chorus" form, used primarily in the Big band context, depends on timbral contrast and careful manipulation of harmonic and rhythmic elements to build tension throughout the piece. We have examined a few basic prototypes of each of these in actual practice in order to prepare for our subsequent discussion in Chapters 7 and 8 of various extended works.

ASSIGNMENTS

1.) Listen to the music discussed in this Chapter.

2.) Bring in examples of each of the following for in-class analysis:

· an example of an AABA or ABAC 32-bar tune

· an example of one of the common variants of AABA or ABAC ("AA'BC", "through composed", etc.)

· an example of a "chorus" form arrangement or composition

· an example of a "compound" form composition

· do an aural / formal analysis of Horace Silver's "Strollin'" (from the album "Horacescope" – see DISCOGRAPHY), using the text found on page 108 to guide your discussion.

3.) Write a 32-bar tune in standard form (AABA or ABAC).

4.) Write a 32-bar "through composed" tune.

5.) Begin sketching out an extended piece based on compound form.

6.) Analyze all of the through-composed pieces listed on page 110 (both aurally and through the use of available leadsheets) to see how the reiteration of the primary motivic phrases of their respective A sections creates a sense of motivic unity.

7.) Transcribe all part of the A and B sections to "Jacqui" (see pp. 111-112).

Chapter 6

Compositional Uses of Rhythm

This Chapter is not intended to be a discussion of the origins of the rhythmic vocabulary of jazz. Certainly much has been written on that extremely important subject.[1,2] Rather our emphasis will be on the compositional uses of rhythm, or how rhythm is used as an organizing principle in a variety of contexts, both *micro* and *macro*, in jazz composition.

Rhythm As a Factor In Motivic Identity

As we said in Chapter 2, the identity of any *motif* is in large part defined by its rhythm. Thus, for example, this component may be manipulated throughout the piece, independently of its melodic contour.

Ex. 6.1

Harry Carney's baritone line
in the intro of Ellington's "Ko-Ko"

As shown in the above example, the opening rhythmic motif of Ellington's 1940 masterpiece consists of three simple eighth notes (sort of a "bluesified" version of the main theme of Beethoven's Fifth – consilience or signification – see related discussion in Mark Tucker's Duke Ellington Reader). This rhythmic cell is reiterated throughout the piece.

The motif in the valve trombone solo in chorus #1

[1] Schuller, Gunther. *Early Jazz: Its Roots and Musical Development.* Oxford, New York, 1968.

[2] Oliver, Paul. *Savannah Syncopators: African Retentions in the Blues.* Stein and Day, New York, 1970.

The motif in chorus #4, in the saxophones, behind the piano solo (played outside its harmonic context of E♭ minor, this sounds like a quote of "When the Saints Go Marchin' In" in the relative major):

The motif in the trumpets in chorus #5 (the pickup note changes from chord to chord, but the *motivic identity* is retained):

Interestingly, each of these iterations targets a different note in the harmony. The baritone targets the tonic (in the introduction), the valve trombone the third (first full chorus), the saxophone background to the piano solo the seventh, and the trumpets the ninth.

The reiteration of rhythmic motifs is pervasive in jazz composition, regardless of style, era, or the ensemble for which the piece is conceived. Revisiting Bud Powell's "Un Poco Loco", we can see how the "clave"– based rhythm established in the first two bars of the A section (and of course complemented in the underlying rhythmic accompaniment and parallel Lydian chord voicings) recurs throughout:

Ex. 6.2

Clave figure iterations in the A section

Note how this *reiteration* of the *clave* continues in the following excerpt from the bridge of the same piece, first appearing in the counterline (ms.B3 and 4), then later in the main melody itself (ms.B9-11):

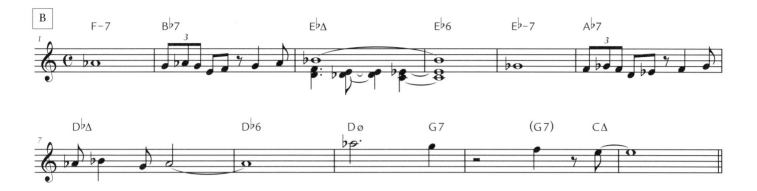

Clearly this piece is extremely sophisticated harmonically, yet there is no doubt that it derives its underlying sense of organization from the reiteration of this rhythm.

As a Stylistic Marker

Rhythm also has an important role to play in terms of its stylistic implications. The main types of rhythm used in jazz are those that are "swing" based and those that are "clave" based.

Swing based rhythms exploit the inherited characteristic in jazz rhythm of the coexistence of duple and triple *subdivision* of the same beat. This coexistence should not be confused with either *polyrhythm* or *polymeter* (to be discussed shortly). Swing might be considered to be a way of playing and phrasing in which pairs of eighth notes are shaded so as to put more weight on the first of the pair, articulating consecutive eighth notes in connected fashion as well. Another important element of *swing phrasing* is that notes that are off the beat, or those that precede rests (frequently they are the same), are accented. Similarly the second and fourth beats (aka the "backbeats") normally receive accents. However, the degree of differentiation between the duration of the first and second eighth notes in a pair is not absolutely consistent from player to player or from tempo to tempo. The inability to accurately account for these distinctions of phrasing represents perhaps the single greatest notational problem faced by jazz composers. Because jazz is an aural tradition, swing phrasing is a learned art. However, the individuality of expression we associate with the great jazz players is also a factor that the composer may exploit. By writing for particular players with a given sound identity the jazz composer is working with a known quantity (more about this later when we discuss the notion of "individuality of voice"), and rhythmic phrasing is certainly a defining factor in an individual player's identity.

Basslines in "swing" tend to involve full-value (connected), "walking" quarter notes, while the drums employ a typical swing beat, articulating the swing eighth note pairs on the ride cymbal, while playing the hi-hat cymbal on 2 and 4 (the "backbeat").

Ex. 6.3A

Typical swing beat in the drums and walking bassline

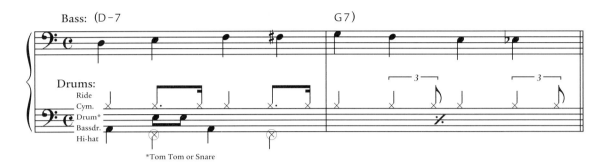

However, written examples are obviously insufficient in fully illustrating this principle. Listen to the Count Basie / Sarah Vaughan version of Freddie Green's "Until I Met You" to hear these various factors at work, both melodically and in the underlying accompaniment.

Clave-based rhythms exploit the rhythm that Jelly Roll Morton described as the "spanish tinge"[3].

Ex. 6.3B

Although there is no question that it can be found in other musical cultures as well (in Spain this rhythm is called "Habanera" for example), as used in jazz the clave based rhythm is primarily associated with Afro-Caribbean and Afro-Brazilian antecedents. In terms of rhythmic phrasing the eighth notes in this style are generally played straighter than in swing based practice. Another important characteristic of *clave-based* styles is that the underlying rhythmic accompaniment originated with a group of percussionists playing relatively static, *complementary* roles, which combined to create the given beat. Thus the jazz drummer has reduced this multiplicity of individual parts to that which can be played in four limbs. This is of course an example of adaptation as well (see Chapter 7).

[3] Dapogny, James. *Ferdinand "Jelly Roll" Morton: The Collected Piano Music.* Smithsonian Institution Press (G. Schirmer). Washington, D.C., 1982, p. 510

The study of Afro-Caribbean and Afro-Cuban rhythms is another undertaking that has been the subject of much study, and one which we cannot hope to undertake thoroughly here[4]. However, it is worthwhile at this point to compare a typical "Latin" beat as played by a percussion section with its adaptation to the jazz drum set. Ex. 6.4A shows an idealized "Mambo" as performed by complementary percussion parts, using what is known as a "2/3" clave as the underlying pulse, while Ex. 6.4B shows this basic beat as adapted to the jazz drum set.

Ex. 6.4A

Typical Mambo

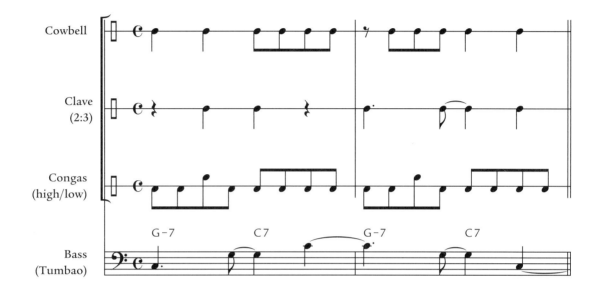

Ex. 6.4B

An idealized version of the basic beat played by drummer
Roy Brooks on the introduction to Horace Silver's "Yeah"

[4] Roberts, John Storm. *Black Music of Two Worlds, Second Edition.* Wadsworth/Thomson Learning (Schirmer), Belmont, CA.

In the excerpt from which Ex. 6.4B was taken, the rest of the rhythm section also reinforces the *clave* in typical fashion.

Ex. 6.5

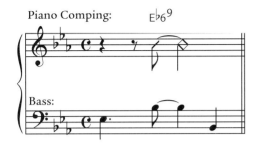

The bassline in Ex. 6.5 might be found in either *Mambo*-based music, like "Yeah", or *Baião* or *Samba*-based music from Brazil.

Ex. 6.6

Bassline from Introduction to Hermeto Pascoal's "Bebê"

In *Bossa Nova*, this rhythm frequently appears in the comping rhythm as well. Both of these rhythms can be seen working together, displaced by one eighth note, in the introduction to Hermeto Pascoal's "Bebê" (of course, in Bossa Nova, this would be notated in 2/4 [5]).

Ex. 6.7

If you are seriously interested in composing in Afro-Caribbean or Afro-Brazilian styles a separate study of these individual disciplines is certainly warranted (see BIBLIOGRAPHY). In fact it does a disservice to these styles to learn no more about them than the few primary characteristic traits that have been largely homogenized in jazz composition and pedagogical practice.

As mentioned previously in Chapter 4, many jazz composers have combined elements of "Latin" and "swing"-based rhythm in the same composition as a way of achieving contrast. Most typically, as in for example "Nica's Dream" (Horace Silver), this involves juxtaposing a "Latin" A section with a swing bridge, although there are also many examples of pieces in which the "Latin" rhythmic feel supports a melody whose phrasing is definitely swung (such as Kenny Dorham's "Blue Bossa").

[5] Pascoal, Hermeto, Ed. Jovino Santos Neta, Tudo E Som. *The Music of Hermeto Pascoal*, Universal Edition, UE 70045, 2001, p. 16

2/4 Rhythmic Feel and Stop-Time

In early forms of jazz, prior to the establishment of *swing* as the dominant rhythmic paradigm, the music retained the underlying duple meter that characterized *Ragtime*. This can be readily heard in recordings from the 1920's. Another important characteristic of early jazz is the "break" or the use of "stop-time". An example from "The Stampede", discussed in the previous Chapter, illustrate the former principle at work.

Ex. 6.8A

Use of the "break" for a soloist as seen in last four bars of "The Stampede"

Another example showing the use of "stop-time" integrated with that of "call and response" in a small group compositional context.

Ex 6.8B

From the A section of Bobby Timmons' "Moanin'"

The "two feel" is used as a dramatic device, as a way of setting off one section of the form from another. It is typical, for example to begin a tune in "two", then switch to 4/4 at the bridge or for a subsequent chorus (this is often accompanied by a switch from brushes to sticks by the drummer). This is another example of the use of a common practice performance device that can be recreated in the compositional context. Thad Jones' "Quietude", from his album "Central Park North" illustrates this well, though again this is best conveyed through listening, not through the use of a notated example.

Before leaving this topic it is important to acknowledge that throughout its history, jazz composers have made use of currently popular dance beats (especially those based on *Rhythm & Blues* and *Rock & Roll*) as a way of making the music more accessible and commercially viable. Such '60's pieces as Ramsay Lewis' "I'm in with the In Crowd", Herbie Hancock's "Watermelon Man" and "Cantaloupe Island", Lee Morgan's "The Sidewinder" (based on a "twist" beat), Thad Jones' arrangement of Nat Adderley's "Jive Samba" (based on a *boogaloo* beat), and Joe Zawinul's "Mercy, Mercy, Mercy", are among numerous examples that illustrate this trend. Of course, this concept is central to the much of the work of Miles Davis from the "Bitches Brew" album forward, and the entire "fusion" style generally. Given the diminishing audience for jazz and the commercial success of Rock based styles, it is not surprising that this attempt was made, and that it continues to this day, blurring the lines between jazz and its more popular cousins.

Rhythm As a Means of Recontextualization

Just as *reharmonization* changes the *tonal* context of an established melody, so a change in meter or time-feel can do the same, personalizing the arranger's mark indelibly on the piece. Thus, when we hear the Coltrane version of "My Favorite Things", it sounds dramatically different than the original version from "The Sound of Music". Although the piece retains the same meter (3/4), the underlying rhythmic feeling is drastically different as a result of the emphasis on duple *subdivision* in the *reiterative*, *modal*, and *ostinato*-based accompaniment. Similarly, Ellington's version of the overture of Tchaikovsky's "Nutcracker Suite" changes its rhythmic context from a light, cut time feel, to that of a heavy, medium *swing* feeling of roughly half the original tempo, with a great emphasis on the *backbeat* (see also Chapter 8).

But this technique is useful to composers as well as arrangers. In "A Tone Parallel to Harlem", Ellington frequently changes the rhythmic context for his thematic statements, often creating the effect of a rhythmic cadence. At around measure 50 there is a saxophone soli with clarinet in the top voice that leads to the return to the motto theme at almost exactly half the tempo. Again, the nuances involved must be heard in order to be fully appreciated. This also brings another concept into play that is not typically thought of as being relevant in jazz performance: that of the conductor's influence (see also Chapter 8).

Ex. 6.9

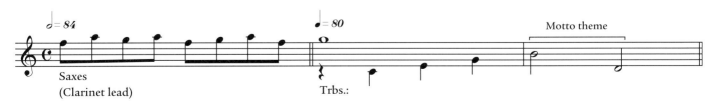

The coda of Billy Strayhorn's "The Hues" similarly recasts its *recapitulation* of the main theme, playing it first at the original, medium up tempo (around ♩= 184), then using a 2-bar drum *break* to prepare its repetition at half the original tempo as a sort of a 12/8 "bump and grind". After playing the theme at half tempo twice in this manner, the drums again get a two-bar break to return the band to tempo primo for the final statement of the theme (this piece can be found on the Dutch Radio Orchestra's "Portrait of a Silk Thread").

A change in rhythmic context emphasizes the duality of function for the "Flirty Bird" theme from Ellington's 1959 "Anatomy of a Murder" film score. The theme first appears as a sultry ballad associated with Lee Remick's character in the film. Later the identical theme returns (albeit in a different key), this time as a medium tempo instrumental *Blues* in a jam session lead by Ellington (and attended by Jimmy Stewart's character, who "sits in" with the band). Although the melodic intervals and harmonic accompaniment remain intact, the new rhythmic context for the piece makes it nearly unrecognizable (see end of Chapter ASSIGNMENTS).

Mary Lou Williams reworked her 1940 "Scratchin' in the Gravel" in similar fashion in its 1968 version, entitled "Gravel/Truth". Instead of a medium swing tempo, the A theme of is given a drastically reharmonized, slow ballad treatment, while the bridge is converted to a waltz.

EX. 6.10

The original theme of "Scratchin' in the Gravel", in medium swing treatment

The "Gravel/Truth" statement of the same theme as a ballad

Ex. 6.11

The bridge of the shout chorus of the original version of "Scratchin' in the Gravel"

The bridge of "Gravel/Truth" as a waltz

In "The Shoes of the Fisherman's Wife Are Some Jive Ass Slippers", Charles Mingus revisits his initial plaintive, 3/4 theme later in the piece as a typical *uptempo swing* theme. Compare the following two iterations of the main theme of the piece (see also Chapter 8, p. 217-218).

Ex. 6.12

Initial statement as a slow waltz

Uptempo 4/4 presentation of the theme

The devices of thematic reiteration and transformation are of course not unique to jazz composition per se, but restating the theme or deriving motifs from it for the purpose of supporting a soloist has certainly become an important and idiomatically distinctive developmental technique in the music; and Mingus was hardly the only composer to have availed himself of this device. As we have seen elsewhere in this text, examples in the Ellington Canon abound, including such pieces as "Lightnin'", "The Tattooed Bride", and, although there is no improvisation called for on the part of soloists, arguably his most effective longform composition, "A Tone Parallel to Harlem". However, thematic restatement as a background for soloists is not confined exclusively to large ensemble extended compositions.

Thelonious Monk routinely incorporated motivic material from his original compositions into his accompaniment to varying degrees, sometimes deconstructing the melody and using the resultant fragments as background riffs, and often repeating entire melodic phrases for this purpose... (listen to his accompaniment to "Well You Needn't", discussed in Chapter 2, for example).

Achieving Contrast Through the Use of Meter, Groove and the Vamp

There are some pieces that are instantly recognizable due to their meter and/or *groove* (this often, though not always, has to do with the use of the related devices of *ostinato* or *vamp* figures, which we will discuss more thoroughly in a moment).

For example, we know Dave Brubeck's "Take Five" the moment we hear its characteristic introduction. Herbie Hancock's "Maiden Voyage" conveys a similar sense of *motivic identity* from its basic signature rhythm. Though it is in 4/4, each different key center visited by the piece appears in the same rhythmic vamp.

Ex. 6.14A

The "Maiden Voyage" groove

An *ostinato* (repeating bass or rhythmic figure) can be effectively used to help to structure introductions and codas.

Geoff Keyser's "Auntie Matter" begins with a vamp in 13/4 (6 + 7), then moves into 4/4 for the *bridge* (the quarter note remains constant). These two events so clearly dominate the form that the thematic material is almost secondary in importance (though the stark voicings, comprised primarily of fourths, fifths and seconds, combined with the bass clarinet doubling of the bass ostinato and use of mallet percussion, also greatly personalize the composition). Indeed, changes in meter or the underlying groove can work to the composer's advantage in creating formal landmarks, a ubiquitous trademark in jazz composition, used by composers like Horace Silver in alternating from "Latin" to "swing" feels between A and B sections.

Ex. 6.14B

A section ostinato to "Auntie Matter"*

* Complete scores available at www.reallygoodmusic.com

Mary Lou Williams' arrangement of John Stubblefield's "Free Spirits" (see end of Chapter Assignments and Discography) is another such example.

A layered ostinato occurs when multiple ostinati work together to create a composite rhythmic framework (as in the Ex. 6.14B above). As mentioned earlier, most rhythm sections in Afro-Caribbean ensembles create what is in effect a layered ostinato to define each individual dance beat. Here is a typical example of a Cha-Cha (for further such examples, consult Rebeca Mauleon's "The Complete Salsa Guidebook").

Ex. 6.15

Example of a Cha-Cha

Therefore it is not surprising to find arrangements or compositions using this basic rhythmic vocabulary that make use of this concept. Clare Fischer's "Gaviota" includes a distinctive *vamp* that functions initially as an introduction, but is actually included in the form.

Ex. 6.16

The vamp from "Gaviota"

Of course there are numerous other examples of layered *ostinato* to be found in arrangements and compositions of virtually all style periods. Consider the coda vamp from the famous Gil Evans arrangement of "Will O' The Wisp", from Miles Davis' "Sketches of Spain".

Ex. 6.17

Concluding vamp from "Will O' The Wisp"

Ex. 6.18

An example from Mvt. 3 of "Portaculture", by the author, showing a 12-tone vamp produced from complementary hexatonic scales (see also Chapter 8)

Another example of *layered ostinato* may be found in Dave Holland's "Shadow Dance", in which the technique might be said to be the composition's primary developmental device (see end of Chapter Assignments and Discography). And many of the pieces by bassist and bandleader Drew Gress employ the concept of slowly evolving layered ostinato patterns, accompanied by tempo and meter shifts in a compositional process that at times seems to reflect the influence of *minimalism* (see Discography).

Aggregate Rhythms Derived From Combined Parts

Closely related to both the concepts of *layered ostinato* and the *riff* is the notion of *aggregate rhythm*. An aggregate rhythm is produced when a combination of individual notes and/or layered riffs or ostinati creates a new rhythm that does not exist in totality in any individual part. For example, Duke Ellington's "Braggin in Brass" is based on one such signature motif. Note the overlapping 3/8 metric units that begin on beat 2:

Ex. 6.19A

The individual parts

The resulting aggregate rhythm and melody (note also the *diatonic* planning):

Ex. 6.19B

The author used this effect as well in a recent composition.

Ex. 6.20A

The individual parts

Interestingly, the aggregate rhythm that results creates the illusion of a medium swing tempo that feels more or less like a double time of the metric pulse, with the quartuplet "taking over" the beat for the duration of the ostinato.

Resultant aggregate rhythmic pulse when the layers of 6.20A are played together:

Ex.6.20B

Polyrhythm

Jazz may be considered to be innately *polymetric*, due to the implicit coexistence of duple and triple meter that is inherently a part of swing. Yet examples of real polymeter in jazz are relatively rare. It is not uncommon to find two meters coexisting to create a layered ostinato (as in Ex.'s 6.20 above), and this effect is normally achieved with reference to a common downbeat and therefore referred to as a *polyrhythm*. One such example would be the ostinato to Mongo Santamaria's "Afro Blue".

Ex. 6.21

Rhythm pattern to "Afro Blue"

These last two examples illustrate the coexistence of different subdivisions of a common beat. This technique may also manifest itself as what is known in classical music parlance as *hemiola*, by superimposing 3/4 rhythmic phrases over a measure of 4/4. When this happens in jazz, it is usually an instance of composers recreating improvisational practice. For drummers (especially when "trading fours"), it is common to create the illusion of playing in 3/4 by subdividing a 4-bar phrase in 4/4 (16 beats) into four bars of 3/4 plus one of 4/4 instead. Oliver Nelson made use of this device in his arrangement of "Down by the Riverside" in the solo backgrounds.

Ex. 6.22

Brass background/shouts from "Down by the Riverside"

(These chords actually work like a break than a background, interrupting the soloist as it were, and/or creating a "call" for him to respond to. The rhythmic impact of these interactive background figures is enhanced by the harmonic content of the voicing itself. Nelson has voiced the entire Eb dorian scale, primarily in seconds, above a single G natural in the Baritone sax, creating an outrageously dense and arguably *bitonal* sound, providing an example of a strikingly synergistic relationship between the use of strong rhythmic figures combined with secondal harmony.)

Ex. 6.23

The voicing of Nelson's interactive backgrounds

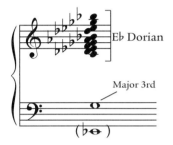

Of course, as noted earlier, Nelson's rhythmic background figure (Ex. 6.22 above) is actually an adaptation of an iconic common practice *polyrhythm* frequently employed in drum solos, in which 5 bars of 3/4 are superimposed over a four-bar 4/4 phrase (in this case a further element of surprise occurs due to the addition of an extra quarter rest separating the final two iterations of the figure, on the downbeat of the fourth measure). Billy Strayhorn's famous arrangement of his composition "Take the A Train" employs a similarly *hemiolic* polyrhythm to create tension just before it modulates from C to Eb at the conclusion of the trumpet solo. This can be heard at 1:37 - 1:42 of the famous Blanton-Webster version of the piece (see end of Chapter ASSIGNMENTS).

Ellington's "Depk" from "The Far East Suite" (1966) provides a good example of real polyrhythm (not to mention asymmetrical phrase lengths[!]). Of particular note is the ensemble section following the piano solo, which seems to superimpose a broad 3/2 meter over the underlying 4/4 swing that continues below the theme (between 1:31 and 1:50, or beginning at measure 85 – also see End of Chapter ASSIGNMENTS).

Perhaps Sun Ra's "Space Is the Place" is an example of real polyrhythm at work, with the signature lyric of the piece repeating in 4/4 over a bass *ostinato* in 10/4, with which it theoretically shares a common downbeat only every 40 beats. It's hard to imagine a better musical metaphor for interplanetary relationships than the way these meters intersect (see end of Chapter ASSIGNMENTS).

Use of the Riff

Mundane though it may seem, there is no denying the capacity for rhythmic development, reiteration and contrast that is implicit in every *riff*. (A riff is a simple, repetitive, and predominantly rhythmic idea, generally of improvisational character and provenance and comprised of only a few notes, that is repeated as background and/or as thematic material.) Complementary background riffs, often created by the players behind soloists, form the backbone of many swing era arrangements (not to mention the composed variety employed so effectively by Charles Mingus). For example, Count Basie's "Jumpin' at the Woodside" and "One O'Clock Jump" are among many riff-based compositions featuring *call and response* melodies between the brass and saxophones as a chief component of its melodic statement. Here is an example in that style showing a unsion melodic riff answering a harmonized one in typical "call and response" format (likely featuring contrasting instrumentation as well, for example brass vs. reeds):

Ex. 6.24

Thad Jones' composition "Big Dipper" uses a simple background riff derived from the main theme of the piece behind the soloist, therefore imparting to it a developmental and organizational quality.

Ex. 6.25

First phrase of main theme of "Big Dipper"

Ex. 6.26

A background riff derived from the theme

Of course in more extended pieces the background riffs are often derived from the theme, or they actually (are) the theme (using the theme as a background to an improvised solo was a favorite Ellington trick). In "The Tattooed Bride", for example, Ellington also uses his spare, zigzagging two-note main motif as a background for soloists (and it seems that Ellington and Strayhorn were unquestionably thinking along these lines[6] – see also End of Chapter ASSIGNMENTS). And as mentioned earlier, in the 1959 filmscore for "Anatomy of a Murder", often cited as an example of economy of means in the exploitation of thematic material, Ellington uses rhythmic *recontextualization* to recast "Flirty Bird" as "Pie Eye Blues".

Thelonious Monk frequently wrote melodies whose rhythmic component seemed more important than either the harmony or melody of the piece. For example, in "Evidence" (his *contrafact* on the standard "Just You, Just Me"), the melody is primarily rhythmic, and very definitely "rifflike" in quality.

Ex. 6.27

"Evidence" A section

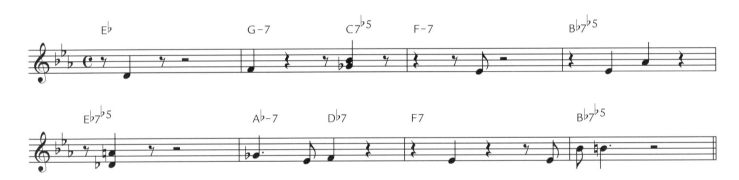

The bridge continues similarly. Two frequently heard elements of Monk's compositional style are at work here. For one, the contrafact, "Evidence", virtually falls in between the cracks of the melody of "Just You, Just Me" (play them together – see also Ex. 6.38). Secondly, Monk often *fragments* an idea from the A section melody to create his B idea (other such examples are "Well, You Needn't", "Straight No Chaser", and "Rhythm-a-Ning").

The bridge of "Evidence"

[6] Boyer, Richard O. *"The Hot Bach", in Tucker, Mark. The Duke Ellington Reader.* Oxford, New York, 1993, pp. 214-245

In much of the repertoire of Art Blakey and the Jazz Messengers, elements of "stop-time" and "call and response" were integrated into the compositional structure using *riff*-type elements. The following example employs these concepts in a manner similar to Benny Golson's "Whisper Not". See also end of Chapter ASSIGNMENTS and DISCOGRAPHY.

Ex.6.28

The master of the use of riff-based layered *ostinato* to create tension was Charles Mingus. For example, in "Haitian Fight Song" he uses four complementary riffs concurrently.

Elision and Asymmetry

Another technique found frequently in the music of Charles Mingus was the use of *asymmetric phrase* structure. Like Strayhorn, Mingus often created phrases which were not periodic. For example, in "Slop", Mingus creates a 9-bar A section.

Ex. 6.29

"Slop" A section

(This is then followed by a 3-bar interlude and a 10-bar bridge!).

Mingus' poignantly beautiful "Self Portrait in Three Colors"[7] is structured as follows: A 5 1/2 bar 4/4 phrase, eliding into a 9-bar bridge via the use of a 2/4 bar at the end of the A section. The piece does not include improvised solos, just the layering in of the three melodies one at a time. It is essentially *through-composed*, with a final 2-bar ending, and although it its use is not as much as in the forefront, as say in "Slop" or "Haitian Fight Song", Mingus is definitely employing a variation of the technique of layered *ostinato* here as well, though in this case the layering involves entire melodic statements. The most striking aesthetic effect conveyed by the piece is not this asymmetry or *counterpoint* however, but its simple beauty. The listener is never left with a sense of *dissonance* or tension (notwithstanding some harmonic clashes – see Chapter 4) or rhythmic instability. It all flows naturally.

* Two such examples are Strayhorn's beautiful ballads "Love Came" and "Passed Me By", both interpreted in a duo setting with Strayhorn at the piano, accompanying vocalist Ozzie Bailey on his "Lush Life" album (see DISCOGRAPHY). The *asymmetric phrase* lengths found in these two compositions are clearly the result of subservience of the musical accompaniment to the lyrics.

SELF-PORTRAIT IN THREE COLORS

Charles Mingus

[7] Mingus, Charles, Ed. Andrew Homzy. *Mingus: More Than a Fakebook*. Hal Leonard, Milwaukee, 1991.

Elision is the process by which the end of one phrase becomes the beginning of the next. For example, in John Coltrane's "Giant Steps", measure 8 is not only the last bar of the second 4-bar phrase, but also the first bar of the *sequential* B section.

Ex. 6.31

The elision in "Giant Steps"

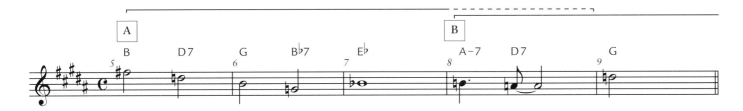

Mingus' "Fables of Faubus" is another example of a piece with non-standard phrase lengths. It also is an excellent example of a piece where changes in the underlying rhythmic feel characterize the various sections of the form, and in which elision is employed to connect them. Although the piece remains in 4/4 throughout, it reinforces all of its formal boundaries by changes in the underlying rhythmic feel.

Ex. 6.32

The formal structure of "Fables Of Faubus"

· Intro: 8-bar introduction sets up *ostinato* over 2-feel.

· A Section "stop-time" horn theme enters (also rifflike in quality) and plays twice over continuing bassline = ms. 9-16, or 2x 4 bars.

· Underlying feel changes to Swing for 6 bars, followed by 5-bar first ending, in which the lst two bars also include the return of the introductory ostinato (an example of elision).

· Following a 5-bar second ending, a 16-bar bridge, divided 8 + 8, with the second 8 bars changing to an underlying "double time" feel for 4 bars, followed by a "stop-time" tritone figure in the bass to lead to the A section going directly to the second ending.

FABLES OF FAUBUS

Charles Mingus

[8] ibid.

Bass & Drums double time

To A w/2nd ending

Bass

Yet these are not just notes and chords in the abstract. Mingus is working with particular musical voices in realizing his harmonic and melodic ideas, and using these does serve to reinforce the form as well. The introductory line is handled by tenor and trombone in unison, with bass fills in a "two feel". The alto and trombone play the melody at A, while the tenor continues the obligato from the introduction. When the time feel switches from *ostinato* to swing at the 9th bar of the A section the melody becomes octave unison. In the B section, by contrast, the melody is in the tenor, with the trombone and alto providing commentary.

Another example of asymmetric phrase structure can be found in "100 Hearts"* by the late pianist and composer Michel Petrucciani. Like Mingus' "Self Portrait", the lyricism of this *through-composed* piece is such that we are left only with the primary impression of its beauty. The 9 and 3-bar phrases it contains are completely logical in context (see DISCOGRAPHY). Wayne Shorter's "Infant Eyes" is also built out of (three) 9-bar phrases.

Yet another example of asymmetric phrase structure is Scott LaFaro's "Gloria's Step", which is comprised entirely of 5-bar phrases (see DISCOGRAPHY and ASSIGNMENTS).

* The leadsheet to this composition can be found in the *Michel Petrucciani Songbook: Compositions Originales*, pp.66-7

Of course, Monk's music contains many examples of *asymmetry*. "Trinkle Tinkle", for example, has a 7 and 1/2 bar A section* during the melody (the result of a final 2/4 bar).

Ex. 6.34

"Trinkle Tinkle" A section

Rhythmic Displacement

No discussion of the uses of rhythm in jazz composition, or of the music of Thelonious Monk, would be complete without an examination of the technique of *rhythmic displacement*. Two of Monk's signature pieces illustrate this. The first is his famous Blues "Straight No Chaser".

Ex. 6.35

"Straight No Chaser"

Monk's use of *displacement* and elongation of the 'A' idea each time it reappears confounds our expectations of typical AAB Blues *phrase structure*.

* "Coming on the Hudson" does as well.

Monk's (or is it Mary Lou Williams', or possibly even Duke Ellington's? – see Chapter 7) "Rhythm-A-Ning" also illustrates the use of *rhythmic displacement*. Notice how in measures A 3 and 4 he repeats the same phrase, first on the downbeat (in measure A-3), then on the third beat (in measure A-4). It is as if for a moment the downbeat of the phrase has been shifted, defying the barline's standard role.

Ex. 6.36

Rhythmic displacement in the A section of "Rhythm-A-Ning"

Unlike many Bop era "Rhythm" tunes, Monk's "Rhythm-A-Ning" develops this consequent idea from the A section in sequence over the standard bridge chord changes, including an unexpected extension of the idea's final iteration using the standard device of the *whole tone* scale (although he startlingly eschews the *consonant* whole tone scale in favor of the *dissonant* one; in other words where F7 first occurs in the 7th measure of the bridge in the box below, the scale used actually implies C7, or V7/V, then resolves to F7 on the downbeat of B-8).

Ex. 6.37

The bridge of "Rhythm-A-Ning" showing the use of the "wrong" whole tone scale in ms.B-7

In Monk's version of "Just You, Just Me", he plays five notes beginning on the second beat of a measure of 4/4 and ending on the downbeat of the next (Monk loved to play tuplets that started on weak beats and transcended barlines). This phrase seems to contradict the arbitrary boundaries of meter and barline, almost defying notation. Such examples must be heard to be fully appreciated, and reinforce the fact that in matters of phrasing and interpretation at least, some things simply cannot be notated.

"Just You, Just Me", arranged by Thelonious Monk, ms.A1-4

Finally, just as Monk frequently reversed the paradigm vis a vis the relationship between *neighbor tones* and their expected *target* (see Ex. 4.50D), so Ellington's "Diminuendo and Crescendo in Blue" achieved that same effect, but with regard to notions of *climax* and *development*. This was accomplished in large part by the means of the interdependent use of the devices of *rhythmic displacement* and *asymmetric phraselength* in the jarring, deliberately disjunct first half of the piece. Some examples follow.

Ex. 6.39

Opening phrase

Displaced "response" in third chorus

Finally it should be noted that Monk's influence on his colleagues in terms of his emphasis on rhythm and angularity cannot be overemphasized. A well-known "Rhythm" variation by Bill Evans, entitled "Five", illustrates the use of both *rhythmic displacement* and *polyrhythm* (see end of Chapter ASSIGNMENTS), and demonstrates musically Evans' oft-stated admiration for Monk.

Conclusions

There are many compositions in which rhythm may be said to be the dominant factor in characterizing the mood, style, and even content of the piece. Beyond obvious stylistic implications (i.e. "Latin","Swing", "stop-time", etc.), the rhythmic content of the piece may be a definitive musical characteristic. Rhythm and meter may also be used creatively to recontextualize thematic material in much the same way as reharmonization does. Changes in the underlying rhythmic feeling may help to delineate and contrast sections of the form. Vamps, ostinatos and riffs may be used as introductions, codas, backgrounds and/or thematically. Asymmetric phraselengths may result from elision of themes.

ASSIGNMENTS

1.) Listen to all of the music discussed in this Chapter (including, if possible, the filmscore from "Anatomy of a Murder", see discussion, page 135, 146).

2.) Find examples of the following and bring them to class for discussion:

· Polyrhythmic phrases (listen together to Ellington's "Depk" from the "Far East Suite" – count the measures of each phrase and listen carefully to the polyrhythmic moment referred to earlier in the text);

· Use of ostinato or stop-time;

· Ostinato or layered ostinato-based vamp;

· Riff-based composition;

· Composition using rhythmic displacement;

· Composition in an AABA songform alternating Latin and Swing sections;

· An example of an arrangement or composition where changes in underlying rhythmic feel and/or meter recontextualize thematic presentation;

· A composition employing asymmetry in its phrase structure;

· Transcribe the rhythms of the melody of Bill Evans' "Five" (see DISCOGRAPHY);

· Transcribe the opening four bars of Benny Golson's "Whisper Not" and examine its use of concerted call and response (cf. also Ex. 6.28);

· Listen to "Gloria's Step" by Scott Lafaro (found on the "Bill Evans Trio Complete Village Vanguard Recordings, 1961", see DISCOGRAPHY);

· Listen to the polyrhythmic cadence in Strayhorn's "Take The A Train" referred to on page 144;

3.) Write a 32-bar composition based on a motif that is primarily rhythmic in character;

4.) Write a 32-bar composition in AABA form that alternates between Latin and Swing from the A to the B. Also include an ostinato based introduction;

5.) Write a Ballad with asymmetric phrase structure. Consider the Strayhorn ballads referred to on page 148 as you do so.

CHAPTER 7

Appropriation & Adaption

In this Chapter we will discuss the myriad implications of the related compositional notions of *appropriation* and *adaptation* as applied to composition in the jazz idiom. These include, but are not limited to, those of:

· Signification (in this case by employing various means of *recontextualization* of existing work);

· Creation of *contrafacts* and other forms based on pre-existing compositions;

· Personalizing one's approach to appropriated materials by creation of a "signature sound" in harmonic and orchestral vocabulary.

· (Adaptation of European Classical Forms and techniques will be addressed separately in Chapter 8.)

Not surprisingly we will see that these principles are rarely found in isolation, and that many of examples selected therefore illustrate the carefully balanced juxtaposition of complementary musical elements.

Quoting and Paraphrase

There are innumerable examples of *quoting* in both improvised and composed jazz. Further, the notion of quoting from extant material is much older than the jazz idiom in the history of music. The complex notion of "signification", described by Henry Louis Gates (see BIBLIOGRAPHY), describes the use of the interdependent elements of *repetition*, *adaptation*, and *appropriation* to create commentary, often under the guise of imitation. For jazz musicians, quoting particular standards in the context of improvisation has been perhaps the best known manifestation of this tradition. Some musicologists have attempted to impute the improviser's motivations for the quoting of melodies associated with particular lyrics in instrumental performance practice[1]. Whether or not such speculation is wholly correct, there is no doubt some truth to the notion that a given quotation or *paraphrase* may at times have specific extra-musical meaning for the jazz composer or improviser (for example, Clifford Brown's introduction to his performance of Bud Powell's "Parisian Thoroughfare" is directly appropriated from Gershwin's "American in Paris" – see end of Chapter ASSIGNMENTS). Often, however, the gesture is done for its own sake, because the quote in question fits the chord changes, and is known to the audience, whether the listener being targeted is in the audience or a fellow musician.

[1] Beeson, Ann. *"Quoting Tunes": Narrative Features in Jazz"*, in Collectanea: Papers in Folklore, Popular and Expressive Culture 1 (1990)

Examples from this latter category may seem relatively mundane and are ubiquitous. Horace Silver, along with Sonny Rollins, Thelonious Monk, Sonny Stitt, Charlie Parker, Dexter Gordon, and virtually every other jazz improviser, frequently quotes other melodies in his solos. For one such example, the spiritual "Down by the Riverside" (also known by the title "Ain't Goin' to Go To War No More" in its sacred version[2]), is quoted over the bridge of his solo on "Nica's Dream" (see end of Chapter ASSIGNMENTS).

Another instance of an improvised solo packed full of quotes is Johnny Griffin's final chorus on Monk's "Rhythm-a-Ning", from "Live at the Five Spot", in which he quotes "Jumpin' with Symphony Sid", "Fascinatin' Rhythm", and "Would You Like to Swing on a Star" in close succession, concluding the solo with Mendelssohn Bartholdy's "Wedding March".

Ex. 7.1

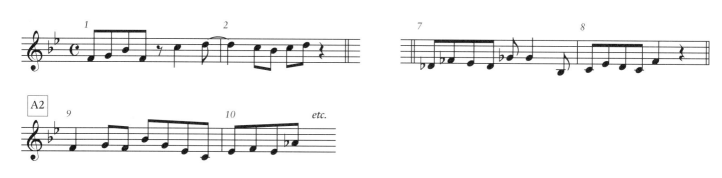

Ex. 7.2

(While the Silver quote referred to above doesn't exactly fit the bridge chord changes to "Nica's Dream", Griffin's quotes imply substitutions for the *standard* changes). There are other sorts of quotes that have acquired a meaning among practicing musicians, whose origins, like those of the use of certain "alternate" chord changes on particular standards, are hard to pinpoint precisely. One such frequently heard quote, originally from "The King and I" ("The March of the Siamese Children"), fits major chords and implies a lydian (#11) sound.

[2] Burleigh, Harry T. *The Spirituals of Harry T. Burleigh.* Warner Brothers, Miami, 1984, p.68

These sorts of quotes seem to be used because they *can* be, meaning in the technical sense that they "fit the changes". Some *quotes* are heard more often because they fit so well over commonly used progressions. In any event, melodic fragments from iconic standards and/or mundane popular songs may be "worked out" in different keys so as to be available to the improviser or composer, just as any melodic pattern might be (any solo by Johnny Griffin, Sonny Rollins, or Dexter Gordon is sure to feature a few such quotes!). What well-known American folk tune is being worked out in the following example?

Ex.7.4

As with any other improvisational practice in the jazz idiom, quoting may be used as a compositional device as well. This may be done in a way that imbues it with a specific contextual meaning as well. For example, Ellington's "Black, Brown and Beige", according to the composer, is a tone poem intended to depict the history of the struggles and achievements of African-Americans. Additionally, its form was based on a poem authored by the composer[3]. Therefore, when he quotes such patriotic tunes as "Yankee Doodle" in Movement 2 ("Brown") of the piece, his meaning is related formally to the poetic content of the piece.

Ex. 7.5

"Yankee Doodle" quoted in "Brown"

Given the year in which the piece was written (1943), and Ellington's famously articulated attitudes about the issue of African-American patriotism and military sacrifice in the face of continuing discrimination in American society[4], the sense of irony that accompanies such a quote is inescapable.

[3] Peress, Maurice. *"My Life with Black, Brown and Beige"*. Black Music Research Journal, Vol. 13 (2), 1993, pp. 155-57

[4] Ellington, Duke. *"We Too Sing America"*, in Tucker, Mark. *The Duke Ellington Reader*. Oxford, New York, 1993, pp.146-8

An earlier example of contextualized *quoting* can be heard in Ellington's use of the Chopin Funeral March in "Black and Tan Fantasy" in 1929. This reference is particularly dramatic when one sees it used in the shortfilm of the same title, reminding us once again that for Ellington music often painted a picture. In terms of absolute music "Black and Tan Fantasy" is sort of a blue-sified version of the Chopin, but in the film score this use has a further, dramatic context[5].

Ex. 7.6

The "Chopin Funeral March" in "Black and Tan Fantasy" (ms.5-8)

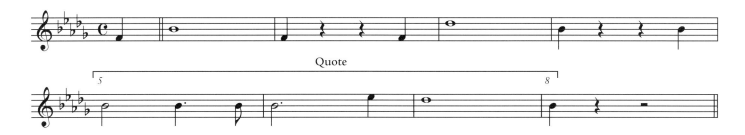

(The quote is reiterated as a *consequent* phrase in ms.11 and 12.)

The important thing that we learn from such examples is that the pervasive practice of quoting in jazz can be done with various degrees of meaning.

Appropriation

The notion of appropriating and recycling the ideas of others or of one's own has also been common practice among jazz composers. For example, as Mark Tucker has point out, Billy Strayhorn seems to have appropriated a line from a Johnny Hodges solo on "Clementine" and expanded on it to create the theme of his "Raincheck"[6].

Ex. 7.7

Hodges solo fragment

(Compare the above solo fragment with Strayhorn's "Raincheck" theme, found on the same recording.)

[5] Black and Tan, 1929, in *"Duke Ellington and His Orchestra: Classics"*, 1929-52, Amvest Video

[6] Tucker, Mark. *Liner Notes for "The Blanton Webster Band"*, RCA Bluebird 3-CD set

Ellington did the same with what was, according to Clark Terry, a warm-up exercise of Cootie Williams', to create the famous "Concerto for Cootie"[7]. As Terry correctly notes, the exercise might have remained just that had Ellington not imagined a way in which to develop it into a fullblown composition, one that not only fit Williams' musical persona, but actually characterized it. This well-known composition is analyzed more fully in Chapter 8.

John Coltrane frequently borrowed and recast the material of others through the prism of his own musical personality. One of his best known compositions, "Impressions", is actually constructed entirely from pre-existing musical materials. As Lewis Porter and others have observed, the A section of the theme comes from Morton Gould's "Pavanne", while the bridge melody bears a strong resemblance to a melodic phrase found in Ravel's "Pavane Pour Une Infante Défunte". (Of course, the chord progression is identical to that of Miles Davis' "So What".) Such was the strength of Coltrane's musical personality that in his hands these materials combined to form "Impressions" (perhaps the title is a nod to Ravel) and became one of his signature pieces[8].

Ex. 7.8A

Excerpt from Ravel's "Pavane" (begins at ms.8)

Ex. 7.8B

Bridge of "Impressions" (approximate / idealized rhythms based on various live performances, as opposed to the published version of the melody found in the Hal Leonard "Music of John Coltrane", see also BIBLIOGRAPHY and DISCOGRAPHY)

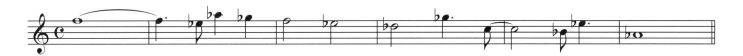

[7] *A Duke Named Ellington, PBS American Masters*, Produced A & E, 1988

[8] Porter, Lewis. *John Coltrane: His Life and Music.* Michigan, Ann Arbor, 1998, p. 218

Coltrane's "India" provides another such example. This time the source was an LP of world music thought with which Trane was said to have been familiar. The LP, entitled "Religious Music from India"[9], contains an example of Vedic chant that is partially transcribed below, with the main theme to "India" following it.

Ex. 7.9A

Vedic chant excerpt from "Religious Music of India"

Ex. 7.9B

Main theme for "India"

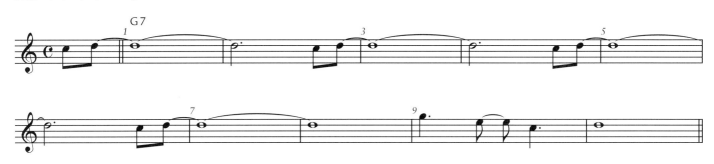

Playing the two excerpts back to back (the spot most closely resembling "India" occurs on the Folkways LP at about 2:38-2:45) provides a striking comparison indeed.

Of course, as with "Impressions", the fact that the thematic material was borrowed does not diminish the powerfully individualistic transformation of the material in Coltrane's hands.

"Giant Steps" (see also Chapter 8) is another example of Coltrane's ability to rework the material of others. In this case, the source is the introduction to Nicolas Slonimsky's "Thesaurus of Scales". The example in Slonimsky's introduction, entitled "Tonal Harmonization of a 12-Tone Pattern"[10], shows a striking similarity to both the key relationships and melodic material of the second half of "Giant Steps".

[9] "Religious Music of India", Folk ways LP 4431

[10] Slonimsky, Nicolas. *Thesaurus of Scales and Melodic Patterns.* Scribners, New York, 1947, p. vi.

Example from Slonimsky Introduction referred to above

The A phrase of "Giant Steps" is constructed from the *hexatonic scale* (of which there are four, produced by the alternation of 1/2 steps and minor thirds, also described by some jazz theorists as the "Augmented" Scale). This *symmetric scale* was also used frequently by Bartók, another composer whose work was surely familiar to Coltrane[11].

Ex. 7.10B

"Giant Steps" melody

Although the "hexatonic scale" is not so named per se by Slonimsky, it does appear in his book[12]:

Ex. 7.11A

Example of a Hexatonic Scale, as found in Slonimsky
(see "Ditone Progression" #181 in The Thesaurus of Scales)[13]

Ex. 7.11B

"Giant Steps" melody showing hexatonic relationships

Hexatonic source

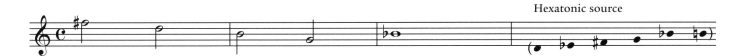

[11] Porter, p. 125
[12] Slonimsky, p. 27
[13] ibid.

Just as Ellington and Strayhorn frequently retitled or excerpted extant compositions (Strayhorn's famous "Isfahan" was originally entitled "Elf" for example, and existed prior to the "Far East Suite" of which it subsequently became such a famous part[14]), so Coltrane frequently reused his signature harmonic devices and melodies in later work. This is a particularly personal form of "signification", in which elements of Coltrane's "signature sound" (use of third related harmony; extended, often modally-based solos; and his uniquely personal voice on the saxophone) are combined. For example, the album "Coltrane's Sound" is an entire recording whose primary premise is the adaptation of Coltrane's signature "three-tonic system" to standards (of course he'd previously employed this system in his solos). When we hear 'Trane's version of "Body and Soul", the interpolation of the "Giant Steps/Countdown" harmonic progression at the end of each phrase of the bridge is obvious.

Ex. 7.12

Coltrane's version of bridge of "Body and Soul"
showing interpolation of "Giant Steps" changes

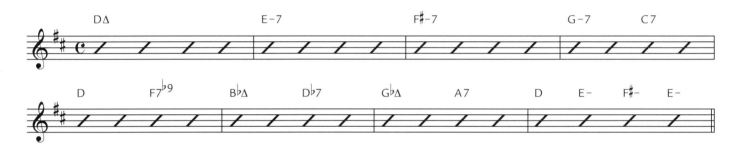

In Coltrane's arrangement of "But Not For Me" (from the "My Favorite Things" album), he divides the form of the ABAC tune essentially in half, juxtaposing the two complementary whole tone scales to support "Giant Steps" changes in the A sections[15] (over a "two" feel), then using the standard chord changes to swing the B and C sections. The implicit contrast is striking. After soloing for several choruses over these changes, Coltrane goes on to play for an equal amount of time over an extended, primarily diatonic, turnaround (actually the chord changes here are ii−7 to V7 followed by iv−7 and ♭VII7). During this second part of his solo Coltrane gradually deconstructs his improvisation until the final melodic phrase of the Gershwin tune is 'revealed' just prior to the break leading to the piano solo. Also of interest, 28 bars prior to the conclusion of the solo 'Trane quotes "Giant Steps", though given the harmonic constraints, the quote is diatonic, not literal. Still, it is undeniable (start listening to the recording at around 3:10 to hear this paraphrase, which is contained in the 28th and 29th measures from the end of the solo).

[14] van de Leur, Walter. *Something to Live For: The Music of Billy Strayhorn.* Oxford, New York, 2002, p. 268

[15] see also Coltrane, John, Ed. Demsey, Dave, *John Coltrane Plays Giant Steps (Introduction)*, Hal Leonard, Milwaukee, 1996.

Reharmonized chord changes and bass line
in Coltrane arrangement of "But Not For Me"

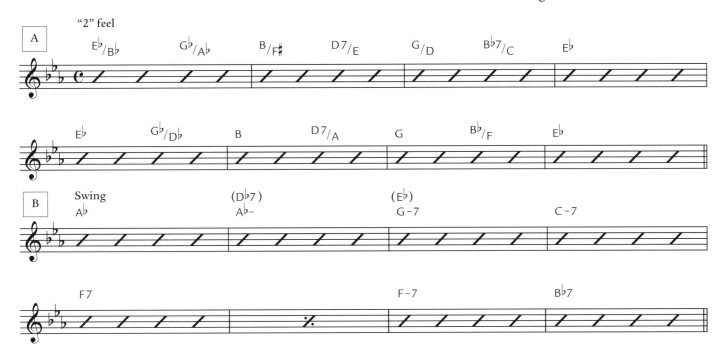

And perhaps Ellington was acknowledging Coltrane's interest in major and minor third relationships when he composed his Blues "Take the Coltrane" for their joint album. The melody of the piece (as well as its harmonization in the second melody chorus - indicated parenthetically) is comprised entirely of major and minor thirds!

Ex. 7.14

Theme to "Take the Coltrane"

The notion of "consilience" (scientifically this term refers to the independent corroboration of a principle or a generalization from widely different inductions), as discussed in Chapter 1, may be applied to apparent instances of appropriation or commentary. Communality of musical style and language may often cause such relationships to become difficult to document. In other words, sometimes what sounds like a quote or a paraphrase may be a coincidental result of the use of ubiquitous common practice materials.

Consider for example the famous Gershwin theme "I Got Rhythm". This theme bears great similarity to the opening theme of the third movement of William Grant Still's "Afro-American Symphony", shown below (the Gershwin piece is dated 1930[16], Still's 1931, and the two composers are said to have worked together[17]). How do we assess the similarity between these two pieces? Given the "common practice" (i.e. pentatonic) nature of the thematic material, is there really an issue of appropriation here? (In other words, couldn't the theme have plausibly been arrived at independently by the two composers?)

EX. 7.15A

"I Got Rhythm" theme excerpt

EX. 7.15B

"Afro-American Symphony" theme excerpt

The same question may be asked with reference to the harmony of "I Got Rhythm", based as it is on common practice devices that can be found throughout the era in which it was written. The A sections of Ellington's "Rockin in Rhythm", to cite but one example, are also based on the I-vi-ii-V7 turnaround, yet who would say that Gershwin appropriated his harmony from Ellington, even though they had worked together circa 1930 as well![18]? This seems to be yet another example of the evolution of consilient ideas resulting from a common musical environment.

Another case of possible appropriation is Thelonious Monk's "Rhythm-A-Ning". Monk's well-known "Rhythm Changes" *contrafact* bears great similarity to both Ellington's "Ducky Wucky" (1929) and Mary Lou Williams' "Walkin' and Swingin'", yet scholars for various reasons feel that the latter composition is the more likely source of the *appropriation*[19]. Whether the similarity is due to appropriation or *consilience*, it is nonetheless undeniable.

[16] Jaffe, Andy. *Jazz Harmony*. Advance Music, Rottenburg Germany, 1996, p. 149

[17] Author's conversation with Dr. Horace Clarence Boyer, 2002

[18] Hasse, *Beyond Category*, p. 122

[19] Tucker, Mark. "Mainstreaming Monk: The Ellington Album", *Black Music Research Journal*, Vol. 19 (2), Fall '99, p. 236

"Ducky Wucky" first ending

Ex. 7.15D

"Walkin' and Swingin'" excerpt

Ex. 7.15E

"Rhythm-A-Ning"

Regardless of the source of the material, however, it is what Monk did with it, particularly in terms of rhythmic treatment and development, and performance (see also Chapter 6) that made it indelibly his own.

The Contrafact

Many writers on jazz composition have asserted that the *contrafact* is one of the most important processes by which new music is created in the idiom. The word contrafact dates to the Renaissance, when it originally meant to write new words to an existing melody[20]. In jazz practice, the term has been adapted to mean the process of writing a new melody on the chord changes to a well-known standard. While the disproportionate emphasis on the preeminence of its importance within the compositional realm is problematic (mostly because such a facile, formulaic approach deemphasizes other important compositional factors), there is no doubt that this process has been an important one. Though this process has perhaps stereotypically been primarily associated with Bebop it has by no means been restricted exclusively to that style. Jazz composers have recycled existing chord progressions throughout the history of the music. Composers have done this for a variety of reasons, some pragmatic, some philosophical. For one thing, by composing a new melody to a pre-existing set of changes, one has created a "copyrightable" piece of one's own, enabling the composer to own the rights to the new piece. During the Bebop era, composers also wrote new lines on the changes to standards as a means of creating a "coded" repertoire that not only provided them ownership of the music in a legal sense, but which also enabled them to keep others from sitting in.

Examples of contrafacts from earlier periods incude Ellington's "Stompy Jones" (1934) which is based on the New Orleans standard "Panama", and Benny Moten's "Moten Swing", based on the standard "(You're Drivin' Me) Crazy". Another example from Ellingtonia would be his use of the chord changes to "Tiger Rag" for the harmonic foundation of the saxophone soli in "Daybreak Express". From the Bebop era, Dizzy Gillespie's "Groovin' High" is a recasting of the 1920's "Whispering". Miles Davis' "Donna Lee" is based on the changes to the World War I era standard "Back Home in Indiana". And of course there are literally hundreds, if not thousands, of contrafacts based on Gershwin's "I Got Rhythm", collectively referred to as "Rhythm Changes" tunes (Parker's "Anthropology", Davis' "The Serpent's Tooth", even the theme song to the popular TV comic "The Flintstones", among many other examples). By examining these pieces in context we learn about the nature of common practice in the period which they were written, as well as something of the composer's stylistic traits and influences. Again, it is never enough to study just the work of a given musician. Only by studying "what they listened to" can we begin to fully understand them as a product of the musical culture in which they existed, and only by breaking down their compositional process can we begin to fully understand how they achieved their "signature sound".

[20] *Harvard Dictionary of Music, Second Edition.* Harvard University Press, Cambridge, Massachusetts, 1969, p. 203

One particular subgenre of the *contrafact* involves what is known as "scat vocalese". In this practice, used in the Bebop era and since, vocalists compose lyrics to solos or tunes by instrumentalists. For example, Eddie Jefferson's version of "Moment's Notice" eulogizes John Coltrane by adding lyrics to his famous composition. Sheila Jordan similarly composed lyrics to Miles Davis' "Little Willie Leaps" (itself a contrafact on Bronislau Kaper's "All God's Children Got Rhythm"), and of course Jon Hendricks adapted entire big band compositions for three voices and rhythm section (examples being his adaptation of Juan Tizol's "Caravan", and the entire album "Sing a Song of Basie").

The Sonic Signature

Various musical elements combine in the work of a mature musician to create his or her *signature sound*. For the jazz player, this may have to do with the particular combination of technical resources employed, such as the kind of mouthpiece, reed or mute used. Elements of phrasing, articulation and tone quality may be important. For the jazz writer (and in this case the disciplines of composition and arranging are indistinguishable), elements of harmonic and rhythmic vocabulary, orchestration, and intervallic configuration of chord voicings may be factors. One thing we all have in common is the fact that our musical personality reflects in large part our listening experience, and as such is always subject to change and evolution, reflecting our aural input and consequent musical development.

Returning to Coltrane's music, his *sonic signature* and particular combination of influences are both in evidence in his arrangement of "My Favorite Things"(rec. 1960). He has not changed the meter of the piece, though the underlying rhythmic pulse is as much duple as it is the standard waltz time of the original piece from the Broadway show "The Sound of Music" (at the time of Coltrane's recording the film version was not yet released[21]). Combined with this subtle change in rhythmic approach is a pedal tone in the bass. Extended *modal* solos, perhaps reflective of the influence Indian music had on Coltrane[22], alternate between parallel major and minor modal explorations, and are set off by Rondo-like statements of the main tune. The net effect is a transformation of the piece from a popular Broadway showtune to a deep spiritual journey. Merely using this unique combination of technical devices does not make it so of course. The chemistry between the players and their unique aggregate musical personality is clearly critical and must be factored into the equation as well. Still, interpretive elements aside, Coltrane definitely used such devices as modality, *pedal point*, *ostinato*, and solos of long duration to personalize his approach to *standards*.

[21] Porter, pp. 181
[22] Porter, pp. 210-11

Often he employed his "three tonic system" as well, as in the album "Coltrane's Sound", or his arrangment of "But Not For Me" (described earlier in this Chapter). The influence of "world music" sources on Coltrane is also undeniable in this piece, as it is in others such as "India" (discussed previously) and "Ole". Although his embrace of non-Western influences was important due to his enormous personal influence and popularity (which came eventually to appeal to a much broader group than just the jazz audience), it was not unique among jazz musicians. While Coltrane had become one of the first "schooled" jazz musicians (benefiting from the GI bill to study in a conservatory-style setting[23]), other musicians had also become aware of non-Western music and trends in contemporary composition through extensive listening and study.

Such was also the case for Miles Davis and Gil Evans, who, like Coltrane, became enamoured of Spanish music, both traditional and formally composed. One result was the famous "Sketches of Spain" recording (1959), in which Evans reworked Rodrigo's "Concierto de Aranjuez" and other Spanish pieces to feature Miles Davis. Evans' work with Davis on this recording established a process in which he would transfer the main solo lines of the piece to Davis' distinctively plaintive harmon mute sound. Open sections were then added to the form for Davis to improvise on. While the main thematic and harmonic material remains primarily intact, Evans personalizes his version of the piece in part by transforming it into a feature for Davis' distinctive solo voice. In this sense the musical personalities of the arranger and soloist are inexorably intertwined, as was so often the case with Ellington and his players. Evans' extensive autodidactic study of 20th century repertoire, as well as his formative experience writing for the Claude Thornhill band in the early '40's, formed the basis for his evolution into an orchestral pioneer in jazz, liberating the music from the constraints of the sound palette of big band instrumentation. Thornhill's band had featured two clarinets in addition to the traditional saxophone section, as well as French Horns and Tuba (these instrumental timbres had reappeared in the reduced instrumentation for the rehearsal band co-led by Davis and Evans that led to the influential "Birth of the Cool" sessions of 1949). Evans' explorations expanded further in "Sketches of Spain" to include bassoons, harp, and additional woodwinds and characteristic Iberian percussion (castanets). While the use of these instruments can hardly be said to have been "new" to Evans' work, the influence it had was indisputable. This became another aesthetic change associated with the "modal" era: the emphasis on timbre for its own sake among many of its composer arrangers. The following examples are illustrative of Evans' characteristic emphasis on timbre and interval in creating his *signature sound*.

23 Porter, pp. 50-51

Brass and Flutes in parallel diatonic harmony in a passage from
"Sketches of Spain" (supported by improvised Harp arpeggios)

(Of course further study of the scores of "Birth of the Cool" [now published[24]] and Evans' contributions to the Thornhill Orchestra [see also Chapter 8] will be of interest to the aspiring jazz composer as well.)

Just as Monk had done in the rhythmic realm, Evans exerted a powerful influence on subsequent writers in terms of orchestration, and the expansion of the timbral palette of the music. Clare Fischer is one composer whose vocabulary routinely includes unison lines combining muted brass and flutes (for example, in "Miles Behind", from the 1969 album "Thesaurus" – see end of Chapter ASSIGNMENTS). Evans' influence in the timbral realm reverberates today in the work of such composer/bandleaders as Maria Schneider and John Hollenbeck (see DISCOGRAPHY), whose work exploits timbral nuance, combined with a reiterative use of rhythm reminiscent of the minimalist composers, to create a distinct orchestral sound.

Contrapuntal Textures and Linearity

Another important aspect of the Evans sound, also found in the writing of Oliver Nelson, Clare Fischer, Bill Hollman, and others, is the use of unison and octave unison textures in both linear and contrapuntal backgrounds, as a means of creating development. For example, as David Baker has observed[25], Evans' Big band arrangement of Thelonious Monk's "Straight, No Chaser" (1959) essentially creates its development without resorting to any harmonization. Motivic manipulation of the melody is the primary factor here.

[24] Davis, Miles. "Birth of the Cool: Original Scores", Hal Leonard, Milwaukee, 2002
[25] Liner notes to "Great Jazz Standards" (BlueNote)

Summary of Gil Evans arrangement of Monk's "Straight, No Chaser"

The first two choruses of the arrangement feature piano and saxophone tremolos while the rhythm section plays straight time over a 12-bar *Blues*. Then, in the third chorus, the melody appears in octave unison, employing Evans' characteristic Thornhill-influenced use of the tuba to state the theme. After the melodic statement follow solos for trumpet, soprano sax and trombone. Behind the last improvised solo (trombone), the following unison background is added and played twice (p/f), in multi-octave unison, but is now presented in flute, harmon-muted trumpets, and tuba:

Ex. 7.17

In the recapitulation, the melody is presented again in unison as it was previously, then adding a harmony a third above, then further thickening the texture by adding the melody in *inversion* in the trumpet as well:

Ex. 7.18

Recapitulation of the theme

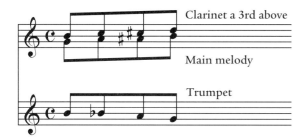

Finally the two-note background theme that earlier accompanied the trombone solo is reiterated and the piece then fades out with tremolos, just as it began, creating a sense of formal balance.

In summary, Evans personalizes this chorus form arrangement through the use of several of his signature orchestral devices. These include:

· Assigning melodic statements to the low brass (see also his reworking of the John Lewis fugue "Concorde");

· The use of "metallic" unison lines (i.e. those mixing flutes with brass, see also Ex. 7.17 above, and Herbie Hancock's "Speak Like a Child", Chapter 8), and

· An impeccably balanced sense of the form, achieved in this case by his *recapitulation* of all of the elements he introduces. There is nothing superfluous here, and, to reiterate, *not one traditional ensemble chord voicing to be found in the entire piece.*

Billy Strayhorn's "Northern Lights" (from the 1960 "Queen's Suite") also uses *counterpoint* freely in "call and response" fashion, over an extended *pedal point*, to create a large portion of its thematic material.

Ex. 7.19

Measures A3 and 4

In his 1946 arrangement of "It Don't Mean a Thing If It Ain't Got That Swing", Ellington used "hocket" style melodic imitation to create a contrapuntal texture.

Ex. 7.20

Three-part vocal statement (1946 arrangement)

Mary Lou Williams and Billy Strayhorn were also experimenting with fugal forms in the 1940's[26] (see also Chapter 8 for analysis and discussion of the John Lewis Fugue "Concorde" and other adaptations of European Classical forms).

Oliver Nelson's arrangement of "Down by the Riverside" also uses the device of counterpoint to thicken the texture, though in this case he does so in a way that specifically simulates improvised New Orleans style 3-part counterpoint. Early New Orleans ensemble dynamics stereotypically featured trumpet playing the melody, with antiphonal and complementary contrapuntal melodies being improvised in the clarinet and trombones. These roles became the foundation of much of the sectional writing of early big band music (see also Chapter 5, "The Stampede"), so Nelson's reference to it, albeit through the use of more modern melodic vocabulary, reminds us once again of the efficacy of recreating idiomatic improvised or interactive instrumental dynamics as a part of the compositional or arranging process.

[26] Buehrer, Ted. "Lonely Moments? The Anatomy of Mary Lou Williams' Oft-Recorded Tune", IAJE Research Papers, 2003, pp. 52-63

Ex. 7.21

The three parts of the "Down by the Riverside" counterpoint

Nelson also popularized a number of important orchestral concepts in his influential early 60's recording "Blues and the Abstract Truth". Perhaps most important among these was his use of an intervallically based vocabulary of voicings. In his 1960 composition, "Stolen Moments", his harmonically complete four-voice texture emphasizes the inner voice-minor second created by replacing the root with the ninth:

Ex. 7.22

The use of these techniques for both small and large ensemble reinforces several important principles:

1.) There is always a small band within the large ensemble. A three or four horn scenario may always be extracted from the larger ensemble for the purposes of stating a melody or creating sectional solo backgrounds.

2.) It is possible to isolate combinations of instruments across sections (i.e. mixing winds and brass in unison statements or voicings), and

3.) Techniques and principles that are effective for small ensembles may be used when writing for large ensembles, and vice-versa. As we will see in Chapter 8, this is equally true with regard to underlying principles used to structure extended works as it is in terms of voicing techniques.

Common Practice Voicing Techniques
Open and Closed Position 4-Part Chords

Although this is not an arranging text per se, we should acknowledge that the use of the type of *close-position* 4-part structures heard in "Stolen Moments" has become an important part of the common practice vocabulary of composers and arrangers working in all sorts of ensemble contexts. In this style of writing, the *4-part chord* nearly always includes the "quality tones"(i.e. third and seventh) of the chord, as well as its root (possibly replaced by the ninth) and fifth (possibly replaced by the thirteenth). Whether or not the roots and fifths are replaced with their respective color tones depends on such variables as what note appears in the melody, and resultant inner-voice intervals. The companion piece to "Stolen Moments", also from the "Blues and the Abstract Truth" recording is entitled "Yearnin'". Whereas "Stolen Moments" featured closed position chords using inner voice color tones, "Yearnin'" employs the technique of what are known as *open voicings*. Open voicings may be thought of as having been created by "dropping" one (sometimes two) of the tones from a four-part *close position* structure down one octave. This might be done for several reasons:

· first, to put the quality tones below the color tones, and to thereby avoid potential harmonic clashes resulting from the conversion of inner-voice 1/2 steps into "inadvertent ♭9" intervals;

· secondly, in order to redistribute the voices of the chord into ranges that are compatible for the instruments or voices involved (i.e. SATB format);

· thirdly, in order to emphasize a given intervallic structure, and

· finally, to create space between adjacent voices.

In the opening measures of "Yearnin'", we can see the use of open voicings, featuring the 13th in the second voice (instead of the 5th). Because the piece is a Blues (indeed the entire album is in effect Nelson's personalized take on the standard Blues and "Rhythm Changes" forms), its *tonic* chord is a dominant seventh. Because the root of the chord is in the melody, it is not replaced by a ninth (of course the need for harmonic completeness in every voicing need not always be slavishly adhered to – more about that in a moment).

Ex. 7.23

Opening chords of "Yearnin'"

Ex. 7.24

To reconstruct the *close position* chord from which the primary voicing of Ex. 7.23 was created, move the bottom voice up an octave.

Note that it would have been a less appropriate choice to have "dropped" the 13th instead of the seventh of the chord, resulting in an "inadvertent ♭9" interval (this is why, as mentioned earlier, in conventional usage *open voicings* generally have thirds and sevenths in the lower voices). The spacing between voices is not as desirable in this example either.

Ex. 7.25

Regardless of whether or not the voicing structures involved are derived "mechanically" (a term sometimes used to describe this process), their intervallic content is certainly the preeminent factor in their sound. Frequently, especially in post-modal period composition and arranging, we find examples of a given voicing being transposed in parallel (also known as "planing"[27]), giving even more emphasis to its reiterated intervallic content. In "Sameeda", from Abdullah Ibrahim's 1985 album "Water from an Ancient Well", we find a series of open, "a cappella" voicings for four saxophones being used in this fashion to striking effect (see end of Chapter ASSIGNMENTS and DISCOGRAPHY).

Of course compositionally there is more here than mere effect. The improvised solos that follow the melodic statement are also based on the melody, this time used as a bassline or unaccompanied harmonic foundation.

Parallelism based on quartally-based intervallically constructed voicings is also quite common. *Quartal voicings* (those built in intervals of fourths – see also Ex. 7.16) are quite effective for this purpose.

Ex. 7.26

Quartal Voicings in Coda of "Yearnin'"

Note that in the above example the devices of pedal tone and Blues-based melody are also being used.

27 Wright, Rayburn. *Inside the Score.* Kendor Music, Delvan, N.Y., 1982, p. 186

Soli Writing

Before leaving the topic of common practice four-part chord voicings it is important that we also discuss the topic of *soli* writing.

A *soli*, as the term implies, is a harmonized melodic line. Generally in jazz ensemble writing this has meant an improvised-sounding line, more often than not in eighth notes, that is harmonized sectionally. The most common scenario has been the saxophone soli, though of course this technique may be transferred to other instrumental sections and/or mixed groups of instruments or voices as well (Strayhorn's "Timperturbably Blue" from the 1959 Ellington album "Jazz Party" features a mallet percussion soli[!]). The following example illustrates the typical Swing Era use of this technique in Gil Evans' 1942 arrangement of Tchaikovsky's "Arab Dance".

Ex. 7.27

Excerpt from "Arab Dance" soli

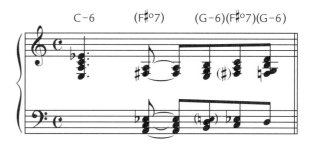

Notice that the fifth voice is essentially a doubled version of the melody one octave lower, so that in effect there are actually only four discrete voices. Also note that the *passing notes* (i.e. those that are inherently less emphasized rhythmically due to their unaccented placement in relationship to the beat) are frequently reharmonized so as to produce motion in each voice to complement that which occurs in the melody line. Note as well the use of the common technique of employing passing *diminished seventh chords* to harmonize these passing tones.

Of course reharmonization techniques are commonly used to deal with non-harmonic tones or *approach notes*. The following example illustrates the use of the *substitute dominant* seventh chord for this purpose.

Ex. 7.28

From shout chorus by Mary Lou Williams ("Scratchin' in the Gravel")

Revisiting Oliver Nelson's "Yearnin'" (Ex. 7.23 above) we can also see that chromatic reharmonization is effective when used in parallel to support chromatic *approach notes*. Although the primary chords in Ex. 7.23 are dominant (because it's a Blues), there is no reason that reharmonization needs to use dominant function chords exclusively. Basically, a reharmonization can be created in any way that will allow each of the individual voices in the chord to approach the parallel voice in the upcoming ("target") chord in a melodic way. Here is another way to reharmonize the first two notes of "Yearnin'" (see Ex. 7.29):

EX. 7.29

And many other possibilities exist as well. Once you have identified the appropriate note(s) to reharmonize (common sense should tell you which notes are approach notes and which need to be harmonized with the primary chord of the measure), you can prioritize the melodic component in choosing voices to support the approach note.

Here is a good list of steps to take in reharmonizing a given melodic line:

· Determine which notes *must* be harmonized with the given chord of the measure (these are obvious chord tones, accented notes, etc.)

· Harmonize these first.

· Then work backwards from the harmonized chords to reharmonize the notes that are left. These will be the *approach notes*, and are generally found on weaker beats or prior to accented notes. Create good melodic lines and avoid excessive leaping and extreme registers in the supporting voices to approach the chords you have already voiced.

· Keep denser voicings in the midregister (around middle C). Don't write too low or too high.

· Finally, note that in "Yearnin'", the approach note was on, rather than *before* or *between*, the beats, a relatively less common but nonetheless possible scenario.

EX. 7.30A

Ellington and Strayhorn developed an idiosyncratic adaptation to the standard 4-part soli writing technique in order to exploit the powerful sound of baritone saxophonist Harry Carney. In this adaptation, the standard 4-part structure was combined with the open voicing concept to produce a hierarchy of voices within the saxophone section in which the melodic doubling was actually *above* the "dropped" voice. For example, the following standard *4-part voicing* in "double lead" format (like the "Arab Dance" example we saw earlier) would normally be voiced as in Ex. 7.30A:

However, it is also possible to voice the same chord in the following manner if the "dropped" voice is placed below the melodic doubling (see Ex. 7.30B).

(Transcribe the saxophone soli to either "Cottontail" or "Lay-By", from "Suite Thursday" to check this technique out.)

As noted by Ellington scholar Dick Domek of the University of Kentucky, Ellington and Strayhorn also occasionally used the standard *closed position* 4-part structure to generate parts for an entire Big band[28]. They accomplished this by distributing the notes of a 4-part close position chord from top to bottom within the appropriate register for the given section. It is certainly an expedient technique, and it became an easily identifiable part of their sound from the mid-50's on. In the following example written using this concept, we can clearly see how this works, with the 4-part close position chord of origin (in either the saxophones or trumpets in this case) generating the trombone parts by doubling the top three voices an octave lower, and the baritone voice by doubling the melody an octave lower. Note that the trombone parts chosen from the 4-part structure yield triadic sounds.

Ex. 7.30B:

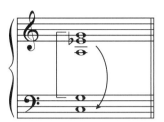

Ex. 7.31

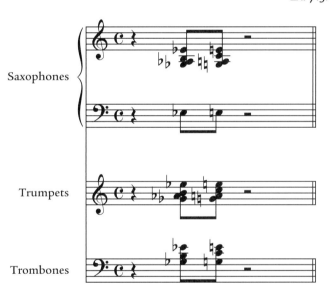

Saxophones

Trumpets

Trombones

[28] Domek, Richard. "Compositional Characteristics of Late Duke Ellington Works", IAJE Research Papers, 2001

Voice-Crossing

The concept of Voice-Crossing, also found most commonly in the work of Ellington, challenges the convention of ordering of saxophones (or other instruments) within the section from highest to lowest. Traditionally, of course, in terms of the saxophone section, the standard order would place the two alto saxophones on top, followed by the two tenors, then the baritone on the bottom. However there are numerous examples in Ellington and Strayhorn's writing where this order is disrupted and/or not kept consistent within a given phrase. This technique generally is associated with situations involving consecutive close position chords.

Ex. 7.32

Example from "Half the Fun"(from "Such Sweet Thunder")

Note that "A." stands for alto, "T." for tenor, "Cl." for clarinet, and "Bar." for baritone (reduction of Ellington's full score).

There has been a great deal of discussion about the origin of this technique. Some trace it to the addition of Ben Webster to the band in 1940 to add a fifth voice to the saxophone section. Refer to Ex. 4.49C to see an example of a distinctive Ben Webster fifth saxophone part. (There has been much discussion about the second tenor voice in this example having been 'added' to what was a pre-existing 4-part structure when Webster joined the band. Whether it was added by Ben Webster or Ellington, however, hardly changes its musical effect, in which the voice-crossing technique creates interwoven inner parts whose independently moving lines still create the identical harmonies while avoiding awkward repeated notes.)

Examples of the voice-crossing technique being used in open position or mixed open and close position situations are also found occasionally, though the application of this technique in open voicings is potentially problematic due to wider ranges of and more extreme melodic contours that result. (In the Ellington /Strayhorn arrangement of "Morning Mood" from their arrangement of Grieg's "Peer Gynt Suite" this technique is employed, see also Ex. 7.33 below). The incredibly personal sound qualities Ellington and Strayhorn were so fortunate to be able to work with among their personnel made this technique all the more effective when realized by their orchestra. (This once again reinforces the notion of the necessity in jazz composition of writing for a particular set of individuals rather than for a generic set of instruments!)

Compare the following example to Ex. 7.32 above, then listen carefully to the reharmonization of the melody to "Morning Mood" that occurs between 3:06 and 3:16 of the Ellington/ Strayhorn arrangement from the "Peer Gynt Suite" referred to above (see also end of Chapter Assignments):

Ex. 7.32 (above) has been reworked below (Ex. 7.33) in an alternate realization using open voicings and the same instrumentation. Play each voice individually to fully appreciate the resultant change in melodic contour. Of course various melodic permutations of the five voices in Ex. 7.32 could be used. When distributing voices using this technique care should be taken to create independent and melodic lines from among the available choices.

Ex. 7.33

Three Horn Voicing Techniques

Finally, we come to techniques that have evolved to accommodate the three horn frontline in ensembles such as Art Blakey and The Jazz Messengers. Other than the obvious use of two-part writing (by doubling one part in unison or at the octave), the *3-voice* frontline has been harmonized in this style either by eliminating one voice from the standard *4-voice structures* outlined above, or by resorting to some sort of triadic formulation as outlined in Chapter 4. If for example, we eliminate the lowest voice from the opening chord of "Stolen Moments" (see Ex. 7.22 above), we obtain the following sonority.

EX. 7.34

Major third and half step voicing

The resultant chord still "works" on a C–7 chord, though it no longer contains its complete chord sound. Exploitation of the modal relationships outlined in Chapter 4 enables the composer/arranger to develop an entire range of intervallically and modally-based sonorities that fit the given harmony without defining it, in the process creating a sound that is:

· *differentiated* (i.e. less redundant between the rhythm section and the horns and inherently more "orchestral" in nature), and

· *harmonically ambiguous* (meaning that the lack of complete chord sound in the frontline voices leaves the chord quality undefined).

Although the "major third and a 1/2-step" sound from Ex. 7.34 is most frequently used to represent the minor chord, it can also fit a variety of other harmonic situations. As such it can become a potential anchor for a harmonic progression in which the given chords are organized through its *reiteration*, rather than by traditional functional relationships.

EX. 7.35A

EX. 7.35B

EX. 7.35C

Another such sound that is frequently heard may be thought of as having been derived from a 4-part dominant seventh chord such as the one found in the bottom three voices of the tonic seventh chord in measure one of "Yearnin'".

Ex. 7.36

This is the so-called "tritone and a fourth" voicing

This "tritone and a fourth" voicing may also have a variety of uses (see also analysis of "Speak Like a Child" to follow in Chapter 8). In effect the lack of harmonic specificity that results from the removal of the fourth voice is what enables these distinctive 3-part sounds to have such a multiplicity of uses.

Ex. 7.37A-D

Common uses for the "tritone and a fourth" voicing

(To review, there is actually a relationship between this set of harmonies. They all are related to modes of Melodic minor. In the specific case of the voicing used in Ex.'s 7.37, the "parent" scale would be E♭ melodic minor, because A♭ is its fourth degree, D its seventh, C its sixth, and G♭ its third. So for example the D7♯9 is related to the D *altered scale*, which is the seventh mode of E♭ melodic minor, and so on for each of these chords. See also Ex. 4.31A, the "Modes of melodic minor".)

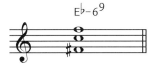

Finally, inverted triads and voicings in pure fourths are also commonly used in three horn writing. The inverted triad often occurs in inversion, since the richer interval of a perfect fourth is not available in root position triads (see also Chapter 4 discussion of "extended triads").

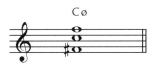

Ex. 7.38

Example of the use of an inverted triad; CΔ♯11 voiced with a D major triad

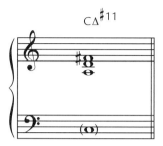

Ex. 7.39

Example of a quartal (fourth) voicing

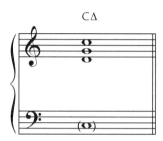

(Note that these voicings are both harmonically incomplete in and of themselves.)

The variety of available harmonic settings for these last two examples is such that it is nearly pointless to attempt to list them all systematically. Suffice it to say that in some of these cases, the result will define the chord...

Ex. 7.40A

Quartal voicing used to express the 3, 6, 9 of a major chord

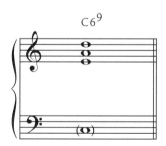

...while in other cases it may yield a sound that includes a combination of chord tones and color tones, necessitating rhythm section support to complete the chord sound.

Ex. 7.40B

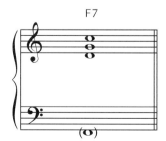

In the A section of Slide Hampton's arrangement of the standard "What's New" from the Dexter Gordon recording "A Day in Copenhagen" (a tour de force for Hampton's three horn writing), we see a combination of the above sounds being used.

Ex. 7.41A

Ms. A-1 illustrates the use of a voicing in perfect 4ths that does not define the chord sound

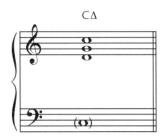

Ex. 7.41B

Ms. A-3 shows the use of an inverted triad in an incomplete chord sound

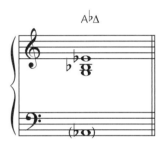

Ex. 7.41C

Ms. A-5 illustrates the use of the major 3rd and 1/2 step voicing

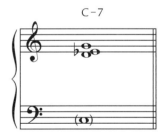

By making use of these characteristic three horn sounds the composer/arranger is placing the value of intervallic timbre above that of harmonic completeness. In other words, choosing sound over function as a means of harmonic organization.

Two final examples reinforce the notion that voicings may be created out of any interval. With the exception of symmetric scales, every scale or mode contains every interval between some two of its notes, and the chord quality associated with that mode may therefore be voiced in such a way as to emphasize any interval of the writer's choosing.

Ex. 7.42A

Example of a *quintal* (fifths voicing) featuring an interlocking 1/2 step

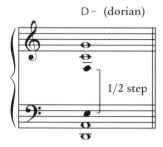

Ex. 7.42B

Example of a *quartal* voicing featuring an interlocking 1/2 step

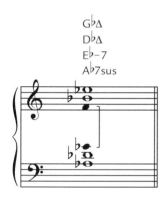

Conclusion

The jazz composer/arranger makes use of a variety of technical and aesthetic resources to personalize his or her own work. These same resources may be used whether one is composing an original piece or arranging the work of others. One's vocabulary of such devices can be referred to as one's "sonic signature", and may become as identifiable as the individual sounds acquired by the great jazz players. The jazz composer/arranger acquires this identity in part by writing for an identifiable group of players, and in part through reliance on specific technical devices, particularly those which are timbrally based, such as unique unison combinations and intervallically based harmonic structures. Such compositional gestures are often combined with devices such as ostinato, pyramid, counterpoint, closed and open position chord voicings, voice-crossing and cross-sectional writing. In order to fully establish one's sonic identity, it is first necessary to understand standard practice before deviating from it. Three horn writing in the modern era has been defined largely by the vocabulary of certain commonly used, intervallically-based yet often harmonically ambiguous, chord voicings.

ASSIGNMENTS

1.) *Listen* to all of the examples discussed in this Chapter.

2.) Find examples of the following for in-class analysis:

- Contrafact;
- Scat Vocalese;
- Appropriation of pre-existing melodic material;
- Personalizing one's arrangement of a standard;
- Use of open and closed position 4-part voicing structures in a soli setting;
- Quoting;
- Use of intervallically-based voicings;
- Use of 3 or 4-part writing techniques inside an arrangement for larger ensemble;
- Timbrally based unison combinations or cross-sectional writing;
- Voice-crossing (non-traditional sectional hierarchy in ensemble voicings);
- Transcribe the first 8 bars of Clare Fischer's "Miles Behind" (see DISCOGRAPHY). What instrumentation is used in the thematic presentation?
- Transcribe the opening A Cappella section of "Sameeda" by Abdullah Ibrahim (refer to DISCOGRAPHY and discussion, page 178).
- Transcribe the reharmonized melodic statement found at 3:06-3:16 of the Ellington/Strayhorn arrangement of Grieg's "Morning Mood" from the "Peer Gynt Suite". Compare it to the technique discussed in Ex. 7.33 (Note: This section immediately follows the baritone saxophone's solo statement of the same theme, which in turn begins at approximately 2:48).
- Listen to Gershwin's "American in Paris" to find the source of Clifford Brown's introduction to "Parisian Thoroughfare" referred to on page 159.

3.) Transcribe two 4-bar examples of saxophone or other instrumental soli. One of the examples should illustrate standard Swing era soli-writing, while the other should illustrate the use of voice-crossing or other non-traditional harmonic devices.

4.) Examine the work of one of the following composers to evaluate what the important elements of their respective sonic signatures are, and who might have influenced them in their development:

- Andrew Hill
- George Russell
- Ornette Coleman

CHAPTER 8

Analysis of Selected Compositions

In this Chapter we will be analyzing in detail several selected compositions. These examples fall into the following categories:

· Adaptations by jazz composers of European Classical forms;

· Through-composed, motivically-based, works;

· Programmatic works;

· Compositions based on alternative harmonic systems; and

· Recomposed versions of pieces from the European Classical Repertoire.

Adaptation of Classical Forms

It is frequently assumed that the influence exerted by European Classical music on jazz musicians began with the so-called "Third Stream" movement of the 1950's. Like all such generalizations, this is of course an oversimplification. In fact, as mentioned in Chapter 5, many jazz composers were aware, *from the very beginnings* of the music, of contemporary trends and repertoire in European Classical music. Late 19th and early 20th century New Orleans musicians are said to have frequently quoted from popular opera arias in their improvisations, and both Scott Joplin and James P. Johnson *wrote* operas. Stride pianists had absorbed the *whole tone scale* as a part of their harmonic vocabulary almost as soon as the device was being used by Debussy and Ravel. James Reese Europe's "Clef Club Orchestra" mixed European and African-American instrumentation. As we will see, Ellington and others were obviously and consciously alluding to such classical forms as Concerto and Sonata long before the '50's (other than the "strain" form as used in Ragtime, itself already a fusion of sorts as was noted in Chapter 5). And although the process of adapting European Classical forms by jazz composers differs from the process of arranging pre-existing European Classical compositions for performance by jazz ensembles, both give evidence of a self-conscious effort to integrate formal elements of the two traditions, as well as of an awareness of the Classical repertoire among jazz composers.

Let's begin by examining two examples of contrasting style written in different periods with different sets of musicians in mind, Duke Ellington's "Concerto For Cootie", and John Lewis' "Concorde".

Concerto for Cootie

Ellington's adaptation of Classical forms in his early period was to some extent tempered by the recording technique of the time, which, as mentioned earlier, limited a given recorded performance to approximately 3 minutes. In considering "Concerto for Cootie", it should be mentioned that it was not Ellington's first use of this form. ("Clarinet Lament" [1936], analyzed in Chapter 5, is generally accepted to have been the first.) Given the three minute constraint, Ellington's adaptation of the form was therefore limited to an application of its general principles in microcosm. As noted correctly by Rattenbury[1], the essential elements of the concerto form as adapted by Ellington were:

· *Thematic exchange* between the featured soloist (in this case Cootie Williams) and the ensemble (this exchange implicitly involves the notion of "call and response");

· Use of *motivic cells from the theme* in the ensemble accompaniment;

· *Changes of key associated with changing themes;*

· Use of Blues-based secondary keys (i.e. IV, ♭VI); and

· *Exploitation of the personal sound* of the featured player, in lieu of the showcasing of virtuosity *per se* that is often found in Classical concerti.

Both "Clarinet Lament" and "Concerto for Cootie" are examples of "compound form" (see also Chapter 5).

Ex. 8.1

The Formal Outline of "Concerto for Cootie"

Introduction	8 bars derived from A strain (key of F)
Songform	AABA form; 10-bar strains; transition/modulation from F to D♭*; A's have muted sound; B the growl sound.
"Sweet" theme	16-bar quasi ABAC form; 2-bar modulatory transition back to F; Open Sound
A varied	10 bars
Coda	Material derived from A

* Note the "extra" two bars inserted prior to the recapitulation of the final A section. These linking measures have a purely modulatory function, a common practice device frequently found in Ragtime and Stride piano compositions as well (and also found in "Clarinet Lament" and "Swampy River" – see also Chapter 5).

[1] Rattenbury, Ken. *Duke Ellington: Jazz Composer.* Yale University Press, New Haven, 1990, Ch.8

Here are examples of the use of thematic material in the accompaniment.

Derivation of the material of the introduction
from the A theme (seventh measure of Intro)*

* Reduction from full score as found in Kingbrand transcription by David Berger

Call and response in the presentation of the A theme

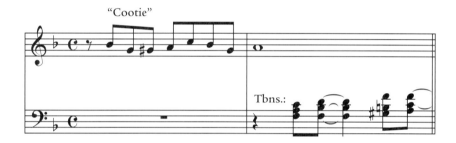

Some other interesting variations include:

· Instead of using the traditional Classical secondary key of V, Ellington uses the more Blues-based and idiomatic "♭VI"(D♭). (In "Clarinet Lament" the secondary key was IV, also Blues-based.)

· He also has honored one of *his* most important compositional principles by associating each theme with a specific sound (i.e. open, muted, etc.) available in the personal vocabulary of the individual soloist for whom the piece was composed.

Ex. 8.3

The principal theme (key of F; muted)

The second theme (key of D♭; open)

Finally, "Concerto for Cootie" provides yet another example of the use of the related principles of appropriation and adaptation, given Clark Terry's previously referenced assertion that the basis for the motif developed by Ellington was one of Williams' own warm-up exercises.

Thus Ellington's adaptations of this form to his own compositional oeuvre succeeded in large part because they honored his own primary compositional principle of respecting and incorporating the sound(s) of an individual soloist, perhaps even developing the soloist's own ideas into full-fledged compositions for them. Elements of the Classical form which he found useful were retained without compromising his personal sound as a composer, and without sounding contrived, unidiomatic or pretentious, adapted to fit into the three-minute form which recording technology of the time necessitated. Interestingly, nothing is improvised in the piece, yet it still swings and embodies the core principles of the music. "The feeling of jazz"* has been successfully communicated in written form. This fact should not be taken as proof that improvisation is not the sine qua non of jazz, however, since there is no question that the writing of Ellington and every other major jazz composer has been conditioned by performance and listening experiences that were based in an improvising tradition. In other words, it may be possible to convey the nuances of improvised jazz music in composed form, but this has yet to be done convincingly by composers who are not grounded in the performance practice of the idiom.

* (the title of an Ellington composition from the Ellington/ Coltrane recording)

John Lewis' "Concorde" (1954) is another example of adaptation of European Classical form by Jazz composers. As Owens has noted, and as mentioned earlier in this text as well, Lewis' were not the first such efforts[2]. Lewis was one of a cadre of musicians, including Gil Evans, Miles Davis, George Russell, and others, whose efforts to fuse elements of contemporary classical music with those of jazz presaged the development of what became labelled the so-called "Third Stream" style. Lewis' *Modern Jazz Quartet* sought to bring the formality, and the concomitant respect, of the concert hall and its "serious" attitude, to the Jazz performance tradition. Like many of the musicians of his generation, Lewis was familiar with the performance practice and repertoire of both the Jazz and European Classical traditions. (As was also mentioned previously, for some composers, for example Dave Brubeck and John Coltrane, this knowledge was acquired through formal study, while for others, among them Ellington, Gil Evans and later Frank Zappa, it was acquired through self-directed listening and score study). It is therefore no surprise that Lewis was successful in merging elements of both worlds in "Concorde", a *Jazz Fugue*.

Fugue, which means "flight" in Latin, is a procedure, fully developed in the Baroque period and most characteristically exemplified in the work of Bach, in which a given theme, or "subject", is developed imitatively through a series of "statements", often accompanied by a "countersubject" (a secondary theme whose appearances are consistently associated with those of the primary theme), in a sequence in which the initial subject appears in at least three voices. These statements are linked by "episodes", in which "free" material that is not directly based on the subject, is developed, often sequentially. The presentation of these thematic statements through all of the individual voices involved is known as the "exposition". Fugues may include single or double expositions presented in this manner. Their harmonic schemes typically involve cycle of fifths harmonic relationships, most commonly featuring tonic-dominant and /or relative minor and major keys (often the second exposition is in the relative minor if the primary one was in the major tonality). Fugues frequently conclude with a "stretto", or series of rapidly overlapping incomplete statements of the subject, featuring its primary motif in fragmentation.

The inherent similarity between the notions of subject and answer on the one hand, and call and response on the other, allows Lewis to successfully accomplish a quite natural and uncontrived adaptation of this form within the context of both compositional traditions, allowing improvisation and composition to seamlessly coexist. Obviously, the following analysis is predicated on the assumption that you will be listening to the piece concurrently.

[2] Owens, Thomas. "The Fugal Pieces of the Modern Jazz Quartet". Journal of Jazz Studies, V.4, 1976, pp.25-46

Ex. 8.4

The Formal Scheme of "Concorde"

Exposition	Ms. #'s	Key area
Subject statement # 1 (in bass)	ms. 1 8	Ab
Answer, and statement #2 of the subject (in piano-accompanied by sequential development of the subject in the bass)	ms. 8-15	A
Statement #3 of the subject in the vibes (accompanied by completion of second statement in piano and "free counterpoint", or quasi "countersubject"/cycle of 5ths bassline in bass)	ms. 16-23	Ab
Statement #4 of the theme (truncated) in the bass	ms. 23-31	A

Some interesting idiomatic details of the Exposition include:

· The traditional second key area of the dominant (Eb) has been replaced here by that of the *substitute dominant* (A). This use of an idiomatic harmonic device is reminiscent of Ellington's use of the Blues-based secondary key (bVI) in "Concerto for Cootie".

· Note also that the first and third statements of the Subject (in the bass and vibes, respectively) include a sequential extension, based on the idiomatic device of the "turnaround", that is not found in statements 2 and 4.

· The theme itself has an "antecedent"/"consequent" flavor that is reinforced by the *blue note* that concludes its primary consequent phrase (see Ex. 8.5A below).

Episode 1	Ms. #'s	Key area
Improvised Piano solo – The piano solo is loosely based on the chord changes to the initial statement, featuring the use of common practice harmonic devices such as cycle of fifths harmony and turnarounds, and accompanied by a background riff derived from the Subject.	ms. 32-56	E-C-Bb
"Stop-time" linking passage – Note that the "stop-time" passage actually begins in the penultimate measure of the solo (55).	ms. 55-57	Eb-Bb
"False" second exposition – This section sounds like it will become a complete second exposition of the subject in the key of E until the incipient third statement of the subject instead elides into an improvised bass solo. Note the "bluesified" quality of the bass part in the second measure. Also note the "mirror" writing between the piano and bass part at letter C (see Ex.'s 8.5B. and C. below).	ms. 57-81	E-Bb

Episode 2	Ms. #'s	Key area
Improvised bass solo – The bass solo ends by cycling to a brief layover in A minor, which serves to set up the second exposition, in B♭ minor.	ms. 73-93	*primarily* B♭-E♭ (I-IV)

Exposition 2	Ms. #'s	Key area
Subject appears in all three voices (but only three this time, unlike the primary exposition in which it made a fourth appearance). Note Lewis' use of elision to link these sections of the form. The second exposition actually begins melodically prior to the resolution to the new key (B♭ minor), in measure 102. Note also the use of another "stop-time" figure in ms.124 and 125. This figure creates transitions that are both harmonic and rhythmic (see Ex. 8.5D below). Also, note that these statements of the subject alternate between B♭ and B minor, i.e. in parallel to the initial statements of the subject in the Major exposition at the beginning of the piece (between A♭ and A). Perhaps it could be said, in jazz theoretical terms, that the second statement of the subject is in the substitute dominant key area in each case.	ms. 102-125	*primarily* B♭ minor

Episode 3	Ms. #'s	Key area
Vibes Solo – Note the use of sequential harmony once again. In comparison with the earlier bass solo (Episode 2), these key centers are much less static, creating a sense of forward motion leading inexorably to the conclusion of the piece. The (probably written) background riff in the piano creates an overarching sense of an AABA' form for the vibes solo, with the A material lasting from ms. 126-133 and then recommencing in ms.138. Note that the riff is derived by fragmentation of the primary theme (see Ex. 8.5E below). * Due to the skillful integration of improvised and written lines it is impossible to know if measures 145-148 in the vibes part were composed or improvised.	ms. 126-144 (or 147)*	G minor, B♭ minor, E♭ minor
Pedal point setting up coda (= last 8 or 9 bars of vibes solo)		D♭

Coda	Ms. #'s	Key area
The coda takes the form of a *stretto*.	ms. 158-end	D♭-A♭ (IV-I)

Some examples of the use of idiomatic devices from the transcribed score follow:

Ex. 8.5A

Blue notes in measure 4 of main theme

Ex. 8.5B

Blues influence in the bass part at C

Ex. 8.5C

"Mirror" writing between bass and piano in C1 and 2

Ex. 8.5D

"Stop-time" in 124 and 125

Ex. 8.5E

Background riff behind vibes solo (rhythm of subject shown above staff)

Comparison of the two compositions

Whereas Ellington succeeded in conveying the idiomatic feeling and ensemble dynamics typical of a jazz performance without employing improvisation to that end, Lewis succeeds by contrast in integrating improvisation within what is arguably a more complete version of the "Classical" form. The two examples show an obvious contrast in content, but share the common denominator of an imaginative and flexible approach to the forms and styles being merged. Clearly the element of surprise implicit in such an unorthodox formal fusion immediately establishes a degree of uniqueness for it. However, creating a more than superficially attractive piece depends upon the composer's ability to combine formal and stylistic elements of the two genres in a manner that does not compromise their integrity. In both of these cases, this is accomplished in large part by the fact that the formal experiment is couched in so many surface elements reflecting idiomatic common practice content (the use of swing, riffs, *call and response, turn-arounds, melodic* and *harmonic sequence, cycle of fifths* harmony, etc.).

In the case of "Concorde", improvised solos fit nicely into the overall form by at once setting *off* and setting *up* the two expositions of the subject. The written thematic material elides smoothly into the improvised sections because the material itself is idiomatic to the style of the improvisers to begin with. This seamless interaction between composition and improvisation could only have occurred if the composer intimately knew the styles of the improvisers for whom he was composing. Like Ellington, Lewis knew specifically for whom he was writing, and provided them material to work with that sounded as convincing when they read it as if they had actually improvised it. Referring to a different composition, Charles Mingus put this concept succinctly, saying that it was written, "so they'd play the compositional parts with as much spontaneity and soul as they'd play a solo"[3]. Lewis also exploits the natural tension and potential for formal contrast implicit in the juxtaposition of major and minor, in this case with parallel expositions and improvised solos in both.

Adaptation of Other Classical Forms

Other forms adapted from the European Classical tradition by jazz composers that we have not yet discussed include Sonata and Rondo form. As with Fugue and Concerto forms, it is more the underlying principles than the formal structures that have proved most important.

[3] Mingus, Charles, Liner notes to "Blues and Roots".

Sonata Form

In Sonata form, there are three main sections: *exposition* (in which the main themes are presented), *development* (in which the motivic content of the themes are developed and interwoven), and a final restatement, or summing up, of the main thematic material, known as *recapitulation*. Most often a movement in this form ends with a brief, additional concluding section known as a coda. The underlying dialectical principle involved follows the familiar literary formula of beginning, middle and end, and as such is similar to small ensemble jazz performance practice, in which the analogue would be the statement of the theme, the solos, and then the final thematic statement and coda. Given this similarity it is easy to see how the principles of Sonata form might be adapted by jazz composers interested in creating extended works. Although extended multi-movement works outside of the "Suite" form are relatively rare in jazz, we should not be surprised that it was Ellington who undertook the challenge of working with Sonata form. As with his adaptation of Concerto form, he did so in a personal way that compromised neither the stylistic integrity of his music nor the authenticity of his source material.

First it must be said that Ellington, as he so frequently did, was appropriating his own ideas to an extent in "Black, Brown and Beige". For many years he had been discussing the notion of creating an extended work depicting the history of African Americans[4]. In fact, in 1935, his dramatic film short, "Symphony in Black", employed some of the same musical and programmatic content which would later resurface in "Black, Brown and Beige" in 1943. The most famous example involves a scene entitled "The Laborers", from the first movement of "Symphony in Black"*, depicting slaves hauling sacks up a flight of stairs in rhythmic unison to the musical accompaniment that would later become the famous "Work Song" in "Black, Brown and Beige".

Ex. 8.6

(*The opening scene of "Symphony in Black" must be seen in order for this musical ancestry to be fully appreciated. Having viewed this dramatic scene, the listener's auditory experience will be conditioned by the image that inspired the music, as such providing an important insight into Ellington's compositional process.)

[4] Hasse, John. *Beyond Category: The Life and Genius of Duke Ellington.* Simon and Shuster, New York, 1993, p. 260

Conversely, Black's other main theme, the "Come Sunday" theme, enjoyed a later incarnation as a separate entity in Ellington's repertoire in an uptempo appearance in his First Sacred Concert as tap-dance number, entitled "And David Danced Before the Lord".

Ex. 8.7A

"Come Sunday" theme excerpt (first appearance – from p.15 of Ellington manuscript score found at the Smithsonian)

(Note that Hodges' much better known treatment of the theme does not occur first. Also note, in comparing Ex.'s 8.7A and B, that the first four bars of the Tizol theme statement are "tritone substitutes" for the "standard" chord changes to the piece [normally V7 and IV7]. Thus Ellington has in a sense presented the reharmonized version of his theme first, a paradigm inversion if ever there was one!)

Ex. 8.7B

The subsequent Hodges thematic statement

The presentation, development, and intertwining of these contrasting themes is not only programmatically meaningful, it also gives form to the entire movement.

After presenting the themes separately, Ellington gradually combines, reharmonizes, reorchestrates and interweaves them throughout the course of the development section. Indeed, Ellington wished, as he made clear in his introductory remarks at Carnegie Hall in January of 1943, to show the connection between the Sacred (as epitomized by the "Come Sunday") and the Secular (the Work theme) in African American life, "to show their close relationship..."[5], as he put it.

[5] Ellington's opening remarks at January, 1943 premiere (1943 Carnegie Hall Concerts).

Here are but a few examples of the ongoing process by which Ellington achieves variety in presenting, developing and in interweaving these themes (due to discrepancies between the manuscript score from the Ellington archives at the Smithsonian and the recorded performances, measure numbers are assigned only for Ex. 8.8A).

Ex. 8.8A

Reharmonizations of the "Work Song" theme
(these ex's found on p. 2,5 of Ellington manuscript score)

Ex. 8.8B

Variation of the "Come Sunday" theme
(= p. 28 of Ellington manuscript)

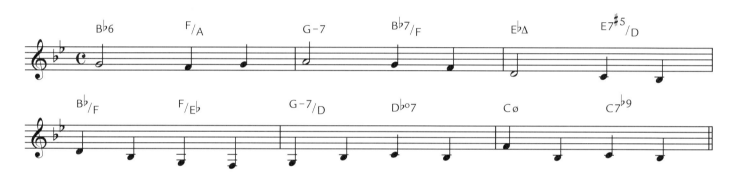

Following the completion of the thematic statement shown in Ex. 8.8B, Ellington interpolates four bars of 3/4 that serve as a metric cadence. The melodic material here could be thought of as being related to the consequent part of either theme, or as a synthesis of the two.

Ex. 8.8C

Following this the piece returns to a medium up tempo 4/4 and immediately combines the two melodies over the chord changes of "Come Sunday", creating a dramatic and inevitable point of arrival that bears out the musical realization of Ellington's introductory comments. Though the melody and harmony of "Come Sunday" are both included here, the elements of the "Work Song" that are used are not just its theme, but also its basic tempo.

Ex. 8.9

Combination of the two themes in the recapitulation of "Black"

"Black" is a formidable study in the art of motivic manipulation and transformation, exploiting every musical and contextual element of the two primary themes to create its development. The examples shown here are only the tip of the iceberg. Further study of the piece will reveal more of its structure to the student. (Note: this can be done equally effectively by careful listening, since Ellington's development of motivic material is almost always audible). It is well worth listening to "Black" with a copy of the formal synopsis of the movement found in Wolfram Knauer's article "Simulated Improvisation in Black, Brown and Beige" – see BIBLIOGRAPHY. Finally, it is interesting to compare the recapitalution in "Black" with that of the last movement in Dvorák's "New World" (9th) Symphony, especially given the relatively small degree of separation between the two composers (see Peress' "My Life With Black, Brown and Beige" – BIBLIOGRAPHY).

Finally, it should not be forgotten that "Black, Brown and Beige" is deliberately programmatic in content as well, not just in the general sense of telling the story in music of the history of African-Americans, but specifically in relation to a poem of the same title authored by Ellington, whose text is depicted in the music. Those who have criticized the piece as being structurally weak (both in 1943 and subsequently) did not have access to the poem (see Maurice Peress' article "My Life with Black, Brown and Beige", BIBLIOGRAPHY). Notwithstanding this fact, however, as is clearly evidenced in the examples cited above, Ellington's introductory remarks provide ample guidance to anyone attempting to follow the form of the piece aurally. (It might also be said that John Coltrane's "Acknowledgement", from "A Love Supreme", as well as Ellington's own setting of the opening stanza of the Bible in the First Sacred Concert ["In the Beginning God"], constitute other examples falling into this "category" of poetically inspired music).

Regardless of the genesis of the form or content of the piece, it is quite clear that Ellington succeeded in creating two contrasting themes of clear identity, and subsequently proceeded to logically develop and interweave them until they were seemingly inevitably merged. This reinforces two important underlying principles that emerge from the analysis of any successful extended composition based on thematic development:

1.) Thematic material needs to be relatively simple, i.e. easily recognizable, and idiomatic, in order to have the flexibility necessary to be able to accommodate the deconstruction and recombination of its core elements in the process of development, and

2.) Just as an artist arranges her palette prior to painting, the composer can similarly anticipate his developmental needs in advance by creating themes whose core elements complement one another.

Rondo

A Rondo is a form in which a simple theme, or refrain (A), continually returns between contrasting themes (ABACA, etc). Ellington made use of this principle in "Rockin in Rhythm" (1930), as Dave Brubeck famously did in "Blue Rondo à la Turk". In Brubeck's composition (whose title alludes to the evocation of elements of Turkish military music "alla Turca" by 18th century Classical composers), the "Turkish" element consists primarily of a 9/8 time signature that characterizes the A theme. Just as John Lewis exploited the common practice small ensemble jazz performance devices of the improvised solo and the turnaround in structuring the "episodes" in "Concorde", so Brubeck resorts to the use of the ubiquitous Blues form in adapting the Rondo to jazz. Brubeck's piece raises two additional important principles in composing extended works in jazz.

· Contrast is everything. Couching a complex formal device in familiar, common practice, surroundings, always provides formal balance and helps assure the accessibility of the piece (in "Blue Rondo", this is achieved through the use of the Blues form).

· Extended works in the jazz idiom need not be written solely for large ensembles (a fact which is evident in much of Coltrane's work as well, see also the analysis of "Blue Train", which follows later in this Chapter).

In Brubeck's adaptation of the Rondo form, the "turkic" A theme insinuates itself into the Blues choruses as well as thematically, and in the process inevitably creates the ubiquitous interactive dynamic of "call and response" as well.

The Rondo theme used in the first chorus
of the alto solo, in bars 3 and 4

Form Analysis

A   The A section establishes the diatonic character (in F major) of the main melodic motif, as well as its characteristic 9/8 meter, which is reinforced in the accompanying counterline. It is 8 bars long, played first in piano, then joined by the alto. It is this A material which will return as a "Rondo theme" throughout the piece, to set off variations of the contrasting B material. It is the also the "hook" of the piece, just as the minor third "motto theme" is for Ellington's "Tone Parallel to Harlem" (see analysis later in this Chapter).

Ex. 8.11A

The A theme and counterline to "Blue Rondo"

B   The B section adapts the primary rhythmic motif to A minor tonality. This is not unlike many Coltrane compositions (for example, "Like Sonny") in its deliberate exploitation of contrasting emphasis between major and minor third relationships in root motion and key areas.

Ex. 8.11B

This juxtaposition continues for the next three repetitions of this basic AB form, carefully developing and changing the B material with each subsequent repetition. (In the first variation the main contour of the melody is inverted, while in the second variation a pedal point appears supporting minor triads, but in every case the 9/8 metric character of the material remains.)

Ex. 8.11C

First B variation showing inversion of melodic contour

Ex. 8.11D

Second B variation showing use of the *pedal point*
to support parallel minor triads

Each of these variations becomes increasingly intense. It is the third variation of B that finally becomes a transitional vehicle, leading us harmonically from A minor, to F major, and G7 before the root motion falls back via F to arrive at the traditional "dominant" note, E. (The final sequence of parallel triads above this root preserves the expected traditional V-I dominant root motion, but eschews the actual dominant 7th chord in favor of modal parallelism). Note especially the introduction of the C♯'s in measure 4 of the third variation in the bassline. These have the subtle effect of presaging the modulation.

Ex. 8.11E

In another compositional gesture related to major and minor third relationships, the climactic concluding cadence of the main thematic exposition is to A major, rather than the previously emphasized A minor tonality. The transition to the Blues choruses is achieved by adding an additional 3-eighth note group to create a measure of 12/8.

Blues solos then follow (in F major), with the first chorus continuing to incorporate the B material to set off the three primary Blues chords until the traditional 12-bar Blues inevitably takes over (see Ex. 8.10 above).

The formal structure of "Blue Rondo à la Turk"
(based on "The Great Concerts", Columbia CD 44215)

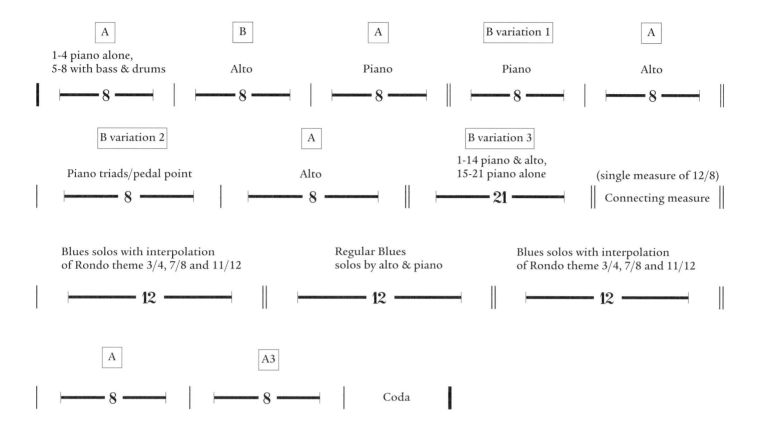

It is interesting to note the adaptability of the Blues to yet another seemingly incongruous setting. The Blues has proven itself to be a favorite foil of Jazz composers, regardless of their compositional goals. This is at least in part due to the implicit potential for contrast and coexistence between major and minor thirds in the Blues. The resolution of the conflict between the major and minor harmonic elements of this particular piece is an important part of its dramatic resolution. So even though there may be a great deal of distinction aesthetically between the music of Ellington, Coltrane, and Brubeck, we find that there is an important communality to be found in their use of the ubiquitous Blues-based resource of major and minor third relationships, both melodic and harmonic.

Arch Form

The notion of arch form is more a *principle* than a particular structure. In an *arch form*, the composition usually has an odd number of movements or sections (as for example in Bartók's Fifth String Quartet). The opening and closing sections tend to share musical content, as do the second and penultimate. Like any other formal concept employed in composition, this may exist in *micro* or *macro* applications. Coltrane's "Blue Train", as we will see later in this chapter, may constitute one example of the latter category, while the second movement of "Black, Brown and Beige" contains a free-standing vocal feature entitled "The Blues" that clearly shows elements of the former.

The Blues

Despite its title, "The Blues" is more about Ellington's take on the emotional content of the Blues than its form *per se* (The "Love Triangle" that it portrays was also presaged in the 1935 filmshort "Symphony in Black"). "The Blues Theme", as it is called in Ellington's shortscore[6], begins with a six measure fanfare, ending on a murkily inverted tonic chord (C−) that provides a melodic cue to the vocalist.

Ex. 8.13A

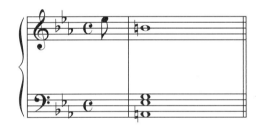

The first line of the melody evolves fragment by fragment over the next several bars. (Instead of establishing a motif or theme, *then* fragmenting it into its component parts, Ellington instead *builds* the line bit by bit).

Ex. 8.13B

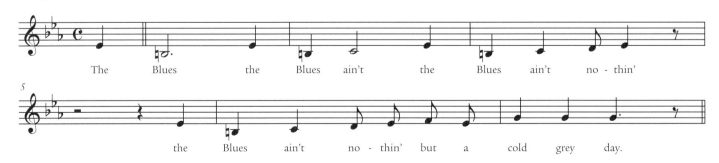

[6] Ellington manuscript score housed at Smithonsian Institution.

And although the 27 measure ABAC vocal theme does not conform to stereotypical notions of Blues *form*, there is little doubt that it succeeds in communicating the emotional content of the Blues, in large part due to the use of idiomatic harmonic and melodic gestures, including the following:

· *Deliberate juxtaposition of major and minor third intervals.* This is central to the opening thematic material, wherein the melody emphasizes the descending *major* third interval from the minor third to the major seventh of the chord (E♭).

Ex. 8.13C

· Use of *Blues-based cadences* (the following cadence supports measures 4 and 20 of the vocal theme – note how the bassline and trombone parts move while the primary chord of the measure, G7, is held in the brass).

Ex. 8.13D

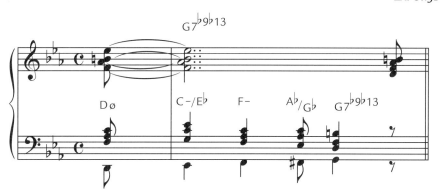

· Use of composed *call and response* (found for example in measures 17 and 18, between the voice and tenor).

Ex. 8.13E

· *Use of Blues-based melodic material to create a cadential effect* (measures 26 and 27). The bassline in ms.26 and 27 is clearly based on C minor Blues, and the *cadence* to the final C minor chord is equally obvious. Yet one would be hard pressed to rationalize this voicing and bassline in a common chord symbol, though their shared function is obvious. This use of the Blues is also a good example of "text painting" (illustrating the lyrics with the music – the lyric here is "The Blues"*).

Ex. 8.13F

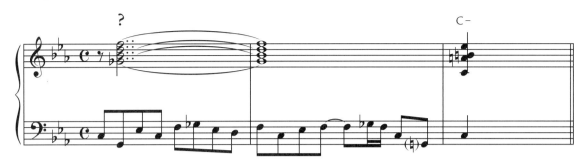

* Other notable examples of text painting can be found in such pieces Billy Strayhorn's "Strange Feeling", Charles Mingus' "Weird Nightmare" and "Eclipse", and Ellington's "Too Good to Title" featuring a wordless vocal by Alice Babs, in which large, leaping intervals, always landing on the flatted fifth of the chord, can be taken to symbolize divinity ("Second Sacred Concert").

The primary vocal statement then elides into a composed 16-bar tenor solo based on a micro ABAA elaboration of the initial 1/2-step motif (i.e. based on the lyrics "Blues ain't"), over what is essentially a cyclic chord progression.

Ex. 8.13G

Tonally, the tenor solo begins by briefly implying the parallel major (using a C7 chord), and ends by converting the new tonic (B♭) to minor, another structural juxtaposition of major and minor, this time used to facilitate *modulation* (This B♭ minor chord is in turn the relative minor of the tonality of the upcoming ensemble chorus (D♭).

Ex. 8.13H

Final two bars of tenor solo

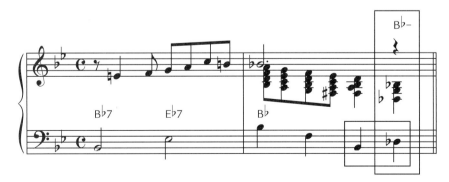

Next comes 12-bar *ensemble Blues chorus* in the AAA strophic structure that deliberately juxtaposes diatonic ("sweet") and Blues-based ("hot") elements in a *call and response* format.

Ex. 8.13I

The voice then returns for a new 8-bar melody that is evocative of the initial vocal statement. Mostly it is connected to the initial statement by the reuse of the lyric motif "The Blues ain't", only this time, instead of implying the minor tonality, the voice begins squarely on the major third (F) of the tonality (now D♭). This is another example of text painting as well – note the syncopation that supports the word "rhyme".

Ex. 8.13J

When the tonality switches back to the relative minor (B♭ minor) in the final two bars of this 8-bar section, the melody modulates to D♭ (still on the words "The Blues ain't")!

Ex. 8.13K

Finally, the initial rubato feeling of the piece returns as the voice sings the lyrics "Sighin', cryin', feels (al)most like dyin'", once again in call and response format with the horns. This is a transitional harmonic phrase as well, moving the piece forward to the original tonality of C minor through the *reiteration* of the augmented triad shared by both the dominant (G7♯5) and original tonic (C minor/major 7th) chords.

Ex. 8.13L

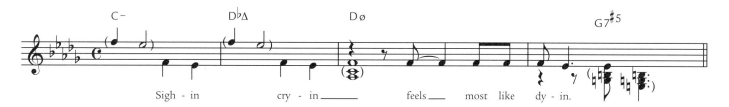

The piece then concludes by recapitulating the first four bars of the vocal melody essentially in reverse order (save that the accompanying response in the horns follows the lyrics "The Blues ain't nothin'" – see also Ex. 8.13D).

Ex. 8.13M

Though Ellington's brilliant miniature may be technically "through-composed", the essential principle at work here is clearly one of palindromic formal symmetry.

Through-Composed Extended Works

Another important category of extended composition might be referred to as *through-composition*. In its most widely accepted meaning, this term more or less suggests that new music appears where formal repetition might be expected, and/or that the piece does not include literal repetitions of entire sections of its form. In this sense it is the opposite of strophic 32-bar songforms or other formal scenarios involving literal recapitulation. What holds a composition together in the absence of such formal repetition? The answer generally lies in reiterative motivic development. We turn to Ellington and Mingus for our examples.

A Tone Parallel to Harlem

In "A Tone Parallel to Harlem" (occasionally entitled more formally the "Harlem Suite"), Ellington masterfully and economically develops the entire piece from the opening "motto theme" of a minor third, "spoken" at its outset by trumpeter Ray Nance employing the characteristic vocalese of the muted horn. (Though this sound may have been popularized by King Oliver, Bubber Miley, "Tricky" Sam Nanton, and others with whom Ellington was familiar early on in his career, he had longsince embraced it as one of his own signature compositional devices). The piece also works as a sonic landscape of its subject, portraying in music the scenes of everyday life in Harlem by means of varying the initial *leitmotif*. As such it might also be referred to as a programmatic or even an *impressionistic* piece. Whatever term is used, there is no doubt that Ellington, as he often stated, frequently composed with a visual particular scene inspiring his work.

It is suggested that this piece be listened to in conjunction with the following transcribed examples as well as the form guide found on page 215.

Ex. 8.14A

The opening minor third *leitmotif*

Throughout the piece, we are constantly confronted with various manifestations of the opening "blue" interval, in every conceivable possible transformation and embellishment (these arbitrarily chosen examples are but a few of many such related thematic statements).

Ex. 8.14B

Ex. 8.14C

Ex. 8.14D

Ex. 8.14E

Even the harmony is impacted by the minor third interval.

EX. 8.14F

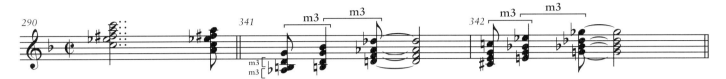

Note also the ability of the minor third to fit and/or reconcile both major and minor tonality, an important property of the Blues generally as noted earlier. In "Harlem" this results in the same theme working in both major and minor tonality.

Ms. 33 showing juxtaposition of major and minor harmony in thematic presentation:

EX. 8.15A

Theme used in a major Blues context:

Further variety is achieved through the presentation of the theme in various rhythmic contexts.

The theme as a "Ballad" (in the "Church Theme"). Note that this is really just an embellished version of the main *leitmotif*, which appears in the second two notes in inversion, and in its original form in the last two:

EX. 8.15B

The theme in an up tempo context (saxophones):

EX. 8.15C

Ellington's development of the slow incarnation of the theme occurs via the device of composed New Orleans style *counterpoint*, building to the dramatic final statement of the theme.

Ex. 8.16

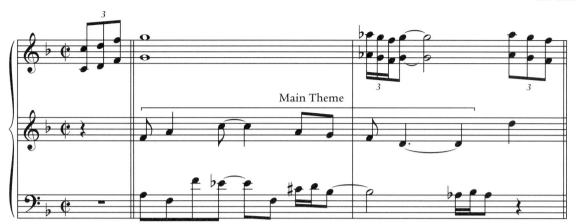

A formal description of the musical events in "Harlem" follows:

Ex.8.17

Form Analysis of "Harlem" (timings based on 1952 "Seattle Concert")
(see DISCOGRAPHY)

PART I – Introduction of Main Theme (stays primarily in key of F)	Ms. #'s	Timing
Introduction (♩ = 84) – mostly rubato	1-10	01:07
Slightly faster theme statement – call and response between saxes and brass	11-18	01:47
Trumpet solo w/brass, drums	19-23	02:08
Clarinet theme presentation	24-42	02:28
Call and response theme statement (♩ = 80) led by trumpet	42-47	03:23
Rubato saxophone soli (clarinet lead)	48-50	03:40
Contrapuntal transition	51-62	03:46
Medium tempo ostinato and theme in baritone	63-75	04:19
Ritard and reiteration of theme (slow/concerted)	76-85	04:44
Composed tenor solo w/backgrounds	86-97	05:07

continued:

PART II – In Tempo (includes discrete Blues choruses and first key changes)	Ms. #'s	Timing
The theme presented as a Rhumba in Minor Blues form	98-125	05:52
The theme presented as a swing Blues	126-137	06:25
The theme presented as a Rhumba	138-147	06:41
Ensemble unison figure (break)	148-149	06:52
The theme presented in swing in trombone accompanied by sax backgrounds derived from it	150-161	06:55
Theme presented in ensemble "call and response"/"shout" format	162-173	07:10
Theme presented as a truncated Minor Blues	174-184	07:25
Modulation and accelerando	184-185	07:34
Ensemble "shout" continues in G (still maintaining Blues-based phrase structure)	186-199	07:38
Antiphonal saxophone and reeds/brass call and response "shout" continues, in A♭	200-209	07:50
Further accelerando	210-211	07:59-08:00
Ensemble unison based on embellished version of the theme	212-219	08:01
Ritard and key change (back to primary key of F)	220-229	08:05
Call and response fanfare leads to *slow* tempo	230-235	08:13

PART III – Church Theme and Recapitulation	Ms. #'s	Timing
Unaccompanied composed clarinet solo	236-239	08:29
Bass/clarinet duet, gradual contrapuntal thickening of texture	240-253	08:40
Motto theme in plunger muted trombones	254-257	09:39
Contrapuntal crescendo and cutoff	255-261	09:42
Reestablishment of slow tempo by slow saxophone ostinato	262-265	09:58
Antiphonal presentation of slow theme, gradually building, in composed "New Orleans counterpoint"	266-289	10:13
Shout statement of main theme in brass in A minor	290-295	11:41
Fermata and contrapuntal transition	296-297	12:02
Uptempo saxophone statement of main theme (ends in F major)	298-307	12:11
Brass choir statement of the main theme (F–)	308-315	12:41
Solo trumpet theme statement solo/counterpoint (C–) over ostinato	316-323	13:08
Contrapuntal transition, and accelerando	324-327	13:33
Crescendo featuring sectional counterpoint	328-342	13:47
Composed drum solo (sets up final tempo)	343-344	14:19
Concerted ensemble statement of main theme (F–)	345-351	14:24
Drum roll/fermata	352	14:40
Antiphonal 3-part full ensemble tutti (piece ends in A♭)	353-362	

Charles Mingus' "The Shoes of the Fisherman's Wife Are Some Jive Ass Slippers" is another example of a monothematic *through-composed* piece*.

Mingus achieves the motivic development, *reiteration*, and transformation that gives form to the piece chiefly by varying the rhythmic setting of the main theme.

Compare the following appearances of the theme:

Ex. 8.18A

Initial chorale-style statement of the theme

As mentioned in Chapter 6, one of Mingus' signature compositional devices is the use of elision, or the overlapping of two phrases so that the end of one becomes the beginning of the next. This occurs at the end of the slow theme, as well as at the conclusion of the entire piece, as the bass clarinet's final theme statement begins prior to the conclusion of the alto statement.

Ex. 8.18B

Mingus' opening theme is inverted, syncopated, and embellished to form a secondary theme that appears in a brighter jazz waltz tempo.

A rapid sixteenth note figure responds to the new theme, itself yet another embellished version of a fragment of the initial theme, which gradually takes over the first section of the piece and brings it to a conclusion.

* (The transcribed examples contained here are based on the Sy Johnson arrangement.)

The theme reappears later, this time in 4/4:

Ex. 8.18c

In Mingus' music, extreme contrast is frequently the rule. In "The Shoes...", this element is brought out by juxtaposing this deliberately structured motivic development with freely improvised interludes.

Aurally obvious thematic manipulation is not the only means employed by Jazz composers in structuring extended compositions however. Sometimes, other non-musical organizational factors can work to structure the piece. As mentioned earlier, programmatic and/or impressionistic content may lead to structure as well. In *Impressionism* (a term originally coined to describe the work of Debussy, Ravel and others), the title of the piece is suggestive of its musical content. As in impressionistic painting, the emphasis is on mood and timbre, rather than on literal representation. Thus, Ellington's "Dusk" evokes the feeling of the setting sun, for example. Many comparisons have been drawn between the work of Ellington and the french impressionist composers. This is not completely surprising given that the era in which Debussy and Ravel were most influential preceded and coincided roughly with Ellington's (and Jazz's) early development. Such technical devices as parallel ninth chords and the use of the whole tone scale were prevalent not just among the Impressionists but also among their counterparts in early jazz composition. While this may be consilient, it is also known that Ellington counted works by the Impressionists among his favorite classical pieces[7].

Ex. 8.19

Parallel 9th chords in "Pavane Pour Une Infante Défunte" by Ravel

[7] Ellington, Duke. "List of Favorites, from Ellington's Silver Jubilee in Downbeat", in Tucker, Mark. The Duke Ellington Reader. Oxford, New York, 1993, pp. 268-9

Parallel 9th chords in "In a Mist" by Beiderbecke

Parallel 9th chords similar to those found in Movement #3 of Ellington's "Reminiscing in Tempo"

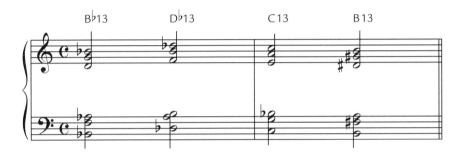

Another concept for organizing a composition around an extra-musical idea is known as *Program Music*. In programmatic works, an external organizational principle is suggested, often by the title. Examples of this structural principle as used in composition in the jazz idiom would be:

· The Suite form: Exemplified by such Ellington/Strayhorn collaborations such as "The Perfume Suite"(1944), "The Far East Suite"(1964), or Mary Lou Williams' "Zodiac Suite", in which the relationships between the discrete movements are loosely suggested by the title (although it would be incorrect to assume, as many writers have, that by employing the Suite form a composer automatically eschews motivic interrelationships between movements – see analysis of thematic content of "The Queen's Suite" later in this Chapter).

· Sacred or liturgical music written by Mary Lou Williams, Dave Brubeck, and Ellington could also be considered to fall into this category as well.

· Film Music: *Leitmotifs* associated with particular characters in a movie may also provide such external guides to musical structure, as seen in Ellington's filmscore for "Anatomy of a Murder" (discussed in Chapter 6).

· Music based on *extramusical systems:* As discussed previously, Sun Ra's signature piece, "Space Is the Place", expresses interplanetary relationships through the coexistence of polyrhythmic ostinati that intersect in predictable "orbits". The "Sonnets" which Ellington and Strayhorn created in "Such Sweet Thunder" (1957) are another such example, in which the Shakespearian form provides the abstract structure for the musical lines (i.e. the music is written in *iambic* pentameter). In any event there are many examples in jazz composition where title dictates content (see also the upcoming discussion of "Giant Steps" contained later in this Chapter).

Expressionism in Jazz Composition

As we have mentioned on several occasions, many jazz composers have been interested in the work of their Classical counterparts in the 20th century. Arnold Schoenberg and his followers developed a system based on so-called "12-tone principles", as this school of composition became labelled. ("Expressionism" because, like the parallel movement in art, it sought to use music to portray the inner workings of the artist's mind, rather than being inspired by an external scene or event.) Coltrane's insatiable musical imagination led him not only to experiment with *dodecaphonic* (12-tone) principles, but with many other manifestations of symmetry in the harmonic, melodic, and formal organization of his music. With these elements he merged his great knowledge of the Blues and standards, his interest in World music, and his incredible sound to create a uniquely personal and influential musical vocabulary.

Coltrane and the 12-Tone Principle

The central tenet of expressionist composition technique embraced by Coltrane was the use of the "tone row". The so-called "12-tone system" was based on the notion that none of the 12 tones in the chromatic scale would be repeated in a composition until all the others had been played in a prescribed order (in a strict application of the technique, rhythmic elements could be similarly "serialized"). Like many other such formal and technical appropriations by jazz musicians, it is unusual to find this one used in its purest form (although there are some notable examples, such as the William O. Smith Clarinet concerto, recorded in the early '60's by "Orchestra USA"). Coltrane was not alone in his use of this technique either. Because jazz in general, and Bebop in particular, makes such extensive use of *chromaticism* to begin with, it is quite easy, at least on the melodic level, to create a line which is rhythmically idiomatic and that uses all 12 tones without repeating any.

Note that because of our conditioning as western listeners, in a given harmonic context we tend to relegate some of the pitches in such a line to the role of *passing notes*, while others are construed as being *consonant*. In the following example, for instance, even without harmonic accompaniment we as jazz listeners tend to hear a C minor tonal center.

Ex. 8.22

Here are some other examples of tone rows as used by Jazz composers, in which the use of the row is similarly contextualized in traditional harmonic and rhythmic practice.

Ex. 8.23

"Row House" by Kenny Barron

Ex. 8.24

"Miles' Mode" by John Coltrane*

* aka "Red Planet" and has also been attributed to Eric Dolphy.

Of course, there are other applications of the principle of using all 12 tones that can lead to interesting harmonic effects. One such principle is the notion of "complementary pitch sets". Its underlying concept is that one group of notes complements another to create an environment in which all 12 tones coexist. One such example would be the coexistence of the two whole tone scales, as for example in the 8-bar A sections of Coltrane's arrangement of "But Not For Me" discussed previously.

Ex. 8.25

Chord changes and bassline to "But Not For Me", (arr. Coltrane)

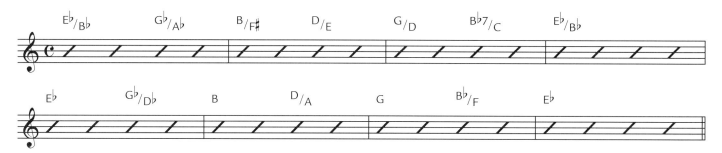

It could be said that this is occurring on two levels in Coltrane's recomposition of Gershwin's "But Not For Me". On the one hand, the basic changes of the tune have been reharmonized using the harmonic third cycles of "Giant Steps", which ordinarily implies a whole tone scale bassline.

Ex. 8.26

However, as indicated in Ex. 8.25 above, Coltrane has the bass alternate between the two whole tone scales during the 'A' sections.

Ex. 8.27

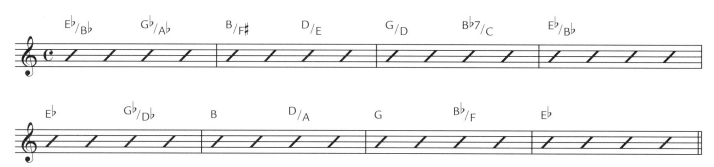

At the same time, he also constructs melody lines in his solos which not only fit over the reharmonized "Giant Steps" chord changes, but which also complement the descending whole tone bassline with which they are ordinarily associated.

Interestingly, this melodic formula also occurs in almost identical form in Coltrane's solos on "Satellite" (1:44) and "26.2" (at the very beginning of the solo). In the first case, the bassline and the melodic line are from the same whole tone scale (as in "But Not For Me"), while in the second instance conventional "Giant Steps" reharmonizations are employed. In any event, it is clear that Coltrane had worked out the use of this whole tone melodic formula, which works over the complementary pitch set of the other whole tone scale (note: Although these solo lines have been transcribed and published in "John Coltrane Plays Coltrane Changes", see DISCOGRAPHY, the basslines that accompany them have not been).

Other Coltrane 12-tone formulas

Other 12-tone formulas of Coltrane's also involve basslines. For example, in his beautiful ballad, "Central Park West", the chord progression is as follows:

ii–7-V7-I in the keys of: B, D, A♭, and F (i.e. the roots of a diminished seventh chord), yielding a bassline with all 12 notes.

This tune's deceptively simple-sounding melodic phrase also illustrates Coltrane's characteristic emphasis on third-based relationships between tonal centers, as well as his emphasis on symmetric relationships (the movement up a minor third from B to D in the beginning of the phrase is mirrored in the descent from A♭ back to F at its conclusion).

In both "Satellite" and the bridge of his version of "Body and Soul" (from the album "Coltrane's Sound" of course), we find the following formula: applying the "Giant Steps" reharmonization to a chord progressions featuring two successive key centers a whole step apart also yields all twelve notes in the bassline:

Original progression:	D–7	G7		C	followed by
	C–7	F7		B♭	becomes...
Bassline with 3-tonic reharmonization:	D–7	(E♭7 A♭ B7 E G7)	C	followed by
	C–7	(D♭7 G♭ A7 D F7)	B♭	

This relationship has its basis in the fact that the "Giant Steps"/ 3-tonic key centers are all diatonic to the same *hexatonic scale* (see earlier discussion). Thus moving the progression down a step produces an identical harmonic sequence based in the complementary hexatonic scale.

Of course, there are as many complementary relationships possible as there are scalar or modal combinations. For example, any *heptatonic scale* or mode (mostly commonly these would be the major or minor scales or any of their modes) may be similarly complemented by a pentatonic scale of some sort. Here are a couple of examples:

Ex. 8.29A

Ex. 8.29B

Of course the resulting vertical relationships may run the entire gamut from *consonance* to *dissonance*, depending on the harmonic context in which the composer places them and the choices of vertical alignment which are made.

Other sets of notes may be treated in similar fashion as well. In a recent composition, the author structured an ostinato out of one of the four "hexatonic" (aka "augmented") scales. The hexatonic scale is constructed by alternating minor third and half-step intervals and is frequently in evidence in Coltrane's solos and compositions (interestingly, the diatonic harmony of the hexatonic scale includes the three tonal centers of his "three tonic system", in both major and minor forms!, and the main melodic phrase of "Giant Steps" may also be regarded as *hexatonic* – see also Ex. 8.30B, which follows). One hexatonic scale is always complemented by another.

Ex. 8.30A

Use of two complementary hexatonic scales in "Portaculture", by the author

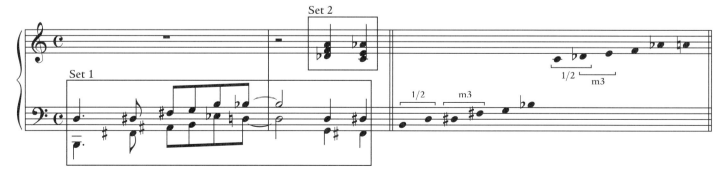

The initial phrase of "Giant Steps" is in fact diatonic to a hexatonic scale.

"Giant Steps" as a 12-tone piece

There are other 12-tone relationships present in "Giant Steps" as well. For example, as pointed out by Dave Demsey in his "John Coltrane Plays Giant Steps"[8], every melody note in the piece is also a bass note. As pointed out by the author in Chapter 13 of "Jazz Harmony"[9], the two sections of the piece (measures 1-7 and 7-15, respectively – measure 7 is shared by both phrases owing to the melodic *elision* it creates, i.e. it is the last measure of the first half of the piece as well as the first measure of the second half - see also Ex. 6.31) each exhibits the characteristic of having their respective tone rows *completed* by significant *absent* notes. In other words, adding the two melodic statements of measures 1-7 together yields 7 of the 12 chromatic notes (each phrase is also hexatonic), with the five remaining pitches comprising a *third* transposition of the same theme:

Ex 8.31

(The concept of complementary pitch sets combining to create all 12 tones is not unique to Coltrane, though the use of unsounded pitches in this way may well be. There are many examples in Bartók's music, for example, of the use of both complementary pitch sets and hexatonic scales — see Gollin article in BIBLIOGRAPHY).

[8] Demsey, Dave. *John Coltrane Plays Giant Steps.* Hal Leonard, Milwaukee, pp. 12-17

[9] Jaffe, Andy. *Jazz Harmony.* Advance Music, Rottenburg, Germany, 1996, pp. 163-172

Doing likewise with measures 7-15 yields 9 of the 12 chromatic notes, with the three remaining, unused notes yielding an augmented triad (C, E, A♭) which describes the major third-based key relationships in the piece. Truly an extraordinary structure!

Coltrane's interest in principles of harmonic symmetry was not always manifest in the identical way however.

The root motion of the chords to Coltrane's "Nita", for example, outlines the tonic chord (B♭Δ) of the piece as it passes through a series of "third-related" modulations (in the primary key, B♭). Thus, the chord sound is expressed in the following series of key centers B♭, D, F and A major[10], while in "Like Sonny" the root motion features (minor seventh chords) moving in root motion of descending *minor* thirds in the first phrase, then in descending *major* thirds in the second eight bars, resulting in two primary keys, B, and E♭, that are familiar to thirds cycle enthusiasts (see end of Chapter ASSIGNMENTS).

"Like Sonny" also shows Coltrane employing third-relations in conjunction with the notion of intervallic symmetry. Further, both "Nita" and "Like Sonny" illustrate the notion that Coltrane's approach to third-related harmonies and concepts of symmetry were not limited exclusively to the use of the specific formulaic chord progressions found in "Giant Steps" and "Countdown".

Yet Coltrane's interest in harmonic and formal experimentation transcended even his obsession with the "three-tonic system".

Coltrane and Formal Experimentation

In "Countdown", his *contrafact* based on Eddie "Cleanhead" Vinson's "Tune Up" (this piece is often erroneously attributed to Miles Davis), Coltrane combines three-tonic reharmonization of a standard ii-V7-I harmonic phrase with an inversion of the paradigm of standard "theme and variations" small ensemble performance practice. In other words, rather than beginning with the statement of the theme, then having solos, then recapitulating it, he begins with a tenor sax solo accompanied only by drums, subsequently adding the piano and bass and stating the completed theme *only* at the end of the piece. In terms of employing one's compositional process as a means of upending traditional performance practice, "Countdown" might therefore be thought of as a companion piece to Ellington's "Diminuendo in Blue"(see also Ex. 6.39). Though these pieces are stylistically contrasting, they have in common this notion of challenging the dominant paradigm of "theme and variations" – based performance practice in jazz. (Ellington does so by starting with the climactic, rhythmically disjunct, shout chorus, then gradually smoothing the piece out and thinning its orchestration, building the piece *down*, rather than *up*).

[10] Porter, Lewis. John Coltrane: His Life and Music. Michigan, Ann Arbor, 1998. p. 116.

Coltrane also wrote extended compositions for small ensemble. His "A Love Supreme" (analyzed concisely by Lewis Porter in his "John Coltrane his Life and Music"), derives all of its melodic material, and the key relationships between the four movements, out of its initial motif (making this piece similar to Ellington's "Harlem" in that regard). The initial motif of "A Love Supreme" that appears in the introduction. It is transposed up a half step to F to begin "Acknowledgement (Mvt. #1)". Notice that the four notes it contains (B, E, F♯, B) represent a symmetrical pattern, similar to that which defines the key relationships in the piece shown in Ex. 8.33 below (see Porter reference cited below for more in-depth discussion):

Ex. 8.32A

Interestingly, this same four-note intervallic shape returns at the end of Part 4, at the very conclusion of the piece, immediately following the famously controversial overdub of the octave C by a second saxophone. Although much attention has been focused on the overdub itself[11], it is interesting that the primary saxophone track follows the overdub immediately with what is in effect a reiteration of the opening motif heard in the introduction, providing yet another example of the many compositional symmetries exhibited by Coltrane's music. If the introduction presages the key relationships and motivic content of the four movements of the piece, this subtle concluding motif reiterates these same relationships.

Ex. 8.32B

Ex. 8.33

Key centers of "A Love Supreme"[12]

Part I	Part 2	Part 3	Part 4
F	(down a whole step to E♭)	(up a perfect fifth to B♭)	(up a step to C)

[11] Porter, p. 248
[12] Porter, p. 236

Coltrane's wideranging musical interests often resulted in the filtering of disparate influences through the prism of his unique personal vocabulary. For example, in his well-known arrangement of "My Favorite Things", the influence of *Raga* can be imputed in the extended modal solos (there is some dispute about how direct this influence actually was, in part fueled by Coltrane's own comments on the subject[13]), while Coltrane's use of Raga principles can be more convincingly postulated in his composition "Alabama", in which the out of tempo statement of the theme prior to the tempo improvised modal solo has both the feeling and formal effect of the *alapana*, or introductory section of the Raga. In addition, there has been persistent speculation[14] (at yet not specifically documented) that Coltrane's "Alabama" is based on a speech by Dr. Martin Luther King (if true this would constitute another instance of his use of the compositional process of "playing" a written text, such as he does with his own poem in "Psalm", the fourth part of "A Love Supreme".) While a thorough examination of both Dr. King's Eulogy for the four girls murdered in Birmingham, as well as the famous "I Have a Dream" speech of August, 1963 yields no such literal representation, there is no doubt that the title of the piece, as well as the same sense of urgency that pervaded Dr. King's remarks, condition both its mood and content.

A Study in the Use of Third Relations in a Multi-movement Structure: "Blue Train"

All of these musical elements, the Blues, preoccupation with major and minor thirds, large scale formal schemes, appropriation, and even the potential for tonal changes to impart psychological impact, can be seen at work in Coltrane's first project as a leader for Blue Note (and only his second as a leader): the 1957 album "Blue Train".

Background and Context

At the outset, it must be stated that the following analysis is based exclusively on the music itself, as opposed to, for example, any documentation surrounding the session or the recollections of any of the principles involved. We do know that on Blue Note, Coltrane had the freedom to record what he wanted (as opposed to the emphasis placed on recording standards requiring little or no rehearsal that was in force at Prestige, his previous label, both as a leader and while recording with Miles Davis). Copyright registrations, for what they are worth as musicological documentation, offer no evidence for the piece having been conceived of as a single entity (i.e. the compositions are registered individually[15], not as a single piece).

[13] Lavezzoli, Peter. *The Dawn of Indian Music in the West.* New York: Continuum International, 2006, pp. 267-296.

[14] Kahn, Ashley. *A Love Supreme: The Story of John Coltrane's Signature Album.* New York, Penguin, 2002, p. 72.

[15] Register of Copyrights, Library of Congress, Washington, D.C.

The following is a formal outline of the album "Blue Train", showing key centers visited and formal characteristics of the individual pieces.

Ex 8.34

The Overall Key Structure of "Blue Train"

Title	Primary Key Centers Visited	Form
Blue Train	E♭	Blues
Moment's Notice	E♭ and G♭	ABAC
Locomotion	B♭	AABA (A sections are Blues, connected by a "Rhythm" Bridge)
I'm Old Fashioned	E♭ and G	ABAC
Lazy Bird	G and E♭	AABA

The individual pieces and the changing emphasis on major and minor thirds:

Blue Train

"Blue Train" is a traditional 12-bar Blues. It begins in unison.

Ex. 8.35A

At the outset of the second chorus, the horns are harmonized triadically, with resulting emphasis on the minor third (G♭) in an idiomatic "♯9" sound.

Ex. 8.35B

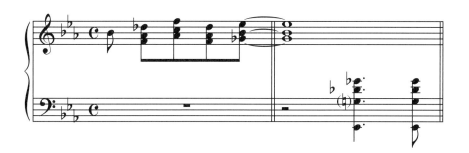

Moment's Notice

"Moment's Notice" begins with the standard device of playing the second half of its ABAC songform as an introduction. Following this, its "clave"-based melodic motif recurs throughout the form, with two notable harmonic landmarks. The first is a secondary key of G♭. The opening motif and the modulation are juxtaposed below for purposes of comparison:

Ex. 8.36A

The second is its *coda*, which features parallel diatonic chords over a dominant pedal preceding the break that leads to solos.

Ex. 8.36B

Coda of first chorus

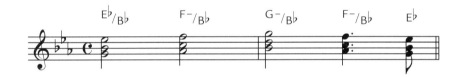

Of note is the variation in the coda that concludes the piece, in which the familiar ♯9 sound from "Blue Train" is reiterated.

Ex. 8.36C

Coda of "Moment's Notice"

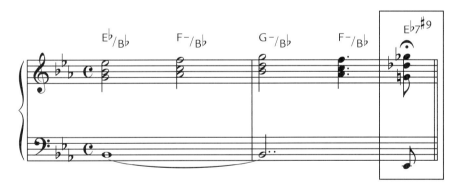

Locomotion

"Locomotion" departs the primary key center of E♭ for its dominant key, B♭. Its form is AABA, with the A's being the 12-bar Blues, and the B section being a reharmonized variation of the "I Got Rhythm" bridge. (In this sense it is also a "compound" form, sort of the reverse of Richie Powell's "Jacqui" – see also Chapter 5).

Ex. 8.37

The form of "Locomotion"

Following the recapitulation of the main tune, there is an interesting coda, in which the other two horns descend in parallel tritones over a series of dominant 7(♭5) chords descending in the *whole tone scale*, beginning and ending on B natural, over which Coltrane solos. It is interesting that this middle piece of the suite is unique harmonically (tonal center of B♭) as well as formally (compound). The harmonic detail of the coda in "Locomotion" is also fascinating: parallel tritones descending the *whole tone scale* from B♭ to B♭.

I'm Old Fashioned

If our argument about "Blue Train" as an extended work is valid, then "I'm Old Fashioned" is an example of a standard being incorporated into a larger form. Ordinarily performed and originally composed in F, Coltrane performs it in here E♭. What could the reasons be for this choice of key, and if it was made deliberately in order to fit the key scheme of the entire piece, how does that work? (While the choice of key certainly could be reflective of Coltrane's well-documented proclivity for playing ballads in E♭, it also conveniently fits the emerging overall "arch form" of the piece). Like its companion piece in the postulated arch form ("Moment's Notice"), "I'm Old Fashioned" has an ABAC form, and uses the second half of the tune as an introduction (in a five movement arch form, the second and fourth movements are related – see Chapter 6). Also, like "Moment's Notice", it features diatonic planing (while this took place in the coda of "Moment's Notice", it is a part of the *bridge* here).

Ex. 8.38

Diatonic planing in the coda of "Moment's Notice"

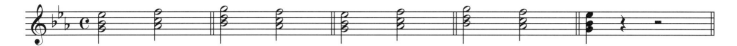

Diatonic planing in the bridge of "I'm Old Fashioned"

And importantly, the secondary key here is G major, a major third as contrasted with the earlier emphasis on the minor third-related G♭.

Lazy Bird

"Lazy Bird" begins with a standard ii−7 to V7 progression in the key of G, then ends in E♭. By the end of the record any reference to the *minor* third, or to the key center of G♭, has disappeared, replaced instead by emphasis on the *major* third. The piece ends on a deceptive resolution to D♭ instead of the expected E♭. The use of the deceptive final resolution to ♭VII instead of I is heard frequently in the music of Monk, and of course the expected tonic, E♭, can still be heard above the ♭VII chord as a triadic extension of it.

Ex. 8.39

The final chord of "Lazy Bird"; the new tonic, ♭VII, w/I chord as extensions

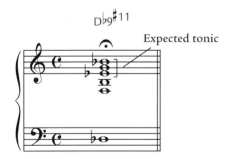

Pantonality

In traditional theory, the term "pantonality" is sometimes thought of being synonymous with that of "atonality". As applied to jazz composition it may be thought of as meaning "not restricted to a single tonality". Many pentatonically based melodies fit this definition, as do their related quartally based harmonies. In the following example, for instance, there are a multiplicity of possible harmonizations for the given melodic fragment.

Ex. 8.40A

Simple pentatonic motif

Ex. 8.40B

Various harmonizations are possible

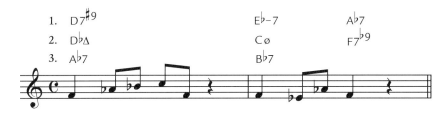

Again, harmonically ambiguous voicings may be used to represent a variety of traditional chord functions (see also Chapter 7, Ex.'s 7.39 and 7.40).

For example, a three-part chord in 4ths...

Ex. 8.41A

...could accommodate various bassnotes and thereby imply many chords:

Ex 8.41B

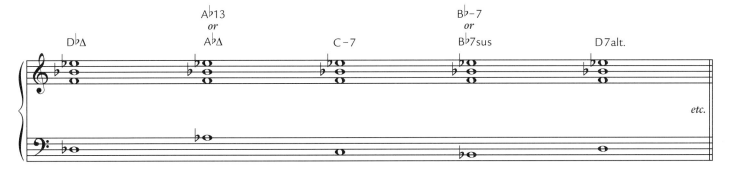

Because of their ability to fit a variety of harmonic situations, simple pentatonic melodies provide flexible (not to mention idiomatic) and manipulable motivic material. Such compositions as "Goodbye Pork Pie Hat" (Mingus) and "Gregory Is Here" (Horace Silver – see end of Chapter ASSIGNMENTS*) illustrate how successfully this sort of idiomatic, Blues-based material, may be wed to sophisticated harmonic support to great compositional effect.

Ex. 8.42

The first two bars of "Goodbye Pork Pie Hat"

* (When you listen to "Gregory Is Here", observe the relationship between the melody notes and supporting chords in the first four bars. As in Ex. 8.42 above, the tonal center of the melody remains static while the harmony beneath it moves to create specific harmonic relationships. It is almost as if harmonies were chosen so that the tune's simple 2-note melody would consist entirely of color tones [aka extensions – see also Ex.s 4.41]. Observe how the motif's relationship to the supporting harmony changes A section develops, becoming progressively *less* rich in relation to the accompanying harmony as it moves forward. Thus the motif is not merely being transposed, it is also being *reharmonized*, and in the process gradually changing character from *antecedent* to *consequent*).

This process may also be used to create structural unity in multi-movement works. As mentioned earlier, Ellington's 1959 "Queen's Suite" provides just such an example. As the following examples show, the characteristic intervallic content of a *pentatonic* scale (whole steps, perfect fourths, and perfect fifths) provides a pervasively reiterative motivic unity in thematic content between the movements of the piece (whether written by Ellington or Strayhorn)[16].

[16] The third movement, entitled "Le Sucrier Velour" was previously entitled "Do Not Disturb" (Private Collection, Vol.1, 1956)

Pentatonically-based intervallic similarities
between themes of "The Queen's Suite"

Movement 1 - Theme

Movement 2 - Theme

Movement 2 - Pyramid

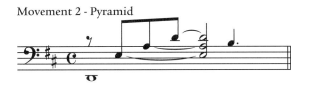

Movement 4 - Tenor sax theme

Movement 5 - Theme excerpt

Movement 3 - Theme

As was also mentioned earlier (in Chapter 7), the same principle can be applied to exploit harmonically ambiguous *voicings*. Using a three-note *quartal voicing* as a point of departure, for example, we could derive a series of harmonically complete and modal sounds that it could represent.

Ex. 8.44

Main 3-note chord (see also Ex. 8.41A)
could be CΔ, FΔ, E–11, B–7, etc.

Once these sounds are *transposed* their potential uses in organizing the harmonic structure of a piece are multiplied. In such a situation the reiteration of the given sound may supplant traditional tonal function as a means of harmonic organization.

This is more or less the process at work in Herbie Hancock's brilliant 1968 piece "Speak Like a Child".

Speak Like a Child

"Speak Like a Child" is a composition for piano trio, augmented by the use of three horns (Flugelhorn, Bass Trombone, and Alto Flute) whose function is essentially more *timbral* than melodic, an orchestration choice that perhaps reflects the influence of Gil Evans. Given the rhythmic context (basically it is a *Bossa Nova*), its pensive medium tempo, and orchestration, the piece is certainly modal in aesthetic character, though not in harmonic technique. The thematic material is not reiterated that forcefully or often, and the form is cyclic harmonically. There are basically two main sections of the form, linked by a two-bar cadence that is reharmonized in its second appearance.

The first section of the form is essentially 20-bars long, based on various transpositions and reharmonizations of the traditional "tritone and a fourth" piano voicing shown previously in Ex. 7.36.

Ex. 8.45

Although Hancock did not always voice this chord the same way, it could nonetheless be said to relate each of the following harmonies used in the first 20 bars of this piece as their underlying structure:

All of the dominant 7ths (for example, the opening D♭7#9)

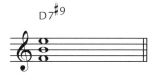

The G♭Δ#11 in measure 13

The G♭°7 which follows it in measure 14

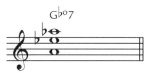

Thus, while the harmonic relationships of the piece do not offer the listener a conventional tonic chord or static key center, the reiteration of this familiar and *accessible* sound (at least 8 times during the first 20 bars) provides that stability instead. Other carefully balanced elements that contribute to the overall effect of consonance in the piece include:

· The *orchestration*, featuring complementary "metallic" sounds among the wind instruments;

· The *time feel*, smooth and not at all rhythmically disjunct;

· A gradual descent in the bassline;

· Assigning smooth, well-blended, and occasionally overlapping *(voice-crossing)* lines to the three horns, as in measure A-9 shown below:

Ex. 8.46

Voice-crossing in measure A-9

· Derivation of the material for the upcoming solo section of the form from within this initial "A" section (the source of this material is first heard in the modal cadence in measures 3 and 4, then developed more fully in measures 23-28):

Ex. 8.47

Ms.3, 4 modal cadence

Ms.23-28 modal harmony

These measures feature a typically repetitive and accessible modal "vamp", back and forth between A–7 and B–7/E (or "E7sus).

The first 20 bars of the piece are linked to the modal cadence occurring in ms. 23-28 by the following two measure connecting phrase in ms. 21 and 22.

Ex. 8.48

Then the harmonic progression repeats, with increasingly active embellishment, especially rhythmically. The following comparative examples juxtapose parallel measures in the first two choruses in terms of their relative rhythmic complexity (these examples show only the three horn parts).

Measures A10-12 of the first chorus

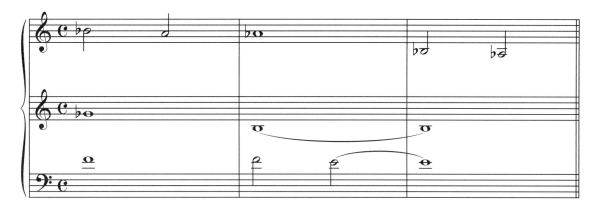

Measures A9-11 of the second chorus

Measures A13-16 of the first chorus

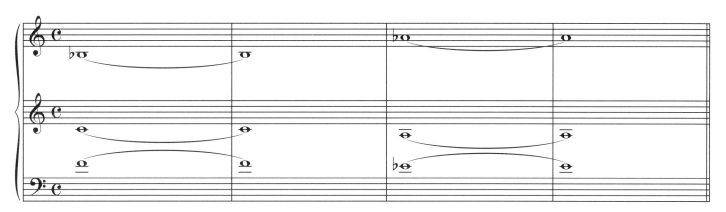

Measures A13-16 of the second chorus

The increased tension brought about by this *rhythmic* activity culminates in a cadence in measures 44-45 that is not only rhythmic, but also harmonically significant in the following ways:

· Measures 45-48 are harmonized differently than the analogous measures (17-20) were in the first chorus;

· This cadence also represents the lowest point in the bassline; and

· *The tritone and a fourth voicing* has appeared in inversion in the three horns (coinciding with their accented, *tutti* attack in measure 45).

Ex. 8.50A

Comparison of harmony of ms. 17-20 and 45-48

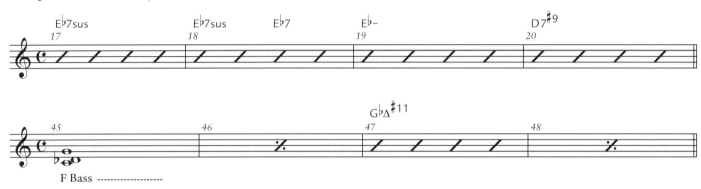

F Bass - - - - - - - - - - - - - - - - - - -

Ex. 8.50B

The voicing in ms. 45

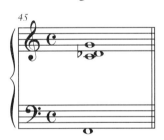

This tension abates only temporarily, returning in ms. 49 and 50 as the linking passage leading to the solo section is reharmonized in a more dissonant fashion (compare Ex. 8.51 with Ex. 8.48 above).

Ex. 8.51

The second linking cadence in ms. 49 and 50

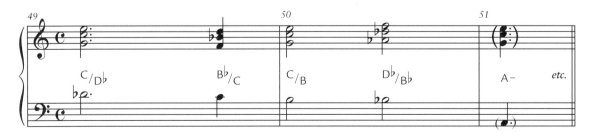

Note that three of the four characteristic "three horn" sounds discussed in Chapter 7 are in use in this piece.

· The "tritone and a fourth" voicing which generated the harmonic structure of the first 20 bars;

· The "inverted triad" sound found in the reharmonization of the linking phrase (shown in Ex. 8.51 above); and

· The "major third and a half-step" sound used in the background horn parts (in measures 55-59):

Ex. 8.52

"Major third and a half-step" voicing at the beginning of the solo section

Conclusion

"Blue Train", "The Queen's Suite", and "Speak Like a Child" all employ common practice devices imaginatively in order to explore sophisticated and original formal concepts.

Recomposition of Classical Pieces

As was mentioned previously, the notion of "Jazzing the Classics" (in fact the title of a CD documenting many such efforts – see Discography) has been around since the beginnings of jazz music. Numerous arrangements and contrafacts of compositions from the European Classical repertoire have been penned by jazz writers participating in a process which was famously championed at the dawn of the era of recorded jazz by bandleader Paul Whiteman. As with any other sort of appropriation, such efforts range in content from the mundane to the profound. Standards such as "I'm Always Chasing Rainbows" (credited to McCarthy and Carroll but clearly appropriated from Chopin's "Fantasie-Impromptu in C♯ minor"), and Jobim's "Insensatez" (equally clearly based on Chopin's Prelude #4 in E minor), among many others, are examples of this process, as are contemporary arrangements of pieces from the European Classical repertoire such as Quincy Jones' 1992 version of "The Messiah". The examples chosen for discussion in this chapter comprise only a small portion of those available, and it is hoped that the reader will endeavor to undertake similar comparative analysis of other works in this genre.

The Ellington/Strayhorn Nutcracker

The Overture: How did Ellington and Strayhorn incorporate their own signature sounds into their adaptation of the original? And most importantly, how did they make it sound like jazz?

This process might be best described as one of *recomposition*.

The Ellington/Strayhorn versions of the "Nutcracker" (1960), and its companion "Peer Gynt Suite" are distinguished from the original compositions in large part by the distribution of thematic material and backgrounds among the distinctive musical voices and sounds available to the arrangers, and through changes in underlying rhythmic feel that create a more *ostinato*- or swing-based context. And although there are many instances of reharmonization in their version of "The Nutcracker", Ellington and Strayhorn generally adhere to the basic form harmony and voice-leading of Tchaikovsky's original movements, opting instead to personalize their treatment by means of converting themes into riffs, and emphasizing melodic material that adapts well to their overall goal of making the piece swing.

Looking at the first movement (the "Overture", written by Strayhorn[17]) in detail, it is clear that one important similarity between the two versions is also a source of great musical contrast. Obviously, the original version had a *function* as a dance piece. Strayhorn's version, based on swing, also shared that function implicitly by virtue of its own musical heritage. Yet there is obviously great contrast between these two styles in terms of this shared element. Tchaikovsky's is in *duple meter*, while the Strayhorn version is in a *medium swing tempo* with the quarter note being almost exactly half as fast. The first movement may be thought of as a study in the stylistic impact of rhythmic context.

Ex. 8.53A

Tchaikovsky Overture, main theme

Ex. 8.53B

Strayhorn arrangement, main theme

[17] van de Leur, Walter. *Something to Live For: The Music of Billy Strayhorn.* Oxford, New York, 2002, p. 275

There are many other idiomatic adaptations that Strayhorn brings to his treatment of the piece. First, he adds an introduction, in which the basic rhythmic elements are established in the walking bassline and standard swing accompaniment in the drums (Tchaikovsky's Overture has no introduction!).

Ex. 8.54

The Strayhorn Introduction

Second, the primary theme achieves a kind of a riff-like quality as a function of the swing phrasing and slower tempo. This is further emphasized when Strayhorn's counter-riff to the primary theme is added as a replacement for Tchaikovsky's more linear and busy *counterpoint*.

Ex. 8.55

Strayhorn riff to accompany principal theme

For the "bridge" theme Strayhorn exploits the uniquely personal voice of Paul Gonsalves (what would the music of Ellington and Strayhorn be without the individual voices for whom they conceived it?). Gonsalves, like Louis Armstrong, Johnny Hodges and Bubber Miley, had a sound whose nuances could not be adequately conveyed in musical notation.

Ex. 8.56

Gonsalves' solo lines

In addition to this melodic exposition, Gonsalves later gets to play an improvised solo over another of Tchaikovsky's 2-note string themes, which has again been converted into a riff by Strayhorn.

Ex. 8.57

Similarly, the brief (2-note) oboe solo which leads to Tchaikovsky's second theme is replaced by plunger-muted trombone in the Strayhorn version, and given greater emphasis by virtue of its being repeated (the slower tempo enables this). This is another example of the use of a vocal and Blues-inflected sound, as well as of the reiterative quality so prevalent in the Blues.

Ex. 8.58

In lieu of a development section, Strayhorn includes a newly composed "shout chorus" not found in the orginal, and then concludes the movement by converting a relatively unimportant string line of Tchaikovsky's into a taglike coda. In Strayhorn's version this material is given more prominence as a result of its reiteration, formal placement, and deft reharmonization.

Ex. 8.59

Strayhorn's Coda

Strayhorn's coda begins with call and response between the saxophones and brass (not all of the harmonic voices in the saxophones are shown here, just the lead lines). Then in the ninth bar of the coda he unifies the ensemble in a concerted statement of his descending scalar tag theme, heavily accenting the backbeat and harmonizing the passage with parallel major triads (F, E, D, etc.), a truly unique and cadentially effective sound.

While space does not permit us to fully analyze the entire Suite, some further examples from its remaining movements follow. These illustrate some of the ways in which Ellington and Strayhorn employ their unique orchestral vocabulary and sense of swing to rephrase Tchaikovsky's original motifs.

Tchaikovsky's "Dance of the Reeds" theme compared with Strayhorn's "Toot Toot, Tootie Toot". Not only is this rephrased rhythmically, the choice of instrumentation is also imaginative. Strayhorn used harmon mutes *over* plunger mutes to create a diffuse, metallic sound for the theme. Note that in addition to change in color, a central principle in the reworking of these themes is to convert them into riffs whenever possible:

Ex. 8.60A

The famous "Waltz of the Flowers" theme is treated similarly, and prepared by an introduction as the Overture was as well. Besides the obvious change from Waltz to heavy Swing (a major transformation to be sure) it also employs the device of *call and response*, trading the theme around between individual voices before bringing in the entire band in a concerted ensemble treatment of the theme:

Ex. 8.60B

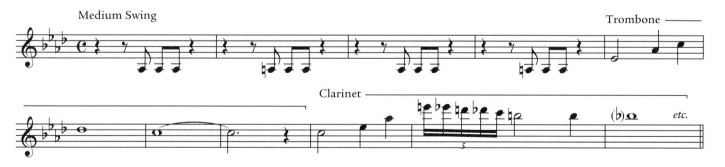

In another striking conversion, "Sugar Plum Fairy" becomes "Sugar Rum Cherry" by slowing the tempo down and using "hand drumming" technique to create a deeply Blues-based mood for the piece. Of course, the theme has a more riff-like feeling as a function of the slower tempo and the new rhythmic accompaniment:

Ex. 8.60c

Certainly none of this music can be fully appreciated without being heard. Notation can only convey so much.

Two versions of Tchaikovsky's "Arabian Dance"

The Ellington-Strayhorn version of the "Nutcracker" reorders the movements, placing "Naibara" (based on the original "Arabian Dance" – "Naibara" is "Arabian" spelled backwards) last. According to van de Leur, this final movement was Strayhorn's as well[18].

The fact that this piece had also been reconstructed some 18 years earlier by Gil Evans in one of his earliest recorded arrangements for the Claude Thornhill band invites comparison between the two versions. (It is unclear as to whether or not Ellington and Strayhorn were aware of the Thornhill version, but it is at least ironic that Evans may have been an influence, given that he once stated that "All I ever did; try to do what Billy Strayhorn did"[19]).

The opportunity to write for the Thornhill band provided a strong influence on the development of Evans' writing style. As mentioned in Chapter 7, one of the main reasons for this was Thornhill's unique instrumentation - a woodwind section featuring the standard five saxophones plus two dedicated clarinet chairs, as well as french horns and tuba to complement the traditional big band brass section. This combination lent a more orchestral sound to the band than was available to most of its contemporaries.

Evans' 1942 reworking of the "Arabian Dance" from the Tchaikovsky ballet exploited this instrumentation, but also deconstructed the original in such a way as to use it as raw material for what was a fairly standard big band treatment of the theme, incorporating such standard idiomatic devices as improvised solos, woodwind soli sections, minor Blues progressions and a shout chorus, in and of itself a radical gesture.

[18] ibid.
[19] Hajdu, David. *Lush Life, A Biography of Billy Strayhorn.* Farrar, Strauss, Giroux, New York, 1996, p.87

Of course Evans took some liberties with the form of the original Tchaikovsky version, beginning with the introduction, in which he uses a pedal tone in the bass and soft tom-toms to evoke an "exotic" mood similar in style to that of Ellington's arrangement of Juan Tizol's "Caravan".

Ex. 8.61A

Evans' treatment of the theme, first in the horns, then subsequently in the brass and woodwind sections, syncopates it in an idiomatically stylized manner. Throughout the piece Evans skillfully creates seamless transitions between asymmetrically structured phrases.

Ex. 8.61B

Evans' version of the first theme remains fairly faithful to Tchaikovsky's

The woodwind statement of the theme elides effortlessly into an eighth-note *soli*, during which the *ostinato* in the bass is abandoned for a walking bassline. Note the frequent use of the common practice device of reharmonization of *passing notes* with diminished seventh chords (see also Ex. 7.27).

Ex. 8.62

The introductory *ostinato* then returns briefly prior to a rhythmically concerted ensemble *shout chorus*.

Ex. 8.63

Following the shout chorus, Evans incorporates a Blues-based chord progression in G minor into the arrangement for improvised solos over the swing rhythmic feel (whereas Strayhorn had Johnny Hodges solo over a progression which only settled in G minor after building tension and dynamics via the use of a prolonged G major ensemble chord).

Ex. 8.64A

Thornhill solo changes

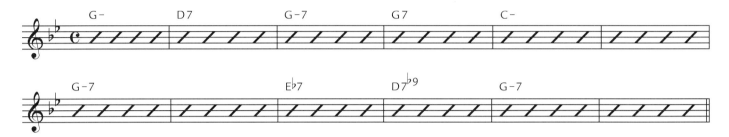

Note that Strayhorn's solo changes for Johnny Hodges don't really have any sort of progression, just an extended background chord (G major, against the prevailing G minor harmony):

Ex. 8.64B

Strayhorn changes

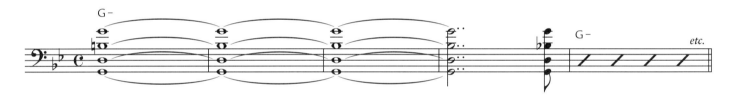

Evans' arrangement follows the clarinet solo with an extended, *riff*-based, layered *ostinato*, leading to a modulation and *reiteration* of the primary thematic material in concerted block harmony.

Ex.8.65

An additional, modulatory shout chorus intervenes prior to the final recapitulation of the theme. One cannot help but note the similarity between this final *shout chorus* and that of Ellington's well-known "Ko-Ko" from just two years earlier – compare the first measure of Evans' shout chorus to the following well-known excerpt from Ellington's "Ko-Ko" (see end of Chapter Assignments).

Ex. 8.66

Ellington's shout chorus

The comparison is striking when the two versions are heard back to back.

While it may be speculative at best to hypothesize that the main motif of Ellington's "Ko-Ko" was intentionally related to Beethoven's 5th[20], there seems to be little doubt, based on the musical evidence, that in this case Evans was doing more than merely trying to emulate "what Billy Strayhorn did", but rather was *appropriating* what his *mentors* had done!

For Ellington and Strayhorn, the placement of "Niabara" last provides a rhythmic complement to the first movement. While the "Overture" began by using the walking bass and ride cymbal to establish the swing feel, "Niabara" begins and ends with a bass *ostinato*, accompanied by the "exotic" device of hand drumming employed so often by Ellington. (Essentially the same device was employed by Evans in the opening of *his* arrangement to the piece.) Thus Strayhorn's arrangements of the outer movements provide a contrasting yet idiomatic rhythmic framework for the entire piece, resulting in a *signification* of sorts on the composers' part. The understated ending is as atypical of Big Band writing generally as it is powerfully dramatic as a consequence.

Ex. 8.67A

Bass ostinato of last movement

Ex. 8.67B

Drum part

Hi-hat

Toms or Timpani

20 Rattenbury, Ken. *Duke Ellington: Jazz Composer.*
   Yale University Press, New Haven, 1999, p. 106

Ellington and Strayhorn use this sort of hand-drumming style as a resource to evoke African drumming traditions and notions of exoticism ("A Drum Is a Woman", "Caravan", "Bakiff", and "Afro-Bossa", to name but a few such examples). Combining the *ostinato* bassline with this drumming style results in a decidedly non-Western rhythmic setting, especially given the use of Timpani in lieu of the more traditional Tom-Toms. The imagery conveyed by this movement made it a perfect underscore for the conversion scene in Spike Lee's film "Malcom X".

To return to the Strayhorn arrangement, following the introduction the main melodic statement is divided among the three trombonists in plunger-mutes, in "call and response" fashion.

Ex. 8.68

The trombone parts

Tchaikovsky's next theme is converted into a background line through the devices of rhythmic *augmentation* and *displacement*.

Ex. 8.69

Certainly the climactic moment of the arrangement comes with the previously mentioned Johnny Hodges solo. Strayhorn manipulates the beginning of its chord progression in such a way as to cleverly juxtapose major and minor key harmony, while concurrently creating further dramatic contrast as a result of a change in the underlying rhythmic feeling, supplanting the prior *ostinato* with *swing* accompaniment. The *ostinato* then returns to support the recapitulation of the theme and end the movement as discussed earlier, a dramatic fade-out to nothing with only a rattling tambourine to mark its conclusion. (This strikingly atypical Big band ending is reminiscent of that of "Amad" as well, which many people feel should properly be considered to be the last movement of "The Far East Suite".)

Comparison of the two versions

Evans' reconstruction of the piece treated the main motif in fairly typical Big band fashion after the mood-setting in the introduction. Evans' rearrangement emphasizes fairly standard elements of big band writing of the time, including a swing-based woodwind *soli* and full ensemble unison *shout chorus*. He also extracts a set of chord changes from the piece for the soloists (though unlike Ellington and Strayhorn he retains the minor key tonality throughout the solos). Although Evans version is therefore more "typical" of big band writing of the time in its use of these standard devices, it also represents a somewhat radical departure in underlying rhythmic feel from Tchaikovsky's.

By contrast, the Ellington-Strayhorn version may be regarded as incorporating an element of "signification" or commentary on Tchaikovsky's original in its use of swing-based and Afro-exotic rhythms, as well as the Blues-based juxtaposition of major and minor tonality in the Hodges solo. The use of *call and response*, plunger mutes, and recycling of the thematic material as background riffs for solos, are all additional devices which are characteristic of the mature style of Ellington and Strayhorn.

Conclusion

In this Chapter we began by studying adaptations of European Classical forms by Jazz Composers. We saw how these adaptations needed to remain idiomatic in order to be musically convincing. We ended the chapter by discussing recomposed versions of pieces from the Classical repertoire, and drew the same conclusion: The musical personalities of both the writer and the ensemble must be taken into account in order to have a convincing result. The expressive possibilities of the music have expanded as composers have challenged set paradigms of performance practice, form, and facile stylistic prescription.

Finally we should note that as jazz has become more a part of the musical mainstream in the larger world, its principles, rhythms, forms, and new orchestral timbres have formed the basis for a number of pieces by composers in the European Classical tradition, including, to name just a few: Stravinsky's "Ragtime" (1918), and "Ebony Concerto" (the latter written for Woody Herman's Orchestra in 1946); Gershwin's "Rhapsody in Blue" (1924); Messiaen's "Quartet for the End of Time" (1941) and "La Creation du Monde" (1923); Donald Erb's "The Hawk" (based on the famous 1939 Coleman Hawkins solo on "Body and Soul"); and Luciano Berio's "Laborinthus II, Part 2" (inspired by Miles Davis; circa 1970), among many, many others.

ASSIGNMENTS

1.) Listen to all of the music discussed in this Chapter.

2.) Bring examples of the following to class for analysis:

· Adaptation of a classical form by a jazz composer;

· Arrangement of a classical composition by a jazz composer;

· An example of a through-composed, motivically-based composition by a jazz composer;

· An example of a multi-movement work by a jazz composer;

· Examine the parallel relationship between melody and harmony in Coltrane's "Like Sonny". Also note the "third-related" intervallic relationships between the roots of the chords.

· An example of an impressionistically inspired jazz composition;

· Transcribe Bill Evans' "Twelve Tone Tune" (see DISCOGRAPHY).

· Listen to the opening measure of the shout chorus found in the Gil Evans arrangement of "Arab Dance" as recorded by Claude Thornhill (see DISCOGRAPHY), and compare it with Ex. 8.66.

3.) *Write* a piece based on pantonal harmonic and/or melodic content.

4.) Do further analysis of the motivic development in either "Harlem" or "Black, Brown and Beige".

INDEX

GLOSSARY

Adaptation: Reuse of an extant form or musical idea in a new formal context (see also "recontextualization").

Aggregate Rhythm: Rhythm produced by a combination of discrete individual parts.

Alapana: Introductory section of a Raga.

Altered Scale: Seventh mode of the melodic minor scale.

Antecedent: First, as in antecedent phrase, an opening or "calling" phrase.

Anticipation: Process of advancing a melody note and/or its associated harmony rhythmically.

Appropriation: Borrowing of musical materials, generally thematic (see also "recontextualization"), and as distinguished from "borrowed *chords*", as in "modal interchange".

Arch Form: Formal design of an extended composition in which odd-numbered discrete sections mirror one another's musical content as they move farther from a unique central movement. For example, in a five-section arch form, the second and fourth, and first and last sections would share material.

Asymmetry(ic):   Formal property of a piece or phrase in which individual sections are not the same length.

Augmentation: Increasing in length, often by doubling.

Aural Tradition: Tradition based on learning by listening.

Backbeat: A 4/4 beat with a heavy accent on 2 and 4, and/or the second or fourth beats in such a rhythm.

Backcycling: Process of moving backward through the cycle of fifths and/or chromatically from a given target chord to find an alternative starting point for the harmonic phrase.

Baião: Brazilian rhythm featuring 3+3+2 subdivision over a quarter note pulse (in 2/4). Also the popular style of music in Northeast Brazil of the same name.

Baser: Exhortative, rhythmically independent improvised bass part in Gospel music.

Bitonal: A harmony with more than one self-contained chord within it (see also "extended" chords).

Blue Notes: Flatted 3rd, 5th, and 7th degrees.

Blues-based Harmony: Chord(s) containing Blue Notes.

Bluesified: Altered by the presence of a Blue Note.

Blues Form: 1.) 12-bar instrumental form and its variants, in which the Tonic chord and/or its substitutes appear in measures 1-4, 7/8 and 11/12; the IV chord and/or its substitutes in measures 5/6; and a cadence (generally compound) in measures 9/10. Melodic format may be AAB, AA'B, riff-based or through-composed.

2.) Strophic vocal (verse) structure consisting of two repeating 4-bar phrases followed by a concluding answering phrase.

Blues Scale:	Commonly used pedagogical term referring to the temperament of the diatonic scale by Blue Notes, resulting in a "scale" containing a mixture of diatonic and Blue Notes, most commonly of the form 1, ♭3, 4, ♭5, 5, ♭7, 1.
Borrowed chords:	Harmonies from parallel modal systems (see also "modal interchange").
Cadence:	Movement from an unstable point to one of relative stability.
Call and Response:	Ubiquitous practice of antiphonal statement and answer between individuals and/or sections.
Chorus Form:	Form in which the primary songform of the melodic statement is repeated with variation.
Clave:	Ubiquitous 4/4 rhythm found in Afro-Caribbean musical styles, based on the alternation of a "3" unit (two dotted quarters followed by a quarter) with a "2" unit (quarter rests surrounding two consecutive quarter notes). May occur in either order ("3/2" or "2/3") alternation.
Close position:	Harmony (generally in 4 voices) wherein no interval is larger than a third.
Color tones:	9ths, 11ths, and 13ths (see also "extensions" and "tensions").
Complementary:	Used most commonly to refer to multiple and mutually exclusive sets of pitches that combine to yield all 12 tones.
Complementary Rhythms:	Rhythm figures which, when combined, form part of a larger rhythmic pattern (see also "Aggregate Rhythm" and "Layered Ostinato").
Compound Cadence:	Cadence involving more than one chord (generally two), moving from the subdominant or one of its substitutes, to the dominant or one of its substitutes, to the tonic.
Compound Form:	Form in which smaller discrete forms are subsumed (aka "form within a form").
Compound Interval:	Interval larger than an octave (i.e. 9ths, 10ths, etc.).
Concerto:	Composition featuring an individual soloist complemented by an accompanying ensemble.
Conjunct:	Stepwise (as opposed to arpeggiated).
Consonnant:	At a point of rest within the harmony (opposite of "dissonant").
Consequent:	Answering phrase (generally complements or responds to an "antecedent" phrase).
Consilient(ce):	Property of shared characteristics that have been arrived at independently (as opposed to through influence).
Consonance:	Quality of harmonic stability (see also "dissonance").
Constant Structure:	Same harmonic structure used in parallel (see also "planing").
Contrafact:	(In Jazz parlance) a new melody composed on an extant set of commonly known chord changes.
Contrapuntal:	Featuring the property of counterpoint, or rhythmically independent melodic lines.

Cross Relations:	Coexistence of conflicting enharmonic descriptions for the same note within a given harmony.
Crushed Note:	Blues piano device in which a single note blues melody is accompanied above or below by a repeating or "drone" tone, played in tutti rhythm in such a way as to reinforce the main rhythmic accents of the phrase (an adaptation from Blues guitar).
Cycle of Fifths (fourths):	Bass and/or associated chordal movement moving in intervals of fourths or fifths, i.e. C, F, B♭, etc.
Development:	Unfolding of a melodic motif through its transformation, also that section of a composition in which this process occurs.
Diatonic:	Containing nothing foreign to the scale.
Diminished Scale:	Synthetic scale constructed of alternating half-and whole-steps (see also "Octatonic Scale").
Diminution:	Rhythmic variation by means of shrinking rhythmic values (opposite of "augmentation").
Disjunct:	Leaping, or non-scalewise, motion (opposite of "Conjunct").
Displacement:	Repetition of a melodic idea beginning on a different or unexpected part of the measure or beat.
Dissonant(ce):	Jarring or unrestful, in the harmonic or psychological sense (opposite of "consonant").
Dodecaphonic:	Synonymous with "twelve-tone", meaning the use of all twelve chromatic tones as a compositional device (see also "Twelve Tone").
Dominant:	7th chord, usually employed to mean the one based on V diatonically.
Double Lead:	Harmony or voicing in which the melody is doubled an octave lower, with the remaining chord tones sandwiched between.
Double Time:	Doubling the speed of the meter, for example changing the pulse from quarter notes to eighth notes.
Double Time Feel:	Creating the illusion of real double time by making the eighth note feel like a quarter note.
Dropped Voice:	In an "open position" harmony, the voice or voices that have been displaced downward by an octave from the original closed position chord.
Elision:	Overlapping of consecutive phrases so that the end of one is also the beginning of the next.
Embellishment:	Decoration.
Enharmonics:	Phenomenon of different names for the same note (i.e. B♭ = A♯).
Exposition:	Initial thematic statement in its entirety.
Expressionism:	Compositional style based on the transformation of abstract intellectual concepts into musical material.
Extended Dominants:	Series of dominant seventh chords moving through the cycle of fifths.
Extensions:	Synonymous with "tensions" or "color tones".

Flamenco:	Indigenous Iberian dance and music tradition whose development was heavily influenced by the Roma.
Fragmentation:	Breaking a melodic idea down into smaller units that are then developed separately.
Fugue:	Formal structure based on contrapuntal restatement of a primary theme in more than two voices.
Gospel:	African-American Sacred vocal style.
Habanera:	Iberian 4/4 rhythm based on two dotted quarters followed by a quarter note (see also "Clave").
Harmonic Rhythm:	Rate of chord change.
Hemiola:	Specific polyrhythm superimposing triple meter over 4/4 time.
Heptatonic:	Containing seven notes.
Hexatonic Scale:	Six-note scale constructed of alternating half-steps and minor thirds.
Hook:	Characteristic and readily identifiable melodic motif of a composition.
Hot:	Rhythmically intense, driving (opposite of "sweet" or "cool").
Hybrid Chord:	Chord created by superimposing a chord over an unrelated bass note.
Impressionism:	Style of composition (originally used to describe the parallel movement in Art) in which the evocation of a specific scene or its associated mood is of primary concern (ex. Ellington's "Dusk").
Interpolation:	Process of inserting additional chords between existing ones.
Inversion:	1.) of a melodic motif; to use it upside down.
	2.) of a chord, to move the lowest voice to the highest (or vice-versa) without changing the hierarchy of the voices.
Key of the Moment:	Temporary key (see also "tonicization").
Latin:	Non-specific term used by musicians to refer to music of Afro-Caribbean or Afro-Brazilian style or origin.
Layered Ostinato:	Complementary rhythm created by the addition of a succession of a series of ostinati.
Leitmotif:	Recurrant motto theme of a piece (ex. the opening minor third of Ellington's "Harlem", which states the title of the composition musically).
Locrian Natural Nine:	Sixth mode of the melodic minor scale.
Lydian Dominant:	Aka "Lydian Flat Seven", or fourth mode of melodic minor.
Major Blues Scale:	Blues scale variant with alternate focus on relative minor (formula is generally 5, [♯5,] 6, 1, 2, ♭3, 3).
Mambo:	A Clave-based rhythm and its associated dance style.
Melodic Minor:	Aka "jazz minor", or the ascending form of Classical melodic minor (i.e. with only a flatted 3rd compared to its parallel major).
Minuet and Trio:	European Classical Form thought to be one of the precursors of Ragtime Form (see also "Strain" form).

Minor Blues:	12-bar form in which the i and iv chords, as well as the cadence, are all taken from some form of minor.
Mirror Writing:	Concurrent use of an idea and its inversion.
Modal Cadence:	Reiterative cadence produced by alternation of the tonic chord with one of its stepwise neighbors in the given mode (for example in dorian, i- followed by either bVII or ii-), often in the presence of an ostinato or pedal tone.
Modal Harmony:	Harmony diatonic to a given mode or modes.
Modal Interchange:	Process of borrowing harmonies from one parallel mode for use in another (generally from parallel minor forms, especially aeolian, into the parallel major). See also "borrowed chords".
Modulation:	Change of key.
Motif:	Main melodic cell of a composition.
Motivic Development:	Unfolding of the music by means of the compositional process of exploiting the rhythm and shape of a given motif, sometimes independently, sometimes interdeptly, through a variety of techniques of recontextualization.
Motivic Identity:	Characteristics of a given motif, usually its distinctive combination of shape and rhythm.
Motivic Transformation:	Metamorphosis of a given motif from its initial form via various developmental techniques.
Non-harmonic tones:	Pitches not contained in the harmony of a given moment.
Novelty Piano:	Genre of Stride piano playing featuring idiomatic pianistic tricks.
Oblique Motion:	Static melody over moving harmonic or contrapuntal accompaniment.
Octatonic:	Containing eight notes, and specifically, the eight-note scale produced by the alternation of 1/2 and whole-steps (see also "Diminished Scale").
Open Position:	Chord structure in which one or more of the voices in the related closed position structure has been displaced by an octave (see also "Closed Position" chords).
Ostinato:	Repeating bass and/or rhythmic figure, frequently employed to structure introductions and codas and especially common in modal compositions and arrangements.
Pedal Tone (Point):	Repeated bass note (less complex than an "ostinato").
Pentatonic Scale(s):	5-note scale whose most common form has the structure: 1, b3, 4, 5, b7 or b3, 4, 5, b7, 1. The former is also known as the "minor pentatonic" scale, and the latter, containing the same notes, but treating the flatted third as the tonic, is also sometimes referred to as the "major pentatonic" (see also "Blues Scale").
Pivot Chord(s):	In a modulation, chord(s) common to both the old and new keys.
Planing:	Parallel harmonic movement, most often diatonic (see also "constant structure").
Polychord(al):	Harmony containing more than one discrete harmony.

Polyrhythm(ic):	Rhythm comprised of more than one discrete concurrent subdivision.
Quartal:	Comprised primarily of intervals of perfect fourths.
Quintal:	Comprised primarily of intervals of fifths.
Raga:	System of modes and rhythms employed in Indian Classical Music.
Recapitulation:	Return to the primary melodic statement.
Recomposition:	Extensive rewriting of an extant piece.
Recontextualization:	Reuse of extant melodic material in a totally new context.
Reharmonize(ation):	Changing the harmony that supports a given melodic phrase.
Resolution (Resolving):	Arrival at the tonic chord following a cadence.
Retrograde:	Backwards.
Retrograde Inversion:	Upside down and backwards.
Rhythm Changes:	Chord progression to Gershwin's "I Got Rhythm", or any of its variants.
Rhythmic Displacement:	See "displacement".
Riff:	Repetitive, simple idea, improvised in character, and often used as background and/or as motivic material.
Rondo:	European Classical form based on the notion of interspering a repeating A idea between contrasting themes or sections.
Sacred:	Music with liturgical or religious content or inspiration.
Samba:	Brazilian dance rhythm and associated musical style.
Saxophone Soli:	Soli using the saxophone section exclusively (see "soli").
Secondary Dominant:	Dominant seventh chord that tonicizes a diatonic chord other than I.
Secondary Ragtime:	3+3+2 rhythm spread over two measures, commonly used device in Ragtime and Stride piano.
Secular:	Music without religious content or inspiration (opposite of "Sacred").
Sequence:	Repetition of an idea at regular intervals, either rhythmic and/or harmonic.
Sideslipping:	Interpolation of cadences a half-step above and directly prior to the primary cadence of a given phrase.
Simple Cadence:	Two chord cadence (from an unstable chord to the tonic or one of its substitutes).
Soli:	Plural of solo, usually taken to mean a melodic passage harmonized in unison rhythm to support the lead part.
Sonata:	European Classical form based on dialectical development of contrasting themes.
Songform(s):	AABA, ABAC, etc.
Spanish Phrygian:	Octatonic variation of the Phrygian mode, characteristic of Flamenco and/or Iberian music, in which both the major third and minor thirds coexist.

Spanish Tinge:	Composer and pianist Jelly Roll Morton's term for "Clave".
Stop Time:	Series of unison ensemble accents interspersed with rests, often used to set off formal boundaries and/or as a platform for featuring individual soloists.
Strain Form:	Form found commonly in Ragtime and Stride piano compositions, in which multiple themes are employed.
Stretto:	Overlapping in quick succession of statements of the subject of a Fugue, usually near the end, to create a Coda.
Stride Piano:	Virtuoso piano style that evolved from Ragtime.
Subject:	Main theme of a Fugue.
Substitute Dominant:	Dominant seventh chord sharing the same third and seventh ("tritone") as the dominant whose root is a tritone (augmented fourth or diminished fifth) away.
Swing:	Rhythmic feel created by the coexistence of duple and triple meters.
Temporary Key:	Synonymous with "key of the moment".
Tension(s):	Synonymous with "color tone(s)" or "extension(s)".
Tertian:	Harmony based on intervals of thirds.
Third Stream:	Term invented in the 1950's to describe the musical process of deliberate synthesis of elements of European Classical forms and instrumentation with those of jazz improvisation.
Three-tonic system:	Harmonic system based on key centers whose roots outline an augmented triad, frequently employed by composer John Coltrane.
Through-Composed:	Not having literally repeated large formal sections.
Tonal:	In a given key or tonality (i.e. major or minor). The opposite of "modal".
Tonicize(ation):	Process of temporarily imputing a sense of tonic to diatonic chords other than I (see also "Temporary Key").
Transitional Modulation:	Modulation in which sequential and/or cadential harmonies are employed, resulting in a period of tonal ambiguity prior to establishment of the new key.
Turnaround:	Simple repeating progression in the form of I - vi - ii - V or any of its many variants.
Tutti:	An ensemble passage in rhythmic unison.
Twelve Tone:	Music based on the notion of giving equal weight to each of the twelve chromatic notes (see also "Dodecaphonic").
Twelve Tone Row:	Melodic lines comprised of all 12 notes without any repetition.
Voice-crossing:	Process of creating independent contours for instruments in a soli or tutti context by changing the hierarchy of voices between adjacent rhythmic attacks.
Voice-leading:	Harmonic motion resulting from the most linear possible movement between parallel voices in adjacent harmonies, characteristic of cycle of fifths (fourths)/tonal harmonic movement.

Voicings: Particular intervallic arrangement of the pitches of a given harmony.

Whole tone scale: Hexatonic scale comprised exclusively of whole steps (of which there are two).

BIBLIOGRAPHY

Adolfo, Antonio. Brazilian Music Workshop. Advance Music, Rottenburg, Germany, 1993.

Arom, Simha. African Polyphony and Polyrhythm. Cambridge, Cambridge University Press, 1992.

Atkins, E. Taylor, Ed. Jazz Planet. University of Mississippi Press, 2003.

Baudoin, Philippe. Jazz mode d'emploi: Petite encyclopedie des donnees techniques de base, Vol. II. Editions Outre Mesure. Paris, 2001.

Beeson, Ann. "Quoting Tunes: Narrative Features in Jazz", from Collectanea: Papers in Folklore, Popular and Expressive Culture 1 (1990).

Berliner, Paul. Thinking in Jazz: the Infinite Art of Improvisation. University of Chicago Press, 1994.

Bernard, Jonathan W. "From Lumpy Gravy to Civilization Phaze III: The Story of Frank Zappa's Disenchantment", in Journal of the Society for American Music: 5, Number 1, 2011, pp. 1-31.

Boyer, Horace Clarence. How Sweet the Sound: The Golden Age of Gospel. Elliott & Clark Publishing, Washington, D.C. 1995.

Boyer, Richard. "The Hot Bach", in The Duke Ellington Reader, Mark Tucker, Ed. Oxford. New York, 1993, pp. 214-45.

Brofsky, Howard. "Miles Davis and My Funny Valentine: The Evolution of a Jazz Solo", in Kirchner, Bill, ed., "The Miles Davis Reader", Smithsonian Institution Press, Washington and London, 1997.

Buehrer, Ted. "Lonely Moments? The Anatomy of Mary Lou Williams' Oft-Recorded Tune". IAJE Research Papers. 2003, pp. 52-63.

Burleigh, Harry T. The Spirituals of Harry T. Burleigh. Warner Brothers, Miami, 1984.

Cole, Bill. John Coltrane. Schirmer Books, New York, 1976.

Coltrane, John, Ed. Alice Coltrane. The Music of John Coltrane. Hal Leonard, Milwaukee, 1991.

Coltrane, John, Ed. Masaya Yamaguchi, John Coltrane Plays Coltrane Changes. Hal Leonard, Milwaukee, 2003.

Coltrane, John, Ed. David Demsey. John Coltrane Plays Giant Steps. Hal Leonard, Milwaukee, 1996.

Coolman, Todd. "The Miles Davis Quintet of the mid-1960's: Synthesis of Improvisational and Compositional Elements". UMI Dissertation Services, Ann Arbor, MI. 1997.

Crease, Stephanie Stein. Gil Evans, Out of the Cool. His Life and Music. A Cappella Books, Chicago. 2002.

Cugny, Laurent. "L'analyse de l'oeuvre de jazz. Spécificités théoriques et methodologiques" (Doctoral Thesis). Sorbonne, Paris. 2001.

Dahl, Linda. Morning Glory: A Biography of Mary Lou Williams. Pantheon Books. New York, 1999.

Dance, Stanley. The World of Duke Ellington. C. Scribner's Sons. New York, 1970.

Davis, Miles. Birth of The Cool. Original Scores. Hal Leonard, Milwaukee, 2002.

Davis, Miles, Bill Kirchner, Ed. Kind of Blue (complete transcriptions). Hal Leonard. Milwaukee, 2001.

Demsey, David. "Chromatic Third Relations in the Music of John Coltrane", Annual Review of Jazz Studies 5 (1991): pp. 145-80.

Dent, Cedric Carl. "The Harmonic Development of the Black Religious Quartet Singing Tradition." UMI Dissertation Services, Ann Arbor, MI. 2002.

DeVeaux, Scott. The Birth of Bebop: A Social and Musical History. University of California Press. Berkeley, 1997.

DeVeaux, Scott. "Nice Work If You Can Get It: Thelonious Monk and Popular Song", Black Music Research Journal, 19 No. 2: 169-86. 1999.

Diaz, Oligario. Latin Jazz Piano Technique. Charles Colin. New York, 1991.

Dietrich, Kurt. Duke's Bones: Ellington's Great Trombonists. Advance Music, Rottenburg, Germany. 1995.

Dobbins, Bill. "Glass Enclosure (Bud Powell)", transcription. The Piano Stylist and Jazz Workshop, October 1989, pp. 1-4.

Domek, Richard. "Compositional Characteristics of Late Duke Ellington Works". IAJE Research Papers, 2001, pp. 120-131.

Ellington, Duke, and Strayhorn, Billy. "Anatomy of A Murder" filmscore. Columbia Feature Film, 1959.

Ellington, Duke. "Black and Tan", in "Duke Ellington and His Orchestra: Classics, 1929-52", Amvest Video (originally RKO), 1929.

Ellington, Duke. "List of Favorites". Downbeat, Nov. 5, 1952: 2-4., in "The Duke Ellington Reader, Mark Tucker, Ed. 268-9. Oxford University Press, New York. 1993.

Ellington, Duke. Introductory Remarks from "Black, Brown and Beige: The Duke Ellington Carnegie Hall Concerts, January 1943." Prestige CD (see also discography).

Ellington, Duke. "Symphony in Black", in "Duke Ellington and His Orchestra: Classics, 1929-1952", Amvest Video (originally Paramount), 1934.

Ellington, Duke. "We too Sing America", in The Duke Ellington Reader, Mark Tucker, Ed. Oxford, New York, 1993, pp. 146-8.

Fernandez, Raul A. From Afro-Cuban Rhythms to Latin Jazz. University of California Press, Berkeley. 2006.

Fischlin, Daniel, and Heble, Ajay, Ed. The Other Side of Nowhere: Jazz, Improvisation, and Communities in Dialogue. Wesleyan University Press, Middletown, CT. 2004.

Fukioka, Yasuhiro with Lewis Porter and Yoh-Ichi Hamada. John Coltrane: a Discography and Musical Biography (Studies in Jazz, No. 20), Scarecrow Press, Metuchen, N.J., 1995.

Gates, Henry Louis. The Signifying Monkey: A Theory of African-American Literary Criticism. Oxford University Press. New York, 1988.

Gioia, Ted. The History of Jazz. Oxford University Press. 1997.

Gillis, Frank. "Hot Rhythm in Piano Ragtime", in Ragtime, John Edward Hasse, Ed.. Schirmer Books, New York. 1985, pp. 220-31.

Givan, Benjamin. "Apart Playing: McCoy Tyner and "Bessie's Blues", Journal of the Society for American Music, Vol 1, #2, 2007. pp. 257-280.

Gollin, Edward. "Multi-Aggregate Cycles and Multi-Aggregate Serial Techniques in the Music of Bela Bartôk," Music Theory Spectrum 20.2 (Fall 2007), pp. 143-176.

Gourse, Leslie. Straight, No Chaser: The Life and Genius of Thelonious Monk. Schirmer Books. New York, 1997.

Hajdu, David. Lush Life: A Biography of Billy Strayhorn. Farrar Strauss Giroux. New York, 1996.

Handy, W.C. Father of The Blues: An Autobiography. Da Capo. New York, 1941 (1969).

Harvard Dictionary of Music, Second ed., Willi Apel, Ed. Harvard University Press. Cambridge, MA. 1969.

Hasse, John Edward. Beyond Category: The Life and Genius of Duke Ellington. Simon and Schuster, 1993.

Hasse, John Edward, Ed. Ragtime: Its History, Composers, and Music. Schirmer Books, New York, 1985.

Howland, John. Ellington Uptown: Duke Ellington, James P. Johnson and the Birth of Concert Jazz. University of Michigan Press, Ann Arbor, 2011.

Howland, John. Jazz Rhapsodies in Black and White: James P. Johnson's Yamekraw. American Music, Vol. 4, #4. pp. 445-509, 2006.

Israels, Chuck. EXPLORING JAZZ ARRANGING Using the Garritan Jazz/Big www.northernsounds.com/.

Jaffe, Andy. Jazz Harmony, Second ed. Advance Music. Rottenburg, Germany, 1996.

Jairazbhoy, N.A. The Rags of North Indian Music. Their Structure And Evolution, Popular Prakashan, Bombay. 1995.

Jobim, Antonio Carlos: Tom Jobim – Site Oficial UOL Personalidades www.2.uol.br/tomjobim

Jones, Arthur Morris. Studies in African Music, 2 Vols. Oxford University Press. New York, 1959.

Jones, Ron. "Jazz Polyrhythms" Jazz Education Journal, 38: #6, pp. 49-51.

Joplin, Scott. The Best of Scott Joplin. A Collection of Original Ragtime Piano Compositions. Charles Hansen. New York, 1972.

Kelley, Robin D.G. Thelonious Monk. The Life and Times of An American Original. Free Press (Simon & Schuster). New York. 2009.

Khan, Ashley. The Making of Kind of Blue. DaCapo. New York, 2000.

A Love Supreme: The Story of John Coltrane's Signature Album. New York, Penguin, 2002.

Kirchner, Bill, ed., A Miles Davis Reader. Smithsonian Institution Press, Washington and London, 1997.

Knauer, Wolfram. "Simulated Improvisation in Duke Ellington's Black, Brown and Beige." The Black Perspective in Music 18: 20-38.

Kubik, Gerhard. Africa and The Blues. University of Mississippi Press, Jackson, 1999.

LaJoie, Steve. Gil Evans & Miles Davis. 1957-1962 Historic Collaborations. Advance Music, Rottenburg, Germany 2003.

Lateef, Yusef. Repository of Scales and Melodic Patterns. Fana Music, Amherst, MA. 1981.

The Latin Tinge. The Impact of Latin American Music on the United States. Oxford. New York, 1985.

Lavezzoli, Peter. The Dawn of Indian Music in the West. New York: Continuum International, 2006.

Lateef, Yusef. "The Pleasures of Voice in Autophysiopsychic Music", unpublished lecture transcription.

Lendvai, Erno, and Bush, Alan. Bela Bartok: An Analysis of His Music. Kane and Averill. London, 1971.

Levine, Mark. The Jazz Piano Book. Sher Music Co., Petaluma, CA. 1995.

Levine, Mark. The Jazz Theory Book. Sher Music Co., Petaluma, CA. 1989.

Levine, Mark. The Drop 2 Book. Sher Music Co., Petaluma, CA. 2006.

Mair, Marilynn. "A History of Choro in Context", http://www.marilynnmair.com/history-of-choro.shtml (originally published in Mandolin Quarterly, March 2000).

Mauleon, Rebeca. The Complete Salsa Guidebook. Sher Music Co., Petaluma, CA. 1993.

Metzger, David. Finale and Jazz Arranging. David Metzger Music. Salem, Oregon. 1993.

Mingus, Charles, Andrew Homzy, Ed. Mingus: More Than a Fakebook. Hal Leonard, Milwaukee, 1991.

Monk, Thelonious, Jim Crockett, Ed. "Thelonious Monk: 1917-82. A Special Section". Various articles, Keyboard Magazine 8, No. 7: 11-30 (including articles by Ran Blake, Chick Corea and others) 1982.

Monk, Thelonious, Ed. Don Sickler. Thelonious Monk Fakebook. Hal Leonard. Milwaukee, 2002.

Morton, Ferdinand "Jelly Roll", James Dapogny, Ed. The Collected Piano Music. Smithsonian Institution Press, G. Schirmer, New York, 1982.

Muccioli, Joe, Ed. The Gil Evans Collection: 15 Study and Sketch Scores from Gil's Manuscripts. Hal Leonard. Milwaukee, 1996.

Murray, Albert. Stomping the Blues. Schirmer Books. New York, 1976.

Nketia, J.H. Kwabena. The Music of Africa. McGraw Hill. New York, 1974.

Nisenson, Eric. Open Sky: Sonny Rollins and his World of Improvisation. St. Martin's Press. New York, 2000.

Oliver, Paul. Savannah Syncopators: African Retentions in The Blues. Stein and Day. New York, 1970.

O'Meally, Robert, Ed. The Jazz Cadence of American Culture. Columbia University Press. New York, 1998.

Owens, Thomas. "The Fugal Pieces of the Modern Jazz Quartet". Journal of Jazz Studies, 4. 1976, 25-46.

Pascoal, Hermeto, Ed. Jovino Santos Neto. "Tudo E Som": The Music of Hermeto Pascoal. Universal Edition, 2001.

Pascoal, Hermeto. Calendario do Som. Editora Senac Sao Paulo: Instituto Cultural Itaú, 2004, Sao Paulo, Brasil.

Pass, Joe. Chord Encounters for Guitar, Book 1: Blues, Chords and Substitutions. Charles Hansen Music and Books. Los Angeles, 1979.

PBS. "A Duke Named Ellington (Video documentary)". 1988.

Pease, Ted. Jazz Composition: Theory and Practice. Berklee Press. Boston, 2003.

Peress, Maurice. "My Life with Black, Brown and Beige." Black Music Research Journal 13, No. 2: 147-160. 1993.

Perrone, Charles. Masters of Contemporary Brazilian Song: MPB 1965-85. University of Texas Press. Austin, 1989.

Petrucciani, Michel. Michel Petrucciani Songbook: Compositions Originales. Francis Dreyfus Music. Paris, 2000.

Porter, Lewis. John Coltrane, His Life and Music. University of Michigan Press. Ann Arbor, 1998.

Priestley, Brian. "Black, Brown and Beige." In The Duke Ellington Reader, Mark Tucker, Ed. Oxford University Press. 1993. pp. 186-204.

Rattenbury, Ken. Duke Ellington, Jazz Composer. Yale University Press. New Haven. 1992.

Ricker, Ramon. Pentatonic Scales for Jazz Improvisation. Studio P/R, Columbia Pictures Publications, Hialeah, FL., 1976.

Riddle, Ronald. "Novelty Piano Music", in Ragtime, John Edward Hasse, Ed. Schirmer Books, New York. 1985. pp. 285-93.

Rinzler, Paul. Jazz Arranging and Performance Practice. Scarecrow Press. Lanham, MD. 1989.

Roberts, John Storm. Black Music of Two Worlds: African, Caribbean, Latin, and African-American Traditions. Second Edition. Thomson/Schirmer. Belmont, CA. 1998.

Russell, George. Lydian Chromatic Concept of Tonal Organization, 4th ed. Concept Publishing Co. Brookline, MA., 2001.

Russo, William. Jazz Composition and Orchestration. University of Chicago Press, 1968.

Schreyer, Lowell. "The Banjo in Ragtime", in Ragtime, John Edward Hasse, Ed., Schirmer Books. New York, 1985. pp. 54-69.

Schuller, Gunther. Early Jazz: Its Roots and Musical Development. Oxford University Press, 1968.

The Swing Era: The Development of Jazz, 1930-1945. Oxford University Press, 1989.

Slonimsky, Nicolas. Thesaurus of Scales and Melodic Patterns. Schirmer Books, New York. 1975.

Sturm, Fred. Changes Over Time: The Evolution of Jazz Arranging. Advance Music, Rottenburg, Germany. 1995

Taylor, Billy. Jazz Piano: a Jazz History. W.C. Brown, Dubuque, IA. 1983.

Thomas, J.C. Chasin' the Trane: The Music and Mystique of John Coltrane. Doubleday, Garden City, NJ. 1975.

Timner, W.E. Ellingtonia: The Recorded Music of Duke Ellington and his Sidemen, 4th Ed. Institute of Jazz Studies and Scarecrow Press. Lanham, MD., 1996.

Tucker, Mark. Ellington: The Early Years. University of Illinois Press. Urbana, 1991.

Tucker, Mark, Ed. The Duke Ellington Reader. Oxford University Press. 1993.

Tucker, Mark. "Duke Ellington, 1940-42." Liner Notes, The Blanton-Webster Band, RCA Bluebird (see also discography).

Tucker, Mark. "The Genesis of Black, Brown and Beige". Black Music Research Journal 13, No. 2: 67-86. 1993.

Tucker, Mark. "Mainstreaming Monk: The Ellington Album", Black Music Research Journal, 19 (2): 227-44. Fall 1999.

Van de Leur, Walter. Something to Live For: The Music of Billy Strayhorn. Oxford University Press, 2002.

van de Leur, Walter. "The 'American Impressionists' and the 'Birth of the Cool'." Tijdschrift voor Muziektheorie. January 2001: 18-26 (translated into English by author).

White, Andrew. The Works of John Coltrane. 10 Vols. Andrew's Music, Washington, D.C. 1973-8.

Wilson, E.O. Consilience: The Unity of Knowledge. Chapter 10 "The Arts and Their Interpretation". Knopf. New York, 1988.

Wright, Rayburn. Inside the Score. Kendor Music Co., Delevan, N.Y., 1982.

Yanow, Scott. Afro-Cuban Jazz. Miller Freeman Books, San Francisco, 2002.

Yudkin, Jeremy. Miles Davis, Miles Smiles, and the Invention of Post Bop. Indiana University Press, Bloomington 2007.

The Lenox School of Jazz. Lenox Library Association, Lenox, MA. 2006.

Zenni, Stefano. Charles Mingus: Polifonie Dell'Universo Musicale AfroAmericano. Nuovi Equilibri, Viterloo, Italy. 2002.

DISCOGRAPHY

CHAPTER 1

Composition	Artist/Composer	Available Recording(s)
Well You Needn't	Thelonious Monk	Greatest Hits: Columbia/Legacy: 65422
The Stampede	Coleman Hawkins	Henderson Days: SAGA 0664422 (Also Smithsonian Collection of Classic Jazz)

CHAPTER 2

Composition	Artist/Composer	Available Recording(s)
Satin Doll	Ellington/Strayhorn	Swingin': BCI Music 469
The Tattooed Bride	Duke Ellington	The Complete Duke Ellington, 1947-52 (Vol. 5; Columbia)
St. Thomas	Sonny Rollins	Saxophone Collosus: APO 7079
Fire Down There	Randy Weston	Get Happy: Original Jazz Classics 1870
Witch Hunt	Wayne Shorter	Speak No Evil: Blue Note 99001
Well You Needn't	Thelonious Monk	see Ch. 1
King Porter Stomp	Arr. Gil Evans	Great Jazz Standards: CDP 74 6822-2
Stolen Moments	Oliver Nelson	Blues and the Abstract Truth: Impulse 154
Thelonious	Thelonious Monk	The Complete Genius: Mosaic MR 4101
Dial 1	Bill Holman	Bill Holman Big Band "LIVE", JazzEdMedia JM 1007.
Heading Home	Joshua Redman	Moodswing, Warner Brothers, 1994
One Note Samba	Antonio Carlos Jobim	The Composer of Desafinado, Plays: Verve 521431
What Price Love	Arr. Gil Evans	Real Birth of the Cool: CBS/SONY 25DP 5321-CD
Arab Dance	Arr. Gil Evans	ibid.
Creole Rhapsody	Duke Ellington	The Duke Ellington Centennial Edition: RCA 24-CD set 09026-63386-2
Tone Parallel To Harlem	Duke Ellington	ibid.

CHAPTER 3

Composition	Artist/Composer	Available Recording(s)
St. Louis Blues	W.C. Handy	Ellington Centennial Edition (cf. Ch. 2)
West End Blues	Oliver/Williams	Swing That Music: EPM (Jazz Archives) 15731-2
Blues For Alice	Charlie Parker	Complete Charlie Parker on Verve: Verve 10-837141-2
Au Privave	Charlie Parker	Essential Charlie Parker: Verve: 314-517173-2
All Blues	Miles Davis	Kind of Blue Columbia/Legacy 64935
Simone	Frank Foster	Leo Rising: Arabesque 124
Ahunk, Ahunk	Thad Jones/Mel Lewis Orchestra	Consummation (Blue Note CD reissue 2002, B0000647MJ)
Creole Rhapsody	Duke Ellington	cf. Ch. 2
Yardbird Suite	Charlie Parker	cf. Ch. 2 "What Price Love"
Goodbye Porkpie Hat	Charles Mingus	This is Jazz 6: Sony/Columbia DIDP087251
Equinox	John Coltrane	Best of John Coltrane: Atlantic 1541-2
Taxman	Lennon/McCartney	The Beatles: Rubber Soul Columbia
Stardust	Hoagy Carmichael	Louis Armstrong and His Orchestra: CBS A 20600
Stars Fell on Alabama	Mitchell Parish	Ella and Louis: Verve 825 373-2

Composition	Artist/Composer	Available Recording(s)
It Don't Mean a Thing If It Ain't Got That Swing	Ellington	Ellington Centennial Edition (cf. Ch. 2)
Backwater Blues	Bessie Smith	Sings the Blues: SONY Music Special products 26422
Creole Love Call	Ellington	Ellington Centennial Edition
Bessie's Blues	John Coltrane	Crescent: Impulse 200
C Jam Blues	Ellington	Ellington Centennial Edition
Sonny Moon For Two	Sonny Rollins	Sonny Rollins Trio Live at the Village Vanguard, Blue Note 45-1698; BLP 1581
Work Song	Nat Adderley	Them Dirty Blues: Cannonball Adderley Capital Jazz 75447
Nostalgia in Times Square	Mingus	Mingus in Wonderland: Blue Note 27325

CHAPTER 4

Composition	Artist/Composer	Available Recording(s)
Nice Work If You Can Get It	Gershwin	Monk: Standards Columbia CK45148
Sophisticated Lady	Ellington	Ellington Centennial Edition (cf. Ch. 2)
Mood Indigo	Ellington	ibid.
I Got Rhythm	Gershwin	Gershwin Plays Gershwin: Magnum Collectors 21
Rockin' in Rhythm	Ellington	Ellington Centennial Collection
Moten Swing	Moten	The Essence of Count Basie: Columbia/Legacy CK47918
You're Drivin' Me Crazy	Lou Donaldson	Bob Crosby "You're Driving Me Crazy": Halcyon 123
Ladybird	Tadd Dameron	Complete Pacific Jazz Live Recordings of Chet Baker Quartet: Mosaic MD3-113
King Porter Stomp	Jelly Roll Morton	Jelly Roll Morton 1923/24: Milestone MCD-47018-2
Carolina Shout	James P. Johnson	Smithsonian Collection of Classic Jazz CDRD-033
Ain't Misbehavin'	Fats Waller	The Joint Is Jumpin': Bluebird 6288 -2-RB
Wave	Antonio Carlos Jobim	Wave: A & M SP-9-3002
Satin Doll	Ellington/Strayhorn	Ellington Centennial Edition
Blue Bossa	Kenny Dorham	Joe Henderson: Page One: Blue Note 98795
What's New	Haggart/Burke	John Coltrane: Ballads: MCA/Impulse MCAD-5885
Waltz for A.	Art Lande	Art Lande and Jan Garbarek, ECM 1038 ST
Round Midnight	Monk	Thelonious Monk: Greatest Hits: Columbia Legacy 65422
In a Sentimental Mood	Ellington	Ellington Centennial Edition
All the Things You Are	Kern	Bird After Dark: Savoy 17135
Along Came Betty	Benny Golson	Art Blakey and The Jazz Messengers: Moanin': Blue Note B21Y-46516
When Lights Are Low	Benny Carter	Benny Carter and the Jazz Giants Fantasy FANCD 66029
Giant Steps	Coltrane	Giant Steps: Atlantic CD 1311-2
Half Nelson	Davis	Workin' with the Miles Davis Quintet: Prestige 7166
Ask Me Now	Thelonious Monk	5 by Monk by 5: Original Jazz Classics 362
Pannonica	Thelonious Monk	Brilliant Corners: Original Jazz Classics 1035622
Who Knows	Ellington	Piano Reflections: Capitol CDP 7 92863
Moment's Notice	Coltrane	Blue Train: Blue Note 41757

Vale Da Rebeira	Hermeto Pascoal	Sergio Mendes: Oceano: Verve P2-32441
Voyage	Kenny Barron	Stan Getz: Soul Eyes, Concord CCD 4783-2
So What	Davis	Kind of Blue (cf. Ch. 2)
Olé	Coltrane	Olé
La Fiesta	Chick Corea	Return to Forever: ECM 78118-21022-2
Gira, Girou	Milton Nascimento	Brasil: A Century of Song: Blue Jackal CD 5004-2
Where You At	Horace Silver	Horacescope: Blue Note 84042
Caravan	Juan Tizol	Twisted: The Best of Lambert, Hendricks & Ross: Sony Music R2 70328/ A 22732
A Night in Tunisia	Dizzy Gillespie	Greatest Hits: Victor Jazz/RCAVictor68499
Un Poco Loco	Bud Powell	The Amazing Bud Powell: Blue Note 32136
Aquarius	Mary Lou Williams	The Zodiac Suite: Smithsonian Folkways SF CD 40810
Recordame	Joe Henderson	Page One
Yeah	Horace Silver	Horacescope
Nica's Dream	Horace Silver	ibid.
Chorinho Pra Ele	Hermeto Pascoal	Slave's Mass: (Missa dos Escravos): WEA BS 2980
Forest Flower	Charles Lloyd	Forest Flower: Rhino 71746
Inner Urge	Joe Henderson	Inner Urge: Blue Note 84189
Speak Like a Child	Herbie Hancock	Speak Like a Child: Blue Note 46136
Just Friends	Lewis/Klenner	Charlie Parker with Strings: Mercury MGC-109, MC-35010; re-release Verve 314517 173-2
Heaven	Ellington	Ellington Centennial Edition (cf Ch. 2)
Bebe	Hermeto Pascoal	A Musica Livre de Hermeto Pascoal: Polygram/Fontana 8246211
Adjustment	Horace Silver	Silver 'N Brass: Blue Note BN-LA 406G
What's New	Arr. Slide Hampton	Jazz Club: Tenor Sax Verve 840031-2
Ugetsu	Cedar Walton	Art Blakey's Jazz Messengers at Birdland Original Jazz Classics 90
Glass Enclosure	Bud Powell	The Amazing Bud Powell: Vol. 2 Blue Note
Strange Feeling	Billy Strayhorn	Ellington Centennial Edition
Northern Lights	Billy Strayhorn	The Queen's Suite: The Ellington Suites Pablo 2310-762.
Nutcracker Overture	Arr. Strayhorn	Ellington Three Suites: Columbia/ Legacy 46825
Ko-Ko	Ellington	Ellington Centennial Edition
Brainville	Sun Ra	Jazz by Sun Ra (retitled Sun Song) Delmark DD-411 (1991, CD)
So You Say	Jaffe	Manhattan Projections: Playscape j012484
Self Portrait in Three Colors	Mingus	This Is Jazz 6 (cf. Ch. 3)
Coming on the Hudson	Thelonious Monk	Monk: The Columbia Years 1962-68
Crepuscule with Nellie	Thelonious Monk	Thelonious Monk Greatest Hits: Columbia Legacy
Evidence	Thelonious Monk	The Complete Genius: Blue Note
Just You, Just Me	Thelonious Monk	Monk: Columbia Legacy
Off Minor	Thelonious Monk	Monk/Coltrane Riverside 946
Dersu	Jaffe	Manhattan Projections
Aguela Valsa	Hermeto Pascoal	Slave's Mass
The Third World	Herbie Nichols	The Third World Blue Note LP BN-LA-485-H2 (reissue on Mosaic: Complete Herbie Nichols on Blue Note)

Chapter 5

Composition	Artist/Composer	Available Recording(s)
Maple Leaf Rag	Scott Joplin	Elite Syncopations/Biograph 30156
King Porter Stomp	Morton	Cf. Ch. 4
Carolina Shout	Johnson	Cf. Ch. 4
In a Mist	Bix Beiderbecke	aka "Bixology": W-81426
Sagittarius	Mary Lou Williams	in Zodiac Suite (cf. Ch. 4)
Nice Work If You Can Get It	Gershwin	Cf. Ch. 4
It Don't Mean a Thing (If It Ain't Got That Swing)	Ellington	Cf. Ch. 4
Our Love Is Here to Stay	Gershwin	Ella Fitzgerald Sings the Gershwin Songbook Verve 3-825024-2
But Not for Me	Gershwin	John Coltrane: My Favorite Things Heavyweight Champion: The Complete Atlantic Recordings Rhino R2 71984
Joy Spring	Clifford Brown	Max Roach/Clifford Brown Quintet: EmArcy 814645-2
All the Things You Are	Jerome Kern	Bird After Dark: Savoy 17135
Stella By Starlight	Victor Young	Stan Getz: Anniversary: Verve 521851
Dear Old Stockholm	Miles Davis	Round About Midnight, Columbia S8649
The Dolphin	Luis Eca	Bill Evans: From Left to Right MGM 31455-4512
Delores	Wayne Shorter	Miles Davis: Miles Smiles Columbia 65682
Speak No Evil	Wayne Shorter	Speak No Evil, Blue Note 99001
Wild Flower	Wayne Shorter	Speak No Evil, Blue Note 99001
Infant Eyes	Wayne Shorter	Speak No Evil, Blue Note 99001
Jacqui	Richie Powell	A Study in Brown: Emarcy 814646
Locomotion	John Coltrane	Blue Train (cf. Ch. 4)
Clarinet Lament	Ellington	Swing, 1930-38, ABC, also Centennial Celebration V.2, Red Hot 625
Basin St. Blues	Spencer Williams	Satch Blows the Blues: Columbia Legacy 86578
Black, Brown and Beige	Ellington	Carnegie Hall Concerts, Jan. 1943 Prestige: 34004
Swampy River	Ellington	The Okeh Ellington, re-release Columbia, 1991 C2K 46177
The Clothed Woman	Ellington	Essential Master of Jazz: Proper Box 18
The Stampede	Fletcher Henderson	Smithsonian Collection of Classic Jazz: cf. Ch. 4
Scratchin' in the Gravel	Mary Lou Williams	Andy Kirk: The Twelve Clouds of Joy with Mary Lou Williams: Living Era AJA 5108 (E)
Lightnin'	Ellington	Duke Ellington and His Orchestra: Classics 626

Chapter 6

Composition	Artist/Composer	Available Recording(s)
Ko-Ko	Ellington	Ellington Centennial Edition (cf. Ch. 4)
Until I Met You	Freddie Green	Count Basie and Sarah Vaughn re-release 1996 (originally 1961 Roulette Records), Blue Note/EMI 753139
Yeah	Horace Silver	Horacescope (cf. Ch. 4)
Bebe	Hermeto Pascoal	A Musica Livre de Hermeto Pascoal (cf. Ch. 4)

Moanin'	Bobby Timmons	Art Blakey and the Jazz Messengers Moanin': Blue Note 95324
The Stampede	Fletcher Henderson	Smithsonian Collection (Cf. Ch. 5)
Quietude	Thad Jones	Central Park North: Toshiba/EMI TOCJ 9458
Tone Parallel to Harlem	Ellington	Centennial Edition (cf. Ch. 3)
Flirty Bird	Ellington	Anatomy of a Murder: Sony Music CD WK 75025
Pie Eye Blues	Ellington	ibid.
Scratchin' in the Gravel	Mary Lou Williams, with Andy Kirk and His Twelve Clouds of Joy (cf. Ch.5)	Mary Lou Williams Cf. Ch. 5
Gravel Truth		No commercially available recording
The Shoes of the Fisherman's Wife Are Some Jive Ass Slippers	Mingus	Let My Children Hear Music: Columbia Legacy 48910
Maiden Voyage	Herbie Hancock	Maiden Voyage: Blue Note B21Y-46339
Auntie Matter	Geoff Keezer	Other Spheres: DIW-871
Free Spirits	John Stubblefield	Mary Lou Williams Trio: Steeplechase 31043
Gaviota	Clare Fischer	Machaca Discovery Records DS-835, 1981
Will O' The Wisp	Arr. Gil Evans	Sketches of Spain: Columbia/Legacy Ck 65142
Shadow Dance	Dave Holland	What Goes Around: ECM 2002 014002
7 Black Butterflies	Drew Gress	7 Black Butterflies, Premonition Records 90767
Portaculture	Jaffe	An Imperfect Storm: MMC Recordings 2132J
Braggin' in Brass	Ellington	Duke Ellington Complete Works 1924-47, Proper Box (UK) re-release 2003 ASIN: B00004LMT0
Afro Blue	Mongo Santamaria	Afro Roots: Prestige 24018
Down By the Riverside	Arr. O. Nelson	James and Wes: The Dynamic Duo Universal UCCU 5079
Take the A Train	Billy Strayhorn	Ellington Centennial Edition (cf. Ch. 2)
Space Is the Place	Sun Ra	Space Is the Place: Impulse IMPD 249
Groove Merchant	Jerome Richardson, Arr. Thad Jones	Central Park North
The Tattooed Bride	Ellington	The Complete Duke Ellington, 1947-52 (cf. Ch. 2)
Evidence	Thelonious Monk	The Complete Genius, Blue Note, re-release Mosaic MR4-101, 1983
Whisper Not	Benny Golson	Dizzy Gillespie Big Band: Birks Works, the Verve Big Band Sessions: 527900, 1995
Haitian Fight Song	Mingus	The Clown: Atlantic
Slop	Mingus	This Is Jazz 6 (cf. Ch. 3)
Self-Portrait in Three Colors	Mingus	ibid.
Love Came	Strayhorn	Lush Life, Red Baron AK 52760
Passed Me By	Strayhorn	Lush Life, Red Baron AK 52760
Giant Steps	Coltrane	Giant Steps (cf. Ch. 4)
Fables of Faubus	Mingus	This Is Jazz 6
100 Hearts	Michel Petrucciani	100 Hearts: Blue Note/Capitol 7243-5-38329-6
Gloria's Step	Scott LaFaro	Bill Evans Trio, Complete Village Vanguard Recordings 1961, Riverside 4443
Trinkle Tinkle	Monk	Monk/Coltrane Riverside 946
Straight No Chaser	Monk	Greatest Hits (cf. Ch. 4), also Monk Legacy Septet, Concord 30095-2, 2006
Rhythm-A-Ning	Monk	Live at the Five Spot
Just You, Just Me	Arr. Monk	Columbia
Diminuendo and Crescendo In Blue	Ellington	Ellington at Newport: Columbia 64932
Five	Bill Evans	Complete Riverside Recordings (original reissue OJC-025)

Composition	Artist/Composer	Available Recording(s)
Nica's Dream	Horace Silver	Horacescope (cf. Ch. 4)
Rhythm-A-Ning	Johnny Griffin	Live at the Five Spot (cf. Ch. 6)
Brown	Ellington	Carnegie Hall 1943 (cf. Ch. 5)
Black and Tan Fantasy	Ellington	RCA Centennial Edition (cf. Ch. 2)
Clementine	Strayhorn	ibid.
Raincheck	Strayhorn	ibid.
Concerto for Cootie	Ellington	ibid.
Impressions	Coltrane	Live at the Village Vanguard: Impulse 251
India	Coltrane	ibid.
Vedic Chant	Anon.	Religious Music of India Folkways LP 4431
	Trilok Gurtu	The Trilok Gurtu Collection, Silva America, 1997.
Pavane Pour Une Infante Défunte	Ravel	Chicago Symphony/ Reiner RCA 60179
Giant Steps	Coltrane	Cf. Ch. 4
Isfahan (aka Elf)	Strayhorn	The Far East Suite (Ellington) Bluebird 07863
Body and Soul	Arr. Coltrane	Coltrane's Sound (incl. In "Heavyweight Champion", Cf. Ch. 5)
Take the Coltrane	Ellington	Ellington/Coltrane, Impulse UCCI 9004
Afro-American Symphony	Still	Chandos CHAN 9154
Rockin' in Rhythm	Ellington	Ellington Centennial Edition
Ducky Wucky	"Symphony in Black" (filmshort)	in Duke Ellington and His Orchestra: Classics, 1929-1952", Amvest Video, (originally Paramount, 1934).
Walkin and Swingin	Mary Lou Williams	Andy Kirk and his Clouds of Joy with Mary Lou Williams (Cf. Ch. 5)
		Twisted: The Best of Lambert Hendricks and Ross, Rhino: R2 70328
Concierto de Aranjuez	Arr. Gil Evans	Miles Davis, Sketches of Spain (Cf. Ch. 6)
A Blessing	John Hollenbeck	John Hollenbeck Large Ensemble Omnitone/ Intuition: 15209 2005
Northern Lights	Strayhorn	Ellington, The Queen's Suite: The Ellington Suites, Pablo 2310-762
It Don't Mean a Thing If It Ain't Got That Swing	Ellington	Ellington Centenniel Edition
Down By the Riverside	Arr. Nelson	Cf. Ch. 6
Stolen Moments	Nelson	Blues and the Abstract Truth, Cf. Ch. 2
Yearnin'	Nelson	ibid.
Sameeda	Abdullah Ibrahim	Water From An Ancient Well, ENJA 8888-12-2
Arab Dance	Arr. Evans	Real Birth of the Cool: Cf. Ch. 2
Scratchin' in the Gravel	Williams	Andy Kirk and his 12 Clouds of Joy
Happy Anatomy	Ellington	Anatomy of A Murder, Cf. Ch. 6
Half the Fun	Strayhorn	Such Sweet Thunder: Columbia Ck 65568 2
Morning Mood	Grieg; Arr. Strayhorn	Peer Gynt Suite, in Three Suites by Ellington, RHCO46709-8
What's New	Arr. Slide Hampton	Jazz Club: Tenor Sax Verve 840031 (cf. Ch. 4)

Composition	Artist/Composer	Available Recording(s)
Concerto for Cootie	Ellington	Centennial Edition (Cf. Ch. 2)
Concorde	John Lewis	Modern Jazz Quartet: Original Jazz Classics 2
Black, Brown and Beige	Ellington	Carnegie Hall 1943 (Cf. Ch. 5)
Blue Rondo à La Turk	Brubeck	Dave Brubeck Quartet: The Great Concerts Columbia Jazz Masterpieces 44215
The Blues	Ellington	Carnegie Hall 1943 (Cf. Ch. 5)
Tone Parallel to Harlem	Ellington	Centennial Edition
The Shoes of the Fisherman's Wife Are some Jive Ass Slippers	Mingus	Let My Children Hear Music, Cf. Ch. 6
Pavane Pour Une Infante Défunte	Ravel	Cf. Ch. 7
Dusk	Ellington	Centennial Edition
In a Mist	Beiderbecke	Cf. Ch. 5
Reminiscing in Tempo	Ellington	Reminiscing in Tempo: Columbia Legacy
Twelve Tone Tune	Evans	The Bill Evans Album: Columbia
Miles' Mode	Coltrane	Coltrane: Priceless Jazz Collection GRP 9874
But Not For Me	Arr. Coltrane	Heavyweight Champion: The Complete Atlantic Recordings of John Coltrane Rhino R2 71984, 1995
Giant Steps	Coltrane	ibid.
Portaculture	Jaffe	An Imperfect Storm: Cf. Ch. 6
Nita	Coltrane	Paul Chambers: Whims of Chambers Blue Note 37647
Like Sonny	Coltrane	Coltrane Jazz: Rhino 79891
A Love Supreme	Coltrane	A Love Supreme: Impulse 155
Blue Train	Coltrane	Blue Train: Cf. Ch. 4
Goodbye Porkpie Hat	Mingus	This Is Jazz 6: Ch. 3
Gregory Is Here	Silver	Return of the 27th Man: in Blue Note Retrospective Box Set (Cf. Ch. 4)
The Queen's Suite	Ellington/Strayhorn	The Queen's Suite: Cf. Ch. 7
Speak Like a Child	Hancock	Cf. Ch. 4
Jazzing the Classics		Living Era: Co AJA 5339
Nutcracker	Arr. Ellington/Strayhorn	Three Suites: Cf. Ch. 4
Nutcracker Suite	Tchaikovsky	EMI Classics: CDBQ 54649 2
Arab Dance	Arr. Gil Evans	Real Birth of the Cool: Cf. Ch. 2

Copyright Notices for Music Excerpts
not in the public domain

Acknolwedgements of Sources Consulted

Although I take full responsibility for the accuracy of the transcriptions presented in this book, I would nonetheless like to take a moment to thank the following valued colleagues who have been so generous over the years in sharing with me many unpublished manuscripts and transcriptions related to the content of this book. In every case I have tried to be faithful to the intent of the composer and to represent the given recordings and compositions accurately (In cases where transcribed excerpts differ from officially published versions of a particular compositions, these distinctions result from transcriptions of a particular recording or performance).

The late Bill Barron for sharing so many interesting musical insights and a varied performance repertoire and manuscripts;

David Berger and Kingbrand Publishing for his many transcriptions of Ellington;

Johanne Cousineau for sharing her Clare Fischer sketches and transcriptions;

Dave Demsey for his invaluable work transcribing and analyzing Coltrane's performances;

Dick Domek for his Ellington scholarship and presentations over the years;

The Drury College Archives, for sharing Gil Evans sketches from the Claude Thornhill Archives;

The Duke Ellington Collection at the Smithsonian Institution in Washington, D.C., curated by Dr. John Edward Hasse and made more accessible to all at its inception due to the invaluable expertise of Annie Kuebler, who now resides at the Institute of Jazz Studies in Newark;

Andrew Homzy for his invaluable work on Mingus' music, particularly in editing "More Than A Fakebook", but also in providing sketches of Mingus' compositions that provided a point of departure for transcribing; also for sharing some of his Strayhorn transcriptions;

Father Peter O'Brien for sharing transcriptions and sketches of Mary Lou Williams' work;

The late Herb Pomeroy for sharing many insights and sketches related to Ellington's music;

Lewis Porter for his incredible scholarship in so many areas;

The late William Russo for sharing so many of his Ellington transcriptions and personal insights about the composer;

Gunther Schuller for his invaluable scholarship and analysis, especially "Early Jazz" and "The Swing Era";

Don Sickler for editing the Monk Fakebook and thereby providing us all access to accurate versions of Monk's compositions;

Fred Sturm, whose seminal work "Changes Over Time" has offered us all a great insight into the comparative study of historically important arrangements of "King Porter Stomp".

The late Mark Tucker for having shared so many insights and transcriptions of Ellington's music, and as well for his incredible scholarship and musicianship;

Walter van de Leur for providing us all with a clearer understanding of the music of Billy Strayhorn;

Among so many others... *thank you all.*

About the Author

Award-winning composer and arranger Andy Jaffe has been active in jazz education worldwide for thirty-five years. He is the author of over one hundred original compositions, ranging from 32-bar songs to works for piano duo and various other jazz and chamber ensembles, large and small. His compositions for sextet, such as those recorded on his CD *Manhattan Projects*, are his best known. He co-leads and is arranger and composer for The Bill Lowe-Andy Jaffe Repertory Big Band.

As an educator, he has taught at the Berklee College of Music (1977-81), Amherst College (1987-99), Tufts University (1990-92), The University of Massachusetts Graduate Program in African-American Music and Jazz (1994-96), The Institut Musical de Formation Professionelle (Nimes, France 1984), and the Tainan National University of the Arts (TNNUA) in Taiwan, as well as having lectured, performed, and done residencies throughout the U.S., Canada, Europe and Asia.

He teaches courses on jazz arranging and composition, the music of Duke Ellington, the Music of John Coltrane, and directs the Jazz Program at Williams College in Williamstown, MA, where he served as Artistic Director of the Williamstown Jazz Festival from 1999-2009.

He may be contacted at http://andyjaffe.com

MARK E. BOLING/EDITED BY JERRY COKER
THE JAZZ THEORY WORKBOOK
· ORDER NO. 11201 (125-PAGE BOOK)

This book is a primer in jazz theory, intended to prepare the student for the serious study of jazz improvisation, arrangement and composition.
Included are many musical examples and written assignments for practice in the theoretical skills. Appropriate exercises are provided to reinforce theoretical concepts by immediate application to the instrument.

JERRY COKER
A GUIDE TO JAZZ ARRANGING & COMPOSING
· ORDER NO. 11310 (78-PAGE BOOK)

This book evolved from 40 years of teaching jazz composition and arranging plus 50 years of personal writing experience in the professional field. It is, therefore, a comprehensive study, covering preparatory activities, philosophical perspectives, listening lists, choice tune lists, all elements of composing melodies and chord progressions, arranging for small and large ensembles, enhanced use of rhythm sections, a sensitive approach to instrumental ranges, textural options, form, and more. Though a self-contained study, the book has the unique feature of leading the reader to other excellent books on the subject.

JERRY COKER/BOB KNAPP/LARRY VINCENT
HEARIN' THE CHANGES
· ORDER NO. 14270 (102-PAGE BOOK)

This is the definite study of chord progressions of hundreds of carefully chosen tunes from the jazz musician's repertoire, comparing them, linking them together by commonalities, and codifying harmonic traits that will clarify the reader's understanding of how progressions "work"! It not only provides the means to learn and memorize tunes more easily, but also becomes the key to acquiring the skill to cognize progressions by ear!

BILL DOBBINS
JAZZ ARRANGING & COMPOSING:
A LINEAR APPROACH
· ORDER NO. 11305 (184-PAGE BOOK W/CD)

Revised edition.

_Many different possibilities for harmonizing the same melody are illustrated and analysed, using techniques by such influential arrangers and composers as Duke Ellington, Billy Strayhorn, Oliver Nelson, Gil Evans and Clare Fischer.

_Techniques of melody harmonization, linear writing and counterpoint for 2, 3, 4 and 5 horns.

_A chapter on writing for the rhythm section clearly illustrates the techniques commonly used by jazz arrangers and composers.

_Six complete scores in concert key are ideal for analysis, for playing the horn parts on the piano or for following the performances on the CD.

_An extensive chapter on form and development deals with extended forms and the use of compositional techniques in writing for the small jazz ensemble.

_A useful discography is included at the end of each chapter.

GIL GOLDSTEIN
JAZZ COMPOSER'S COMPANION
· ORDER NO. 11304 (116-PAGE BOOK)

The book is divided into three main sections: Melody, Rhythm, and Harmony. Dozens of musical examples as well as compositions by Bill Evans (pianist), Jaco Pastorious, Jim Hall, Ralph Towner, Steve Swallow, Pat Metheny, Michael Gibbs, a.o., are included in order to illustrate specific compositional techniques. Plus interviews with Bill Evans, Carla Bley, George Russell, Horace Silver, Pat Metheny, Chick Corea, Lyle Mays, Anthony Davis, Herbie Hancock, Ralph Towner, a.o.

"Gil does a service here on a high level. The concepts he offers impose no style and thus, can be used and extended to enrich any musicians vocabulary. The rest is up to you." (Bill Evans)

PETER HERBORN
JAZZ ARRANGING (E-D)
· ORDER NO. 11301 (186-PAGE BOOK)

Comparable to a course, the reader will be guided step by step from the grassroots to more advanced and complex ways of writing. Here, it is not intended to simply float some apodictic rules that lack proper explanation. On the contrary, the explanations given will cover the questions time and again asked by students as well as the issues arising when working in an artistic situation. Through refined verbalization and a vast number of musical examples this book should contribute to a clear understanding of these guidelines, and foster the student's ability to realize the issues when arranging.

ANDY JAFFE
JAZZ HARMONY (THIRD EDITION)
· ORDER NO. 11203 (200-PAGE BOOK)

Andy Jaffe's *Jazz Harmony*, one of the most definitive texts on the subject, goes into its third edition in 2009. Over the years the book has proven equally useful for students of all backgrounds, whether self-taught, classically trained, or as a useful reference for working professionals. Also appropriate for use as a class-room text.

GARY KELLER
THE JAZZ CHORD/SCALE HANDBOOK
· ORDER NO. 11217 (110-PAGE BOOK)

New, completely revised 2002 edition!

The "Jazz Chord/Scale Handbook" provides a concise yet comprehensive reference source for chord/scale theory.
This is not a "how to" book, but rather a systemized guide to identifying, organizing, and understanding the relationships between virtually all the common (and uncommon) scale/chord relationships used in jazz improvisation and composition. Based on the principle of harmonic systems, the handbook organizes all the modes of major, melodic and harmonic minor, harmonic major, as well as nine different symmetric scales, various pentatonic scales, the blues scale(s) and more. Most importantly, each scale is presented with appropriate modal and functional chord voicings, information about common usage, and examples from the recorded jazz literature.

STEVE LAJOIE
GIL EVANS & MILES DAVIS:
1957-1962 HISTORIC COLLABORATIONS
· ORDER NO. 11315 (432-PAGE BOOK)

The collaborations of Gil Evans and Miles Davis over the five year period from 1957 to 1962 produced some of the finest jazz albums of all time, including "Miles Ahead", "Porgy and Bess" and "Sketches of Spain". Their music reached beyond jazz to a wider audience and its influence has been felt in jazz writing ever since. For the first time, this book offers a detailed analysis of the major works by Gil Evans and Miles Davis, examining their collaborations in their historical context and assessing the importance of their collaborations to jazz ensemble literature.Their use of the techniques of composition vis-à-vis recomposition and arrangement is discussed in depth and the book includes detailed analysis and transcribed full scores for *Blues for Pablo; New Rhumba; Bess, You Is My Woman Now* and *Will o' The Wisp*. It includes recommendations for further study, a bibliography and discography of issued recordings of the 1957 to 1962 Evans-Davis collaborations. This book is essential study for all musicians interested in the processes of composition and arranging.

DAVID LIEBMAN
A CHROMATIC APPROACH TO JAZZ HARMONY & MELODY
· ORDER NO. 14201 (173-PAGE BOOK)

A CHROMATIC APPROACH TO JAZZ HARMONY & MELODY
· ORDER NO. 14216 (BOOK W/CD)

New revised edition! (2006)

This book should be seen as a method to help the artist to develop his or her own way when trying to improvise chromatically. Through the concepts and examples offered, the improviser should be able to use this material alongside already familiar tonal ideas. Specifically, the book serves as a guide for organizing chromaticism into a coherent musical statement meant to satisfy both the intellectual and emotional needs of artistic creation. The reader will be introduced to more than one way of conceiving chromatic lines and harmonies. There is nothing theoretically complex or new in the text, it is the organization of the material as well as many musical examples and transcriptions (Bach, Scriabin, Coltrane, Shorter, Hancock, Beirach, Liebman, a.o.) which should serve to inspire musicians to expand their usual diatonic vocabulary. In addition the book contains 100 assorted solo lines and 100 chord voicings.

RON MILLER
MODAL JAZZ COMPOSITION & HARMONY, VOL. 1
· ORDER NO. 11303 (142-PAGE BOOK)

The goal of this book is to show the student the means to develop latent creative abilities by offering the unfettered environment of the chromatic-modal system and free asymmetric form. The freedom of the approach will allow the composer to express him/herself in any style: post 50s jazz, ECM, fusion, pop, classical, etc., that is not tied to any harmonic particulars.
Ron Miller is professor of jazz studies at the University of Miami. His compositions have been recorded and/or performed by notable musicians as Red Rodney, "Elements", Jerry Coker, Hal Galper, Ira Sullivan, Joe Lovano and Stan Getz. Composition students of Ron Miller that have attained notoriety include: Pat Metheny, Steve Morse, "T" Lavitz, Bruce Hornsby, Gil Goldstein, Mark Egan, Matt Harris, Denis DiBlasio and Rick Margitza.

RON MILLER
MODAL JAZZ COMPOSITION & HARMONY, VOL. 2
· ORDER NO. 11308 (142-PAGE BOOK)

The goal of Volume 2 is to continue the dissemination of information that presents a path of study for the aspiring jazz composer. Where Volume1 of the book emphasized the preparation of a modal harmonic foundation, this volume will introduce concepts of melody writing and a study of the styles of jazz compositions that are an intrinsic addition to the contemporary jazz composer's repertoire. Also included are chapters on harmonization and reharmonization techniques – as many of the concepts presented reflect an influence of Gil Evans, Duke Ellington and Charles Mingus as well as those of Herbie Hancock – and on pentatonic tunes that are harmonized with a modal harmonic foundation. As with Volume 1, an appendix with additional peripheral information is included for the student desiring theoretical explanation and additional examples.

WAYNE NAUS
BEYOND FUNCTIONAL HARMONY
· ORDER NO. 11225 (111-PAGE BOOK W/CD)

This book/CD set presents a system that creates melody and harmony and allows them to function outside of the normal dependencies governing the principles of diatonic harmony, melody and form. It offers the composer a departure point from the harmonic and melodic characteristics grounded in the principles of tonal, key related or functional harmony. The principles outlined are specifically designed to help examine, analyze and compose music written in the style of today's leading composers of jazz and fusion music.

"A unique approach to writing in the style of contemporary jazz and fusion." (Russell Ferrante, The Yellowjackets)

ADVANCED HARMONIC CONCEPTS
(A NON-FUNCTIONAL APPROACH)
· ORDER NO. 11226 (104-PAGE BOOK W/CD)

"A clear, concise, and beautifully conceived approach to expanding the harmonic possibilities for today's composer". (Russell Ferrante - The Yellowjackets)

"A way to forge a personal creative process which provides structure in a harmonic style that has few boundaries". (Joe Mulholland - Chairman Harmony Department, Berklee College of Music.)

BARRIE NETTLES / RICHARD GRAF
THE CHORD SCALE THEORY & JAZZ HARMONY
· ORDER NO. 11216 (184-PAGE BOOK)

Jazz harmony, as taught at the Berklee College of Music is based on the so called Chord Scale Theory. This method – further developed – is now available as a comprehensive textbook for the first time. Emerged from practice and designed for practical use, it provides theoretical knowledge necessary for improvisation, composing, and arranging.

"Having never had any institutional training in harmony and theory, I have often wondered just how Jazz Harmony came to be? To develop and exist with its so deep well of knowledge that is necessary to the improviser? Where did this come from and how did it develop? The Chord Scale Theory & Jazz Harmony explains this and also goes farther by showing just how this knowledge can be used. My only regret is that I've just found it." (Art Farmer)

"A helpful and organized tool that can surely aid any musician interested in understanding harmony as it relates to the complex subtleties of jazz improvisation." (Michael Brecker)

"This is a fine book, clear, comprehensive, and detailed. I like to think of it as the 'Basics Bible'." (Mick Goodrick)

MIKE ROSSI
CONTRAST AND CONTINUITY
· ORDER NO. 14202 (220-PAGE BOOK)

While nearly all great solos contain a delicate balance of contrast and continuity in the broader sense, (rhythm, range, harmonic interest & variation, dynamics, pacing, etc.) this concept illustrates the way towards creating a diatonic, multi-colored and contemporary language for jazz improvisation.

UNCOMMON ETUDES FROM COMMON SCALES
· ORDER NO. 14206 (112-PAGE BOOK)

Applying melodic contrast to diatonic phrases.

Uncommon Etudes from Common Scales will better equip students and challenge improvisers of all levels with etudes that travel through all keys using common chord types. Also, expand your melodic and creative ability as an improviser and composer by applying Contrast to diatonic phrases! The etudes are suited for C, B♭ and E♭ treble clef instruments. The appendix features the changes for all etudes in the correct transposition to accompany B♭ and E♭ instruments.

ADAM RUDOLPH
PURE RHYTHM
· ORDER NO. 13285 (112-PAGE BOOK /2CDS)

This book is for the instrumentalist, composer, percussionist, student and music educator who aims to expand his or her understanding of rhythm and overall musicianship. It is an applied guide to the fundamentals of rhythm, presented step-by-step from the simple to the complex.

"As open and generous as the author himself, Pure Rhythm is an excellent and essential introduction to world rhythms. Presented step by step in a clear, intelligent and systematic format, this is a long overdue classic in the field." (John Zorn)

"This book is a critical introduction to much of the important creative insight into the whole feeling of movement in music, with a strong implication of both regularity and differentiation.
I recommend this book highly for musicians, on all levels, as a means of nurturing their rhythmic creativity." (Dr. Yusef Lateef)

FRED STURM
CHANGES OVER TIME:
THE EVOLUTION OF JAZZ ARRANGING
· ORDER NO. 11350 (224-PAGE BOOK W/CD)

This book illustrates, through comparative case studies, the dramatic development of rhythmic, melodic, harmonic, orchestrational, and structural variation in jazz arranging from the 1920s to the present. The case studies were narrowed to 35 arrangements of three classic jazz compositions and one American popular standard song: "Jelly Roll" Morton's *King Porter Stomp*, Don Redman's *Chant of the Weed*, Gerald Marks' and Seymour Simon's *All of Me*, and Billy Strayhorn's *Take the "A" Train*. Scores and/or parts representing nine decades were supplied by living arrangers, borrowed from collections, reconstructed from sketches, or transcribed from recordings. Four contemporary masters were ultimately commissioned to create new arrangements of four selected compositions.

LUDMILA ULEHLA
CONTEMPORARY HARMONY: ROMANTICISM
THROUGH THE 12-TONE ROW
· ORDER NO. 11400 (534-PAGE BOOK)

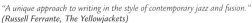

The understanding of the musical techniques of composition can not be reduced to a handbook of simplified rules. Music is complex and ever changing. It is the purpose of this book to trace the path of musical growth from the late Romantic period to the serial techniques of the contemporary composer. Through the detailed analysis of the musical characteristics that dominate a specific style of writing, a graduated plan is organized and presented here in the form of explanations and exercises. A new analytical method substitutes for the diatonic figured bass and makes exercises and the analysis of non-diatonic literature more manageable.
The explanations describing each technique are thorough. They are designed to help the teacher and the student see the many extenuating circumstances that affect a particular analytical decision. More important than a dogmatic decision on a particular key center or a root tone, for example, is the understanding of why such an underdeterminate condition may exist.

"[...] one of the great analytical essays of our century." (Ron Thomas, pianist)

"Contemporary Harmony is one of the finest, most comprehensive texts ever written on the subject." (D. Anthony Ricigliano, Manhattan School of Music, New York)